A1 60130 'Kestrel' backs through Holbeck High Level on its way into Leeds Central to take over the 11.00 Glasgow - Kings Cross Pullman whilst B1 61122 passes with the 16.13 Leeds Central - Cleethorpes. The line to the left of the Pacific is the up loop platform line whilst those to the right of the B1 are, respectively, the down GN goods and the down and up LNW goods lines which ran to Copley Hill marshalling yard and joined the Leeds City - Huddersfield - Manchester main line at Farnley Junction.

Although the Great Northern is often thought of as being little more than a component of the East Coast London - Edinburgh main line, in fact its principal passenger operation was the express service between London and the West Riding of Yorkshire; services from Kings Cross to Scotland being much less numerous in number.

Up to the late 1930's a typical West Riding express would leave London with portions for Hull, Bradford Exchange and Leeds Central (plus, in many cases, a section for York as well). The Pacific would only work as far as Doncaster where it would be replaced by a D49 on the Hull and York portions of the train whilst the West Riding portion (the Doncaster - Leeds line being at that time something of a retirement route for main line engines) would be taken over by an ex-GNR 2-6-0 or a Great Central 4-6-0.

At Wakefield the Bradford coaches would be removed to be taken - usually by an N1 0-6-2T - either down the main line to Ardsley and then over the Tingley branch or else via Dewsbury Central and Batley to Bradford Exchange.

The handful of coaches that eventually arrived in Leeds Central was a far cry from the fifteen coach express that had left London four hours earlier.

The story did not always end at Leeds since a number of services reversed and continued north to Harrogate, transferring to the North Eastern by way of the Geldard spur a short distance outside Leeds Central.

This was the traditional way in which West Riding trains operated from London but by the late 1930's changes were put into affect that were going to have lasting changes.

For many years the viaduct between Sandal and Wakefield had precluded Pacifics from running between Doncaster and Leeds; a circumstance that had caused much head-scratching in the search to find suitable engines for the handful of through workings - chiefly the Pullman expresses - between Leeds and Kings Cross. The results gave lineside observers enough material for three generations of books and articles as strangers such as D10 4-4-0's and Great Central 4-6-0's rubbed shoulders for a while with LNER Pacifics. It was an entertaining rather than enlightening episode which concluded somewhat lamely with large-boilered Great Northern Atlantics holding the fort until the route was finally cleared for Pacifics in 1937.

The newly introduced West Riding streamliner, which was worked in both directions by a Kings Cross-based A4 Pacific, was the first train to take advantage of the clearance whilst the great majority of trains continued to operate in the traditional way until 1948 when the arrival of the postwar A1 class gave the LNER sufficient Pacifics to allow Copley Hill an allocation and to do away with the change of engines at Doncaster. From that time Copley Hill engines and men became a regular feature at Kings Cross with several through services a day.

Most of the Leeds crews working to London lodged overnight but one duty - probably the most arduous on British Railways - involved working the 400-mile return trip in one shift.

Putting Copley Hill on the main line map was not, however, the only major change made to the post-1948 Leeds district.

For years the intensive local service over the nine-mile Leeds - Bradford route had been worked by GN N1 0-6-2 tanks which, by the early 1950's, were showing signs of age. As a stopgap - which smacked almost of panic - a handful of motor-fitted N7 0-6-2T's and push & pull coaches were drafted in but in 1955 a completely new order saw the light of day when the Bradford - Leeds workings became the country's first suburban service to be completely handed over to diesel operation. Thanks to some imaginative diagramming, the new diesels not only took in the Bradford service but also encompassed the Castleford workings together with a completely new service from Leeds Central to Harrogate: a route that had previously only been covered by through trains from Kings Cross.

Leeds Central, which had always been a joint station, also ran an hourly London Midland service to Liverpool Exchange via Manchester Victoria using a mix of 2-6-4T's and Black 5's.

Whether you worked there, used the station or simply stood on its platforms to watch trains, Leeds Central provided as much interest as one was entitled to ask of any location and if this book rekindles memories and answers some questions, it will have served its task.

Thanks for assistance are due to: W. Becket, S. Standbridge, J.Fozard. H.C. Casserley, C. Dymock, I. Fraser, J. Whitaker, R. Pulleyn, E. Firth, D. Hill, A. Baker, W. Halpin and J. Marshall.

WORKING TIMETABLE : DONCASTER/BRADFORD – LEEDS CENTRAL (1957/8)

DOWN

	1	2	3	4	5	6	7	8	9	10	11	12	13	14	15	16	17	18
Train	00.02	20.25			02.25	22.45				02.58	03.15	04.10						06.30
From	Leeds C	Grimsby			Leeds C	KX				D'ter	Sow B	Kirkgate						Horsforth
Route		Kirkgate								Kirkgate		Stanningley						
Class	Pcls	Fish	Light	Light	Light	EP	Light	Light	Pcls	Pcls	Light	ECS	Pcls	Pcls	ECS	ECS	Pass	Pass
No.	435	1282	455	951	433	970	970	3014	3014	463	486	969	324	342	961	481	471	5517
Engine	2MTT	B1	B1	B1	5XP	A3	B1	J50	B1	4MTT	B1	J50	B1	N1	N1	DMU	DMU	3DMU
Diagram		CH26	CH29	CH25		DR14	CH71	CH74	DR80	LM17	CH71	CH10G	AY4	AY2	CH72			
DONCASTER						02.15			02.58									
Bentley Crossing						02/18			03/01									
Carcroft																		
Adwick Jcn						02/24			03/10									
South Elmsall						02/28			03/15									
Hemsworth																		
Fitzwilliam																		
Hare Park Jcn						02/41			03/21									
Sandal						02/43			K									
WAKEFIELD (W)						02.46									04.13			
WAKEFIELD (W)						02.56			03.51				05.30		04.55			
Lofthouse						03.01			03.55				*(To*		05.00			
Lofthouse N. Jcn						03.02			03.56				*Batley)*		05.01			
Ardsley		(23.55)																
Ardsley		00.05				03.06			03.59						05.05			
Wortley S. Jcn		00/21				03/13			04/07						05/14			
BRADFORD										04.28						05.30	05.35	
Laisterdyke											04/21					05/36	05/41	
Stanningley										04/33	04/26					05/39	05/44	
Bramley																		
Armley Moor																		
Wortley W. Jcn										04/38	04/33			05/16		05/42	05/48	
Copley Hill CS												04.44		05.30				
Copley Hill Loco			00.40	01.22			03.20	04.15										
HOLBECK HL						03.15			04.09	04.35								
HOLBECK HL		00/23	00/45	01/27		03.25	03/25	04/20	04.35	04.45	04/40	04/48			05/34	05/44	05/51	
Geldard Jn	00/18				02/39													06/38
LEEDS	00.20	00.25	00.50	01.32	02.41	03.28	03.30	04.25	04.38	04.48	04.45	04.51			05.37	05.46	05.53	06.40
Platform	2	M	4	3	1	2	2	-	3	2	-	4			5	1	6	6
Train works	00.48	-	-	-	-	03.43	-	-	06.22	06.28	-	07.30			07.50	06.00/40	06.20	07.13
Engine works	00.48	01.50	01.05	01.42	03.25	04.00	03.43	06.22	05.00	08.55	06.28	07.32			07.57	06.00	-	-

WORKING TIMETABLE : LEEDS CENTRAL – BRADFORD/DONCASTER (1957/8)

UP

	1	2	3	4	5	6	7	8	9	10	11	12	13	14	15	16	17	18
Train						01.05		22.45			04.10		22.45					
From						Leeds		KX			Kirkgate		KX					
Class	Light	Pcls	Light	Pcls	Pass	Light	Pcls	XP	XP	Light	Light	Pcls	Pass	ECS	Pass	Pass	ECS	Pass
No.	452	458		455	951		455	462	970			324	1582	970	480	1584	5582	484
Engine	4MTT	2MTT		B1	B1	B1	B1	5XP	B1	A3	B1	B1	DMU	J50	DMU	DMU	3DMU	DMU
Diagram	LM20		CH74	CH29	CH25	CH26	CH29		CH71	DR14	DR80			CH73				
Engine arr	23.41	00.20	23.45	00.50	01.32	00.25		02.41	03.30	03.28	04.38			0451				
Stock arr		00.20		22.43	22.43		-	23.41	03.28				23.10	03.28	22.46	05.46	23.36	05.53
Platform	-	2	-	4	3	M	-	1	2	2	4	-	6	M	7	1	A	6
LEEDS	00.15	00.48	01.00	01.05	01.42	01.50		03.25	03.43	04.00	05.00		05.25	05.30	05.47	06.00	06.12	06.20
Geldard Jn		00/50															06/14	
HOLBECK HL								03.28					05.27					06.22
HOLBECK HL	00/17		01/02	01/07	01/44	01/52		03.31	03/45	04/03	05/03		05.27	05/33	05/49	06/02		06.22
Copley Hill Loco			01.05							04.06	05.08							
Copley Hill CS						01.55								05.40				
Wortley W. Jcn	00/19							03/33	03/47					05/16	05/51			06/24
Armley Moor															05.52			06.27
Bramley															05.57			06.31
Stanningley	00/25							03/40	03/53					05/28	P			06/34
Laisterdyke	00/29							03/43	03/56					05/33	06.08			06/39
BRADFORD								04.01						05.38	06.13			06.44
Wortley S. Jcn				01/09	01/46								05/29			06/04		
Ardsley													05.37			06.11		
Ardsley				01.17	01/53								05.37			06.11		
Lofthouse N. Jcn				01/20	01/56								05/39			06/13		
Lofthouse				01.21	01/57													
WAKEFIELD (W)				01.25														
WAKEFIELD (W)				01.50	01/59													
Sandal				K	02/01		K											
Hare Park Jcn				02/05			02/20											
Fitzwilliam																		
Hemsworth																		
South Elmsall				02/17			02/33											
Adwick Jcn				02/23			02/39											
Carcroft																		
Bentley Crossing				02/27			02/43											
DONCASTER				02.30			02.46											
Destination	L. Moor	Leeds C		March	Sheffield		March	M'ter					Castleford			Castleford	Horsforth	
Route		Kirkgate		Kirkgate									Ardsley					

3DMU = 3-CAR Metro-Cammell diesel unit. K = Routed via Wakefield Kirkgate. P = Routed via Pudsey Greenside

WORKING TIMETABLE : DONCASTER/BRADFORD - LEEDS CENTRAL (1957/8)

DOWN

	473	475	153	403	477	5519	961	969	479		483	3018	346	405	5549	5521		495
Train	06.28	04.20	06.37			06.32								07.08	07.30	07.25		
From	Low Moor	Sheffield	Castleford			Harrogate								Castleford	Horsforth	Harrogate		
Route												Kirkgate	Batley					
Class	Pass	Pass	Pass	Pass	Pass	Pass	Light	Light	Pass	Light	Pass	Pass	Pass	Pass	Pass	Pass	Light	Pass
Engine	3DMU	5MT	B1	DMU	DMU	DMU	A3	A1	DMU	J50	DMU	B1	DMU	3DMU	DMU	DMU	B1	3DMU
Diagram		SPT1	CH29				DR14	CH1		CH74		DR77					DR80	
DONCASTER			05.25									06.20						
Bentley Crossing			05/28									06/23						
Carcroft												06.27						
Adwick Jcn			05/33									06/29						
South Elmsall			05.41									06.35						
Hemsworth			05.50									06.42						
Fitzwilliam												06.46						
Hare Park Jcn			06/02									06/56						
Sandal			06/05									K						
WAKEFIELD (W)			06.07									07.08						
WAKEFIELD (W)			06.21									07.11	07.14					
Lofthouse			06/26									07/17	(To					
Lofthouse N. Jcn			06/27	06/50								07/18	Brad	07/21				
Ardsley			06.31	06.54								07.21	ford	07.25				
Ardsley			06.33	06.54								07.22		07.25				
Wortley S. Jcn			06/44	07/00								07/28		07/32				
BRADFORD	06.19				06.40				06.50		07.02							07.45
Laisterdyke	06.26	06.36			06.47				06.57		07.09							07.52
Stanningley	P	06.41			P				07.02		P							07.57
Bramley	06.37				06.58				07.05		07.20							08.00
Armley Moor	06.41				07.02				07.09		07.24							08.04
Wortley W. Jcn	06/42	06/47			07/03				07/10		07/25							08/05
Copley Hill CS																		
Copley Hill Loco							07.00	07.02		07.10							07.55	
HOLBECK HL	06.43		06.46	07.02	07.04				07.12		07.27	07.30		07.34				08.07
HOLBECK HL	06.44	06/49	06.51	07.03	07.04	07/05	07/07		07.12	07/15	07.27	07.31		07.34			08/00	08.07
Geldard Jn						07/07									07/38	07/58		
LEEDS	06.46	06.51	06.53	07.05	07.07	07.09	07.10	07.12	07.14	07.20	07.29	07.33		07.36	07.40	08.00	08.05	08.09
Platform	7	2	1	7	3	3	4	5	6	1	6	3	-	7	7	6	3	5
Train works	07.00	07.55	07.45	07.17	07.22	07.15			07.40		07.36	08.22		08.18	07.43	08.06		08.15
Engine works	-	07.55	07.47	-			07.30	07.50		07.45		08.00					08.22	

WORKING TIMETABLE : LEEDS CENTRAL - BRADFORD/DONCASTER (1957/8)

UP

	3014	275	486	3077	5548	490	5584	1592	492	961	961		496	279	1586	498	153	
Train		06.10							07.05			07.12						
From		Bradford							Bradford			Bradford						
Class	ECS	Pass	Pcls	Pass	ECS	Pass	Pass	Pass	Pass	XP	XP	Light	Pass	Pass	Pass	Pass	ECS	Light
Engine	J50	DMU	B1	DMU	3DMU	3DMU	DMU	DMU	DMU	B1	A3	J50	DMU	DMU	DMU	3DMU	J50	B1
Diagram	CH74		CH71							BJ75	DR14	CH10G					CH74	CH29
Engine arr	04.25	04.45	-	-	-	-	-	-	-	07.10	05.37	-	-	-			07.20	06.53
Stock arr	04.38	04.48	05.46	06.46	06.40	07.09	07.05	07.07			05.37		07.29		07.14	07.40		06.53
Platform	3	-	2	1	7	6	3	7	3	-	4	4	6	-	6	7	1	1
LEEDS	06.22		06.28	06.40	07.00	07.13	07.15	07.17	07.22	07.30	07.32	07.36	07.40			07.43	07.45	07.47
Geldard Jn					07/02		07/17											
HOLBECK HL			06.30	06.42				07.19	07.24									
HOLBECK HL	06/25		06.38	06.44		07/15		07/19	07.24	07/32	07/35	07/38	07/42			07/45	07/48	07/49
Copley Hill Loco											07/40							
Copley Hill CS	06.30																07/52	
Wortley W. Jcn			06/40			07/17			07/26				07/40			07/46		
Armley Moor						07.18			07.29							07.48		
Bramley			06.48			07.23			07.34							07.53		
Stanningley			P			07.26			P				P					
Laisterdyke			07.18			07.30			07.44				07/51			08.04		
BRADFORD			07.23			07.36			07.49				07.56			08.09		
Wortley S. Jcn				06/46				07/21			07/34			07/44				
Ardsley				06.54				07.29						07.51				
Ardsley				06.55				07.29		07/32	07/40			07.51				
Lofthouse N. Jcn				06/58				07/31		07/35	07/43			07/53				
Lofthouse				07.00						07/36	07/44							
WAKEFIELD (W)		06.47		07.04						07.39	07.46			07.54				
WAKEFIELD (W)				07.12						(07.51)	07.51							
Sandal				07.16							07/54							
Hare Park Jcn				07/19							07/57							
Fitzwilliam				07.29														
Hemsworth				07.33														
South Elmsall				07.39							08/07							
Adwick Jcn				07/45							08/13							
Carcroft				07.47														
Bentley Crossing				07/53							08/17							
DONCASTER				07.56							08.20							
Destination				Doncaster	Horsforth	Bradford	Knares	Castleford	Bradford	Combine	KX		Bradford	Castleford				
Route		Batley								Tingley				Batley				

3DMU = 3-CAR Metro-Cammell diesel unit.. K = Routed via Wakefield Kirkgate. P = Routed via Pudsey Greenside.

WORKING TIMETABLE : DONCASTER/BRADFORD - LEEDS CENTRAL (1957/8)

DOWN

	—	407	126	168	497	5586	409	501	3022	352	411	5523	503	5550	3024	936	3024	356
Train	07.41						08.05	08.12		08.17	08.07					04.00	07.50	
From	Castleford						Castleford	Low Moor		Castleford	Knares					KX	Doncaster	
Route			Batley												Kirkgate	Kirkgate	Batley	
Class	Light	Pass	Pass	Pass	Pass	Pass	Pass	Pass	Pass	Pass	Pass	Pass	Pass	Pass	Pcls	XP	Pcls	Pass
No.		407	126	168	497	5586	409	501	3022	352	411	5523	503	5550	3024	936	3024	356
Engine	N1	DMU	DMU	DMU	DMU	DMU	DMU	4MTT	B1	N1	DMU	DMU	3DMU	DMU	B1	A4	B1	DMU
Diagram	CH75							LM14	CH25	AY2					DR89	KX1	DR89	
DONCASTER									07.33						07.50	08.10		
Bentley Crossing									07/36						07/53	08/13		
Carcroft									07.40									
Adwick Jcn									07/42						07/59	08/19		
South Elmsall									07.48						08.04	08.22		
Hemsworth									07.55						08.12		08.32	
Fitzwilliam									07.59									
Hare Park Jcn									08/09						08/34	08/44		
Sandal									08.12								K	
WAKEFIELD (W)									08.16						08.39			
WAKEFIELD (W)			07.56	08.09					08.18	08.26						08.44		09.10
Lofthouse			08.02	(To					08.24	(To						08.48		(To
Lofthouse N. Jcn		07/55	08/03	Brad			08/17		08/25	Batley)	08/29					08/49		Brad
Ardsley		07.59		ford)			08.21		08.28		08.33							ford)
Ardsley		08.00	08/06				08.21		08.29		08.33					08/53		
Wortley S. Jcn		08.09	08/13				08/28		08/35		08/40					08/59		
BRADFORD						07.53	08.05						08.20	08.35				
Laisterdyke						08.00	08/11						08.27	08/41				
Stanningley						P	08/14	08.22					P	08.45				
Bramley						08.11							08.38					
Armley Moor						08.15							08.42					
Wortley W. Jcn						08/16	08/19	08/30					08/44	08/49				
Copley Hill CS																		
Copley Hill Loco	08.00																	
HOLBECK HL		08.11	08.15		08.18				08.30				08.37					09.01
HOLBECK HL	08/05	08.12	08.16		08.18	08/21	08.30	08/32	08.39		08.42		08.46	08/51		09.03		
Geldard Jn												08/44						
LEEDS	08.10	08.14	08.18		08.20	08.23	08.32	08.34	08.41		08.44	08.46	08.48	08.53		09.06		
Platform	-	6	1	-	1	7	7	2	4	-	7	5	6	5	-	5	-	-
Train works		12.17	08.37		08.37	08.28	10.21	08.55	10.09		09.22	08.49	09.01	08.57		09.30		
Engine works	09.30							09.45	09.05							09.31		

WORKING TIMETABLE : LEEDS CENTRAL - BRADFORD/DONCASTER (1957/8)

UP

	969	969	500	—	—	5521	508	1594	285	3083	5586	514	5523	530	5550	534	283	—
Train	07.19					07.25			08.00		08.05		08.07		08.35		09.02	
From	Bradford					Harrogate			Bradford		Bradford		Knares		Bradford		Batley	
Class	XP	XP	XP	Light	Gas	Pass	Pass	Pass	Pass	Pass	Pass	Pass	Pass	XP	Pass	Pass	Pcls	Light
No.	969	969	500	-	-	5521	508	1594	285	3083	5586	514	5523	530	5550	534	283	-
Engine	B1	A1	5MT	N1	B1	DMU	3DMU	DMU	DMU	B1	DMU	DMU	DMU	4MTT	DMU	3DMU	N1	B1
Diagram	BJ76	CH1	SPT1	CH72	DR77					DR80				LM17			AY2	CH25
Engine arr		07.12	06.51	04.51	07.33	-	-	-		08.15		-		04.48				08.41
Stock arr		04.51	06.51			08.00	08.09	07.36		07.33	08.23	08.18/20	08.46	08.34	08.53	08.48		
Platform	-	5	2	5	-	6	5	7	-	3	7	1	5	2	5	6	-	4
LEEDS	07.50	07.55	07.57	08.00		08.06	08.15	08.18		08.22	08.28	08.37	08.49	08.55	08.57	09.01		09.05
Geldard Jn											08/30				08/59			
HOLBECK HL	07.53	07.57					08.17			08.24								
HOLBECK HL	07.54	07.58	08/00	08/02		08/08	08.18	08/20		08.26		08/39	08/51	08/57		09/03		09/07
Copley Hill Loco				08.05														09.10
Copley Hill CS					08.05													
Wortley W. Jcn			08/00			08/10	08/20					08/41	08/53	08/59		09/05		
Armley Moor						08.11	08.22									09.06		
Bramley						08.16	08.26									09.11		
Stanningley			08.07			08.19	P					08.47	08.59	09.05		P		
Laisterdyke			08/11			08/23	08.37					08/51	09/03	09/09		09.22		
BRADFORD						08.28	08.42					08.56	09.08			09.27		
Wortley S. Jcn		07/56							08/22	08/28								
Ardsley		08.03							08.29	08.37								
Lofthouse N. Jcn		08/06							08/31	08/40								
Lofthouse		08/07								08.42								
WAKEFIELD (W)	08.04	08.11							08.38	08.46							09.26	
WAKEFIELD (W)	(08.16)	08.16								08.52								
Sandal		08/19								K								
Hare Park Jcn		08/21								09/08								
Fitzwilliam										09.18								
Hemsworth										09.22								
South Elmsall		08/32								09.28								
Adwick Jcn		08/41								09/34								
Carcroft										09.36								
Bentley Crossing		08/45								09/40								
DONCASTER		08.48								09.45								
Destination	Combine	KX	M'ter				Castleford		Doncaster	Harrogate			Liverpool		Harrogate			
Route	Batley								Batley	Kirkgate								

3DMU = 3-CAR Metro-Cammell diesel unit.. K = Routed via Wakefield Kirkgate. P = Routed via Pudsey Greenside

WORKING TIMETABLE : DONCASTER/BRADFORD - LEEDS CENTRAL (1957/8)

DOWN

Train	08.17	07.50			08.10	09.00			07.00	09.33	07.50		07.50			09.39	07.50	
From	Sow Bge	Doncaster			Bradford	Harrogate			Southport	Harrogate			Doncaster			Castleford	Doncaster	
Route		Kirkgate											Kirkgate			Batley	Kirkgate	
Class	ECS	Pass	Pcls	Pcls	Pass	Pcls	Light	Pass	Pass	Light	Pass	XP	Pass	Pcls	Pcls	Pass	Pcls	XP
No.	971	511	3024	507	517	507	3115	5525	513	971	5552	7	5551	3024	344	413	3024	525
Engine	J50	5MT	B1	B1	3DMU	B1	B1	DMU	DMU	A4	3DMU	4MTT	DMU	B1	B1	DMU	B1	DMU
Diagram	CH74	NH17	DR89	CH71		CH71	DR77			KX39		SB6		DR89	AY1		DR89	
DONCASTER																		
Bentley Crossing																		
Carcroft																		
Adwick Jcn																		
South Elmsall																		
Hemsworth																		
Fitzwilliam																		
Hare Park Jcn																		
Sandal		K																
WAKEFIELD (W)		09.13									(09.13)							
WAKEFIELD (W)		(09.30)									09.30		09.45					
Lofthouse											09.34		*(To*					
Lofthouse N. Jcn											09.35		*Brad*	09.52				
Ardsley											09.40		*ford)*	09.56				
Ardsley											09.50		09.56					
Wortley S. Jcn											09.59		10/02					
BRADFORD				08.10	09.05			09.11			09.31							10.05
Laisterdyke		08.58		08.43	09/11			09.18			09.37	09.46						10/11
Stanningley		09.03		P	09/14						09.42							10/14
Bramley				09.08				09.29										
Armley Moor				09.13				09.33										
Wortley W. Jcn		09/08		09/14	09/17			09/34			09/45	09/54						10/17
Copley Hill CS	09.03																	
Copley Hill Loco							09.15			09.30								
HOLBECK HL				09.16		(09.16)											(10.01)	
HOLBECK HL	09/08	09/10		(09/22)	09/19	09.22	09/20	09/32	09/35		09/47	09/56	(10/13)			10/04	10.13	10/19
Geldard Jn								09/32					09/59					
LEEDS	09.10	09.12			09.21	09.24	09.25	09.34	09.38	09.40	09.49	09.58	10.01			10.06	10.15	10.21
Platform	3	2	-	-	6	1	4	7	5	3	7	2	7	-	-	6	3	6
Train works	10.00	09.45		09.42		12.22		09.38	10.18		09.57	10.55	10.07			11.36	11.12	10.38
Engine works	10.02	09.50		09.43		10.09			10.00		10.55						11.33	

WORKING TIMETABLE : LEEDS CENTRAL - BRADFORD/DONCASTER (1957/8)

UP

Train				09.08	09.00						09.31	09.35		09.33				10.11
From				Bradford	Harrogate						Bradford	Bradford		Harrogate				Bradford
Class	Pass	ECS	Light	Pass	Pass	Pass	Light	ECS	Light	Pass	XP	XP	XP	Pass	Pass	Pass	XP	Pass
No.	1596	936	-		5525	536	-	511	-	5552	971	971	5551	3115	544	1598	546	287
Engine	DMU	N1	A4	DMU	DMU	3DMU	B1	4MTT	5MT	3DMU	B1	A4	DMU	B1	DMU	DMU	DMU	DMU
Diagram		CH75	KX1				CH71	LM14	NH17		AY4	KX39		DR77				
Engine arr		08.10	09.06					09.24	09.12		09.40	09.25						
Stock arr	08.44	09.06			09.34	09.21		09.12		09.49	09.10	10.01		08.41	09.38	08.32	10.21	
Platform	7	5	5	-	7	6	1	2	2	7	-	3	7	4	5	7	6	-
LEEDS	09.22	09.30	09.31		09.38	09.42	09.43	09.45	09.50	09.57		10.00	10.07	10.09	10.18	10.21	10.38	
Geldard Jn										09/59								
HOLBECK HL																10.20		
HOLBECK HL	09/24	09/33	09/34		09/40	09/44	09/46	09/47	09/53			10/02	10/09	10/11	10.21	10/23	10/40	
Copley Hill Loco			09.40				09.50		09.57									
Copley Hill CS		09.40																
Wortley W. Jcn					09/42	09/45		09/49				10/11			10/23		10/42	
Armley Moor						09.47									10.25			
Bramley						09.52									10.29			
Stanningley					09.48	P		09/58				10/16			P		10/47	
Laisterdyke					09/52	10.04		10/02				10/21			10.40		10/51	
BRADFORD					09.57	10.09						10.25			10.45		10.55	
Wortley S. Jcn	09/26											10.04			10/13		10/25	
Ardsley	09.34																10.32	
Ardsley	09.34											10/02	10/10	10/20			10.32	
Lofthouse N. Jcn	09/36											10/04	10/12	10/22		10/34		
Lofthouse												10/05	10/13	10/23				
WAKEFIELD (W)					09.46							10/09	10/16	10/27				10.49
WAKEFIELD (W)												(10.21)	10.21	10.29				
Sandal													10/24	10/32				
Hare Park Jcn													10/26	10/34				
Fitzwilliam																		
Hemsworth																		
South Elmsall													10/37	10/48				
Adwick Jcn													10/43	10/52				
Carcroft																		
Bentley Crossing													10/45	10/57				
DONCASTER													10/48	11.01				
Destination	Castleford							L. Moor		Ripon	Combine	KX		Doncaster		Castleford		Batley
Route			Batley								Tingley							

3DMU = 3-CAR Metro-Cammell diesel unit.   K = Routed via Wakefield Kirkgate.   P = Routed via Pudsey Greenside.

WORKING TIMETABLE : DONCASTER/BRADFORD - LEEDS CENTRAL (1957/8)

DOWN

Train	09.06					10.07		08.32		10.37						08.00		
From	Doncaster					Harrogate		Liverpool		Castleford		Turn				KX		
Route	Kirkgate		Batley		Batley						Batley							
Class	Pass	Light	Pass	Pull	Pcls	Pull	Light	Pass	XP	Pass	Pass	Light	XP	Pass	ECS	XP	Light	XP
No.	3026	19	396	19	362	19	3024	531	535	415	358		541	539	35	948	302	5556
Engine	DMU	A1	DMU	B1	N1	BR 4MTT	N1	DMU	2MTT	DMU	DMU	B1	DMU	DMU	N1	A4	N1	DMU
Diagram		CH2		BJ76	AY2	NE	CH75		LM8			BJ76			CH72	KX3	CH75	
DONCASTER	09.06														10.55			
Bentley Crossing	09.09														10/58			
Carcroft	09.13																	
Adwick Jcn	09/15														11/04			
South Elmsall	09.21														11/07			
Hemsworth	09.28																	
Fitzwilliam	09.32																	
Hare Park Jcn	09/42														11/19			
Sandal	K																	
WAKEFIELD (W)	09.54														11.24			
WAKEFIELD (W)	09.58	10.05		10.30							11.07				11.26			
Lofthouse	10.04	(To		(To								(To			10/31			
Lofthouse N. Jcn	10/05	Brad		Batley)						10/51		Brad			10/32			
Ardsley	10.08	ford)								10.55		ford)						
Ardsley	10.09									10.55					11.35			
Wortley S. Jcn	10/17									11/01					11/40			
BRADFORD				10.15				10.35					11.05	11.09				11.35
Laisterdyke				10/21				10/41	10/47				11/11	11.16				11/41
Stanningley				10/25				10.46	10/51				11/14	P				11/44
Bramley														11.27				
Armley Moor														11.31				
Wortley W. Jcn				10.28				10/49	10/55				11/17	11/32				11/47
Copley Hill CS															11.30			
Copley Hill Loco		10.15					10.31									11.35		
HOLBECK HL	10.19								10.57					11.34				
HOLBECK HL	10.21	10/20		10.30			10/36	10/51	10.59	11.03	11.07	11/19	11.34	11.36	11/36	11/42	11/40	11/49
Geldard Jn					10/35													
LEEDS	10.23	10.25		10.32		10.37	10.41	10.53	11.01	11.05		11.10	11.21	11.36	11.39	11.44	11.45	11.51
Platform	7	M	-	4	-	5	3	7	2	6	-	M	5	3	5	4	M	7
Train works	11.40			10.45		10.45		11.06	11.33	11.18			12.36	12.15	12.30	12.00		11.57
Engine works		10.45		10.47		10.50	11.12		11.45			11.50			12.46	12.02	12.19	

WORKING TIMETABLE : LEEDS CENTRAL - BRADFORD/DONCASTER (1957/8)

UP

Train								11.15		08.00	11.35		08.00			08.00		11.10
From								Bradford		KX	Bradford		KX			KX		Ripon
Class	Pullman	Light	Light	XP	Pass	ECS	Pass	ECS	XP	Pass	Pass	Light	XP	Pass	Light	ECS	Light	Pass
No.	19			548	552	3024	1600	535	556	301	3117	1014	948	5556		948		5555
Engine	A1	B1	BR 4MTT	4MTT	DMU	N1	DMU	B1	DMU	DMU	DMU	2MTT	B1	DMU	B1	J50	A4	3DMU
Diagram	CH2	BJ76	NE	SB6		CH75		DR89				LM8	BJ76		DR89	CH74	KX3	
Engine arr	10.25	10.32	10.37	09.58		10.15			10.15				11.01	11.10		09.10	11.44	
Stock arr	10.32/7			09.58	10.53	10.15	11.05	11.01	10.06		10.23		11.44	11.51		11.44		11.59
Platform	5	4	5	2	7	3	6	2	6	-	7	2	4	7	-	4	4	6
LEEDS	10.45	10.47	10.50	10.55	11.06	11.12	11.18	11.33	11.36		11.40	11.45	11.50	11.57		12.00	12.02	12.06
Geldard Jn		10/52												11/59				
HOLBECK HL				10.57							11.42							
HOLBECK HL	10/47	10/50		10.58	11.08	11/15	11/20	11/36	11.38		11.45	11.47	11/52			12.03	12.05	12.08
Copley Hill Loco															12.01		12.10	
Copley Hill CS						11.19		11.40								12.07		
Wortley W. Jcn				11/00	11.12				11/40			11/49	11/54					12/10
Armley Moor																		
Bramley																		
Stanningley				11/10	11.16				11/45			11/55	11/59					12.16
Laisterdyke				11/13	11/20				11/49			12/00	12/03					12.21
BRADFORD					11.25				11.53				12.08					12.26
Wortley S. Jcn	10/49						11/22				11/47					12/05		
Ardsley							11.29				11.55							
Ardsley	10.55						11.29				11.56					12/12		
Lofthouse N. Jcn	10/58						11/31				11/59					12/15		
Lofthouse	10.59										12.01					12/16		
WAKEFIELD (W)	11.01									11.53	12.05							
WAKEFIELD (W)	11.03										12.11					12/20		
Sandal	11/06										12/15					12/23		
Hare Park Jcn	11/08										12/18					12/26		
Fitzwilliam											12.28							
Hemsworth											12.32							
South Elmsall	11/19										12.38					13/39		
Adwick Jcn	11/25										12/44					13/46		
Carcroft											12.46							
Bentley Crossing	11/29										12/50					13/52		
DONCASTER	11.32										12.55					13/55		
Destination	KX	Turn	City	L'pool			Castleford				Doncaster	L. Moor	Bradford	Harrogate		Carr Loco		Bradford
Route											Batley							

3DMU = 3-CAR Metro-Cammell diesel unit. K = Routed via Wakefield Kirkgate. P = Routed via Pudsey Greenside

B1 4-6-0's handled the majority of stopping trains to and from Doncaster but larger engines made occasional appearances, especially after works visits to Doncaster. A1 60156 'Great Central' of Copley Hill runs into Leeds Central with a stopping train from Doncaster on 24th October 1960. (KRM/J. Marshall)

The distinctive J50 0-6-0 tanks of 1922 were a class 102-engines strong most of which had been allocated to the northern sections of the Great Northern and Great Central, principally engaged in shunting the larger marshalling yards. Other than a handful based on the Great Eastern for shunting Goodmayes yard, the class were not much seen in the South until 1951 when 27 examples were sent to Hornsey as being the only suitable replacements for the J52 0-6-0's which worked the widened lines goods traffic between Ferme Park and the Southern. Rather surprisingly, since the class was essentially for goods use, J50's were employed on station pilot duties at Leeds Central and could be seen at most times of the day shunting stock around the station or hauling trains of empty coaches to and from Copley Hill sidings. 68984 pauses in its duties whilst the Queen of Scots Pullman changes direction in the background. (KRM/J. Marshall)

Overshadowed by a large fleet of Pacifics, the B1 4-6-0's never had the same opportunities for express running on ex-LNER lines that their equivalents on the London Midland had and one of the unanswered questions of railway history was how the B1's would have fared had they had to handle the traffic worked by Black Fives on the ex-LNW and ex-Midland lines. The class were a familiar sight at Leeds Central and were diagrammed to work many of the stopping trains to Doncaster. 61250 'A. Harold Bibby' prepares to leave Leeds for Copley Hill carriage sidings with the empty stock of a Doncaster service. (KRM/J. Marshall)

For sheer dramatic effect, there were few sights that could equal the arrival of a long-distance express at a main line terminus as a Pacific wound its way slowly and regally along the platform to come to an almost imperceptible halt a few feet short of the stops. A1 60134 'Foxhunter' of Copley Hill stands in platform 4 shortly after arriving with an express from Kings Cross. (KRM/J. Marshall)

WORKING TIMETABLE : DONCASTER/BRADFORD - LEEDS CENTRAL (1957/8)

DOWN

No.	35	5555	582	302	329	461	35	382	5588	3030	574	557	5578	5557	40	417	40	390
Train		11.10		09.23	09.40	11.41	11.45							12.36	09.20	12.46	09.20	
From		Ripon		Cleethorpe	Liverpool	Castleford	Harrogate							Harrogate	KX	Castleford	KX	
Route		Harrogate						Batley									Tingley	Batley
Class	Light	Pass	Light	XP	XP	Pass	XP	Pass	Pass	Pass	ECS	Pass	XP	Pass	XP	Pass	XP	Pass
Engine	A4	3DMU	B1	B1	4MTT	DMU	BR4MTT	DMU	DMU	B1	5MT	DMU	3DMU	DMU	A1	DMU	B1	DMU
Diagram	KX1		AY1	IMM54	LM17		NE			DR78	NH17				CH32		AY5	
DONCASTER										11.15					12.15			
Bentley Crossing										11/18					12/18			
Carcroft										11.22								
Adwick Jcn				11/08						11/24					12/24			
South Elmsall				11.16						11.30					12/27			
Hemsworth										11/37								
Fitzwilliam										11/41								
Hare Park Jcn				11/32						11/51					12/39			
Sandal										11/54					12/41			
WAKEFIELD (W)				11.38						11.58					12.44			(12.44)
WAKEFIELD (W)				11.40				12.09		12.06					12.49	12.55		13.05
Lofthouse				11/45				(To		12.12					12/54	13/00		(To
Lofthouse N. Jcn				11/46		11/54				12/13					12/55	12/59	13/01	
Ardsley						11.58				12.16						13.03		Brad
Ardsley				11.50						12.18					12.58	13.03	13/08	
Wortley S. Jcn				11/59		12/04				12/25					13/03	13/09		ford)
BRADFORD			11.40						12.05		12.17		12.35					
Laisterdyke			11/45		11/55				12/11		12.24		12.41					
Stanningley			11/50		11/59				12.15		P		12.44					
Bramley											12.35	12.39						
Armley Moor																		
Wortley W. Jcn			11/55		12/02				12/19			12/40	12/47					
Copley Hill CS											12.28							
Copley Hill Loco	11.45																	
HOLBECK HL											12.27	12.42						
HOLBECK HL	11.50		11/57	12/01	12/04	12/06			12/21	12.30	12/32	12.42	12/49		13/05	13/11		
Geldard Jn		11/57					12/13							13/00				
LEEDS	11.55	11.59	12.00	12.03	12.06	12.08	12.15		12.23	12.32	12.35	12.44	12.51	13.02	13.07	13.13		
Platform	5	6	1	3	2	6	5	-	6	3	1	7	6	6	4	7	-	-
Train works		12.06		12.19		13.55	12.15	12.30	12.28	12.46	12.55	13.22	12.57	13.06	15.35	13.20		
Engine works	12.30		12.22	O/R	12.55		12.38			13.00	13.05				13.50			

WORKING TIMETABLE : LEEDS CENTRAL - BRADFORD/DONCASTER (1957/8)

UP

No.	568	1602	302	582	5588	35	35	570	321		3030		574	5578			5557	1606
Train						12.05	12.08			12.20							12.36	
From						Bradford	Bradford			Bradford							Harrogate	
Class	Pass	Pass	ECS	Pcls	Pass	XP	XP	Pass	Pass	Light	ECS	Light	XP	Pass	Light	Light	Pass	Pass
Engine	DMU	DMU	N1	B1	DMU	B1	A4	DMU	DMU	BR4MTT	N1	B1	4MTT	3DMU	B1	5MT	DMU	DMU
Diagram			CH75	AY1		BJ75	KX1			NE	CH72	Imm 54	LM17		DR78	NH17		
Engine arr						11.45	12.00			11.55	11.39		12.15	12.06	12.32	12.35		
Stock arr	11.36/12.08	08.14	12.03	09.24	12.23		12.15	11.21			12.32		12.35	12.51			13.02	13.13
Platform	6	7	3	1	6	-	5	7	-	5	3	-	1	6	3	1	6	7
LEEDS	12.15	12.17	12.19	12.22	12.28		12.30	12.36		12.38	12.46		12.55	12.57	13.00	13.05	13.06	13.20
Geldard Jn							12/30			12/40				12/59				
HOLBECK HL	12.17	12.19		12.24														
HOLBECK HL	12.18	12.19	12/22	12.28			12/32	12/38			12/49		12/57		13/03	13/08	13/08	13/22
Copley Hill Loco										12.40					13.10			
Copley Hill CS			12.26								12.55							
Wortley W. Jcn	12/20			12/30				12/40					12/59				13/10	
Armley Moor	12.22			12.33														
Bramley	12.26			12.38														
Stanningley	P			P				12.46					13/04				13.16	
Laisterdyke	12.37			12/59				12/50					13/08				13/20	
BRADFORD	12.42			13.41				12.55									13.25	
Wortley S. Jcn		12/21					12/34						12/45					13/24
Ardsley		12.29																13.31
Ardsley		12.29				12/32	12/40						12/52					13.31
Lofthouse N. Jcn		12/31				12/35	12/43						12/55					13/33
Lofthouse						12/36	12/44						12/56					
WAKEFIELD (W)						12.39	12.46		12.58									
WAKEFIELD (W)					(12.51)	12.51							13/01					
Sandal						12/54							13/05					
Hare Park Jcn						12/56							13/09					
Fitzwilliam																		
Hemsworth																		
South Elmsall						13/07							13/24					
Adwick Jcn						13/13							13/30					
Carcroft																		
Bentley Crossing						13/16												
DONCASTER						13.20												
Destination	Bradford	Castleford		Bradford	Harrogate	Combine	KX		Batley		City		Imm	L'pool	Harrogate		Farnley Jn	Castleford
Route						Tingley												

3DMU = 3-CAR Metro-Cammell diesel unit..   K = Routed via Wakefield Kirkgate.   P = Routed via Pudsey Greenside.   O/R = On rear (trailing) of ECS

WORKING TIMETABLE : DONCASTER/BRADFORD - LEEDS CENTRAL (1957/8)

DOWN

Train				13.05	13.05					13.36	12.55	11.30	13.42				10.20	10.20
From				Low Moor	Harrogate					Harrogate	Doncaster	Liverpool	Castleford				KX	KX
Route														Batley				Tingley
Class	Pass	Pass	ECS	Light	Pass	ECS	XP	Light	Light	Pass	Pass	XP	Pass	Pass	Pass	Pass	XP	XP
No.	563	579	3143	1051	5527	948	5558	3143	-	5579	3048	583	465	386	585	589	952	952
Engine	DMU	DMU	J50	4MTT	DMU	B1	DMU	B1	B1	3DMU	B1	4MTT	DMU	DMU	DMU	DMU	A3	B1
Diagram			CH74	LM15		BJ76		CH29	DR78	DR71		LM11					DR4	AY4
DONCASTER											12.55						13.36	
Bentley Crossing											12/58						13/39	
Carcroft											13.02							
Adwick Jcn											13/04						13/45	
South Elmsall											13.10						13.48	
Hemsworth											13.17							
Fitzwilliam											13.21							
Hare Park Jcn											13/29						14/00	
Sandal											13/32						14/02	
WAKEFIELD (W)											13.35						14.05	
WAKEFIELD (W)											13.39		14.02				14.10	14.16
Lofthouse											13.45		(To				14/15	14/21
Lofthouse N. Jcn											13/46	13/55	Brad				14/16	14/22
Ardsley											13/49	13/59	ford)					
Ardsley											13.51	13.59					14/19	14/26
Wortley S. Jcn											13/59	14/06					14/24	(To
BRADFORD	12.49	13.05			13.20		13.35								13.52	14.05		Brad
Laisterdyke	12.56	13/11		13/18	13/27	13/41	13/44					13/53			13/59	14/11		ford)
Stanningley	P	13.15		13/23	13/31	13/44						13/57			P	14.15		
Bramley	13.07	13.18													14.10			
Armley Moor	13.11	13.22													14.14			
Wortley W. Jcn	13/12	13/23		13/29	13/38		13/48					14/01			14/15	14/19		
Copley Hill CS			13.23															
Copley Hill Loco								13.45	13.55									
HOLBECK HL											14.01	14.03			14.17			
HOLBECK HL	13/13	13/25	13/27	13/31		13/40	13/50	13/50	14/00		14.04	14.06	14/08		14.17	14/21	14/26	
Geldard Jn					13/37					14/02								
LEEDS	13.15	13.27	13.30	13.33	13.39	13.42	13.52	13.55	14.00	14.04	14.06	14.08	14.10		14.20	14.23	14.28	
Platform	6	7	3	2	7	M	6	3	M	6	5	2	6	-	7	6	3	-
Train works	13.40	13.36	14.04		14.12	13.57				14.08	15.40	15.55	14.15		14.43	14.36	17.33	
Engine works			18.01	13.55		14.27		14.04	14.25		14.30	15.55					15.00	

WORKING TIMETABLE : LEEDS CENTRAL - BRADFORD/DONCASTER (1957/8)

UP

Train			14.10				13.35		13.36						14.35			
From			Bradford				Bradford		Harrogate						Bradford			
Class	Pass	XP	Pass	Pass	Light	XP	Pass	Pass	Pass	Pass	Pass	Postal	Light	Light	XP	Pass	Pass	Light
No.	584	588	339	586	-	590	5558	3143	5579	592	1608	-	-	-	600	602	5560	-
Engine	DMU	DMU	DMU	DMU	A1	4MTT	DMU	B1	3DMU	DMU	DMU	B1	B1	B1	DMU	DMU	3DMU	A3
Diagram					CH32	LM15		CH29				DR78	BJ76	DR71				DR4
Engine arr					13.07	13.33		13.55				14.00	13.42	14.06				14.28
Stock arr	12.44	13.27		13.15		12.06	13.52	13.30	14.04	13.39	14.10	13.42			14.23	14.20	14.51	
Platform	7	7	-	6	4	2	6	3	6	7	6	M	M	5	6	7	6	3
LEEDS	13.22	13.36		13.40	13.50	13.55	13.57	14.04	14.08	14.12	14.15	14.25	14.27	14.30	14.36	14.43	14.57	15.00
Geldard Jn							13/59										14/59	
HOLBECK HL				13.42			13.57		14.06									
HOLBECK HL	13/24	13/38		13/43	13/52	13.58		14.07	14/10	14/14	14/17	14/27	14/29	14/33	14/38	14/45		15/03
Copley Hill Loco					13.55									14.37				15/07
Copley Hill CS																		
Wortley W. Jcn	13/26	13/40		13/45		14/00			14/12	14/16				14/31		14/40	14/47	
Armley Moor				13.47						14.17							14.48	
Bramley	13.30			13.51						14.22							14.53	
Stanningley	P	13/45		P		14/07			14.18	P				14/37	14/45	P		
Laisterdyke	13.42	13/49		14.02		14/11			14/22	14/34				14/41	14/50	15.04		
BRADFORD	13.47	13.53		14.07					14.27	14.39					14.54	15.09		
Wortley S. Jcn							14/09					14/19	14/29					
Ardsley							14.17					14.26						
Ardsley							14.18					14.26						
Lofthouse N. Jcn							14/21					14/28						
Lofthouse							14.23											
WAKEFIELD (W)				14.48			14.27											
WAKEFIELD (W)							14.30											
Sandal							K											
Hare Park Jcn							14/44											
Fitzwilliam							14.54											
Hemsworth							14.58											
South Elmsall							15.04											
Adwick Jcn							15/10											
Carcroft							15.12											
Bentley Crossing							15/16											
DONCASTER							15.21											
Destination						L'pool	Harrogate	Doncaster				Castleford	Turn	Low Moor				Harrogate
Route				Batley				Kirkgate										

3DMU = 3-CAR Metro-Cammell diesel unit. K = Routed via Wakefield Kirkgate. P = Routed via Pudsey Greenside. O/R = On rear (trailing) of ECS

WORKING TIMETABLE : DONCASTER/BRADFORD - LEEDS CENTRAL (1957/8)

DOWN

Train		14.35					14.46	11.50				13.10		15.38	15.38	15.03		
From	N. Hill	Harrogate					Castleford	KX				Southport		Harrogate	Castleford	Doncaster		
Route							Westgate	Batley										
Class	Light	XP	Pass	Pass	Light	Light	Pass	Pull	Pass	XP	ECS	Pass	XP	XP	Pass	Pass	Pass	Light
No.	58	5560	5559	593	985	3155	421	58	204	597	439	599	57	5562	5561	423	3036	131
Engine	A3	3DMU	DMU	3DMU	A4	B1	DMU	A1	DMU	DMU	B1	DMU	4MTT	DMU	3DMU	DMU	DMU	A1
Diagram	NE				KX3	CH25		CH34			DR78		LM15					CH31
DONCASTER								14/38									15.03	
Bentley Crossing								14/40									15.06	
Carcroft																	15.10	
Adwick Jcn								14/45									15.12	
South Elmsall								14/48									15.18	
Hemsworth																	15.25	
Fitzwilliam																	15.29	
Hare Park Jcn								15/01									15.39	
Sandal								15/03									15.42	
WAKEFIELD (W)																	15.46	
WAKEFIELD (W)								15/05	15.07								15.50	
Lofthouse								15/09	(To								15.56	
Lofthouse N. Jcn						14/59		15/10	Brad							15/51	15/57	
Ardsley									ford)							15.55	16.00	
Ardsley								15/12								15.55	16.01	
Wortley S. Jcn						15/09		15/17								16/01	16/08	
BRADFORD		14.35		14.39						15.05		15.20		15.35				
Laisterdyke		14/41		14.46						15/11		15.27		15/35	15/42			
Stanningley		14/44		P						15/14		P		15.41	15/47			
Bramley				14.57								15.38						
Armley Moor				15.01								15.42						
Wortley W. Jcn		14/47		15/02						15/19		15/43		15/47	15/52			
Copley Hill CS											15.32							
Copley Hill Loco					15.00	15.02												16.07
HOLBECK HL								15.11						15.49		16.03	16.10	
HOLBECK HL		14/49		15/03	15/05	15/07	15.11			15/19	15/36	15/21	15/44	15.50	15/54	16.03	16.12	16/14
Geldard Jn	14/46		15/00													16/00		
LEEDS	14.48	14.51	15.02	15.05	15.08	15.10	15.13	15.21		15.23	15.39	15.46	15.52	15.56	16.02	16.05	16.14	16.17
Platform	M	6	7	6	4	5	7	3	-	6	3	6	1	7	5	7	5	2
Train works		14.57	15.07	15.14			16.46	15.29		15.37	16.13	16.10	17.11	15.59	16.06	16.18	19.32	
Engine works	15.29			15.35	15.40			15.30			17.16		17.55					16.36

WORKING TIMETABLE : LEEDS CENTRAL - BRADFORD/DONCASTER (1957/8)

UP

Train	14.35	13.55		11.50		15.13				15.17		15.35	15.28					11.00
From	Harrogate	Bradford		KX		Bradford				Bradford		Bradford	Harrogate					Glasgow
Class	XP	Pass	Pcls	Pull	Light	XP	XP	Pass	Pass	Pass	XP	Pass	Pass	Pass	XP	Pass	XP	Pullman
No.	5559	1610	341	58	-	985	985	608	349	3155	616	5562	5561	620	439	1612	628	131
Engine	DMU	3DMU	B1	A3	A1	B1	A4	DMU	DMU	B1	4MTT	DMU	3DMU	DMU	B1	DMU	DMU	A1
Diagram		AY1	NE	CH34	BJ77	KX3				CH25	LM11				CH26			CH31
Engine arr				14.48	15.21		15.08			15.10	14.08				O/R			16.17
Stock arr	15.02	15.05		15.21			13.07	15.23		14.06	14.08	15.56	16.02	15.46	15.39	16.05	16.23	16.25
Platform	7	6	-	3	3	-	4	6	-	5	2	7	5	6	3	7	6	2
LEEDS	15.07	15.14	15.29	15.30		15.35	15.37			15.40	15.55	15.59	16.06	16.10	16.13	16.18	16.32	16.36
Geldard Jn		15/31										16/01						
HOLBECK HL										15.42	15.57			16.12		16.20		
HOLBECK HL	15/09	15/15		15/33		15/37	15/39			15/43	15.58		16/08	16.12	16/15	16.20	16/34	16/38
Copley Hill Loco					15.37													
Copley Hill CS																		
Wortley W. Jcn	15/11						15/41				16/00		16/10	16/14		16/36		
Armley Moor														16.17				
Bramley														16.21				
Stanningley	15/16						15.47				16/05		16.16	P		16/41		
Laisterdyke	15/24						15/51				16/10		16/20	16.32		16/45		
BRADFORD	15.28						15.56						16.25	16.37		16.49		
Wortley S. Jcn		15/18				15/39				15/45					16/17		16/22	16/40
Ardsley		15.25								15.53					16.30			
Ardsley		15.25				15/37		15/45		15.54					16/24		16.30	16/46
Lofthouse N. Jcn		15/27				15/39		15/47		15/57					16/27		16/32	16/48
Lofthouse						15/40		15/48		15.59					16/28			16/49
WAKEFIELD (W)			15.29			15.44		15.51	15.59	16.03					16.31			
WAKEFIELD (W)						(15.56)		16.07		16.07					16.33			16/51
Sandal						15/59				16/10					16/36			16/54
Hare Park Jcn						16/01				16/12					16/38			16/56
Fitzwilliam										16.23								
Hemsworth										16.27								
South Elmsall						16/12				16/33					16.54			17/06
Adwick Jcn						16/18				16/39					17/01			17/12
Carcroft										16.41								
Bentley Crossing						16/21				16/45								17/14
DONCASTER						16.25				16.48								17.17
Destination		Castleford	Glasgow			Combine	KX			Doncaster	L'pool	Harrogate			Cleethorpe	Castleford		KX
Route		Batley	Harrogate			Tingley												

3DMU = 3-CAR Metro-Cammell diesel unit. K = Routed via Wakefield Kirkgate. P = Routed via Pudsey Greenside. O/R = On rear (trailing) of ECS

WORKING TIMETABLE : DONCASTER/BRADFORD - LEEDS CENTRAL (1957/8)

DOWN

Train From				11.00 Glasgow	16.11 Low Moor		16.25 Castleford	City		16.33 Harrogate			13.20 KX	13.20 KX	14.30 Liverpool		17.00 Kirkgate	
Route			Batley	Harrogate									Tingley				Westgate	
Class	ECS	Pass	Pass	Pull	Light	XP	Pass	Light	ECS	Pass	Light	Pass	XP	XP	XP	XP	Pass	Pass
No.	3165	603	402	131	640	607	467	70	3167	5563	71	613	70	70	611	5590	222	615
Engine	N1	DMU	DMU	A3	5MT	DMU	3DMU	BR4MTT	N1	DMU	A1	DMU	A3	B1	5MT	3DMU	N1	DMU
Diagram	CH72				BH2				CH75		CH33		DR14	BJ77	LM2		AY3	
DONCASTER													16.21					
Bentley Crossing													16/24					
Carcroft																		
Adwick Jcn													16/30					
South Elmsall													16/33					
Hemsworth																		
Fitzwilliam																		
Hare Park Jcn													16/45					
Sandal													16/47					
WAKEFIELD (W)													16.50	(16.50)			17.04	
WAKEFIELD (W)				16.20									16.55	17.01			17.08	
Lofthouse				(To									17.00	17.06			17.14	
Lofthouse N. Jcn				Brad			16/38						17/01	17/07			17/15	
Ardsley				ford)			16.42										17.18	
Ardsley							16.42						17/04	17/11			17.19	
Wortley S. Jcn							16/50						17/09	(To Bradford)			17.26	
BRADFORD		16.05				16.35						16.43			17.05			17.10
Laisterdyke		16/11			16/25	16/41						16.50		17/01		17/11		17/16
Stanningley		16.16			16/30	16/44						P		17/06		17/14		17.20
Bramley												17.01						17.23
Armley Moor												17.05						17.27
Wortley W. Jcn		16/19			16/36	16/47						17/06			17/10	17/20		17/28
Copley Hill CS	16.13								16.51									
Copley Hill Loco											16.53							
HOLBECK HL												17.08			17.12			17.28
HOLBECK HL	16/17	16/21				16/38	16/49	16/52	16/53	16/58		17.08	17/11		17.14	17/22	17.29	17/31
Geldard Jn				16/21				16/53		16/58								
LEEDS	16.20	16.23		16.25	16.40	16.51	16.54	16.55	16.58	17.00	17.03	17.10	17.13		17.16	17.24	17.31	17.33
Platform	4	6	-	2	1	7	6	5	4	7	3	6	5	-	2	7	4	6
Train works	16.43	16.32		16.36		17.13	17.22		17.16	17.06		17.36	17.19		17.55	17.27	17.50	17.42
Engine works	17.50			16.40	17.11		17.19	18.40		17.33			O/R		17.29	17.46		

WORKING TIMETABLE : LEEDS CENTRAL - BRADFORD/DONCASTER (1957/8)

UP

Train From	16.16 Bradford			16.33 Harrogate				13.20 KX			17.00 Bradford			17.05 Bradford			17.20 Bradford	
Class	Pass		Pass	XP	XP	Pass	Pass	XP	Pass	Pass	Pass	Light	XP	Pass	Pass	Pass	Pass	Light
No.	357	3165	630	5563	640	642	3167	70	1616	71	5590	-	71	646	375	650		3183
Engine	DMU	A3	DMU	DMU	5MT	DMU	B1	BR4MTT	3DMU	B1	3DMU	5MT	A1	DMU	DMU	DMU	B1	J50
Diagram		DR3		BH2		DR78			BJ77			LM2	CH33				DR71	CH10G
Engine arr		O/R		16.40				15.39	16.55			17.16	17.03					17.38
Stock arr	16.20	15.13	17.00	15.52	16.51	16.58	17.13	16.54			17.24			14.28	17.10		17.33	17.38
Platform	-	4	7	7	1	7	4	5	6	-	7	2	3	7	-	6	3	3
LEEDS		16.43		16.46	17.06	17.11	17.13	17.16	17.19	17.22		17.27	17.29	17.33	17.36	17.42	17.45	17.47
Geldard Jn									17/21				17/29					17/50
HOLBECK HL		16.45				17.15				17.24						17.44	17.47	
HOLBECK HL		16.46	16/48		17/08	17/13	17.16	17/18		17.24			17/31	17/35	17/38	17.45	17.48	
Copley Hill Loco																		
Copley Hill CS																		
Wortley W. Jcn				16/50	17/10	17/15	17/18						17/33	17/40		17/47		
Armley Moor				16.51			17.20									17.49		
Bramley				16.56			17.25									17.53		
Stanningley				16.59	17.16	17/20	P						17/38	17.46		P		
Laisterdyke				17.04	17/20	17/24	17.37						17/42	17/50		18.04		
BRADFORD				17.09		17.25	17.42							17.55		18.09		
Wortley S. Jcn		16/48							17/20	17/26			17/37				17/50	
Ardsley		16.56								17.34							17.58	
Ardsley		16.57							17.27	17.34			17/43				17.59	
Lofthouse N. Jcn		17/00							17/30	17/36			17/46				18/02	
Lofthouse		17.02							17/31				17/47				18.04	
WAKEFIELD (W)	16.54	17.06							17.34		17.45		17.50		17.58		18.08	
WAKEFIELD (W)		17.10							17.36		(17.55)		17.55				18.13	
Sandal		17.13							17/39				17/58				18.17	
Hare Park Jcn		17.16							17/41				18/00				18.20	
Fitzwilliam		17.26															18.30	
Hemsworth		17.30															18.35	
South Elmsall		17.36							17.57				18/11				18.40	
Adwick Jcn		17.42							18.04				18/17				18.47	
Carcroft		17.44															18.49	
Bentley Crossing		17.53							18.08				18/19				18.55	
DONCASTER		17.56							18.11				18/22				18.58	
Destination					L'pool			Harrogate	Castleford		Knares	Low Moor	KX					Well St
Route									Batley							Batley		

3DMU = 3-CAR Metro-Cammell diesel unit..   K = Routed via Wakefield Kirkgate.   P = Routed via Pudsey Greenside.   O/R = On rear (trailing) of ECS

Train		17.25					15.30	17.13				18.20	17.44			16.30	18.42
From		Castleford					Liverpool	Doncaster				Castleford	Doncaster			Liverpool	Castleford
Route		Batley							Batley								
Class	ECS	Pass	Pass	Pass	Pass	Pass	XP	Pass	Pass	Pass	ECS	Pass	Pass	XP	Pass	Light	XP	Pass
No.		410	629	425	621	5566	973	3046	414	3185		639	427	5568	3052	962	647	429
Engine	J50	DMU	DMU	DMU	DMU	DMU	4MTT	B1	DMU	DMU	J50	DMU	3DMU	DMU	B1	N1	5MT	DMU
Diagram	CH10G						LM11	DR84			CH74				DR72	CH75	LM2	
DONCASTER								17.13							17.44			
Bentley Crossing								17/16							17/47			
Carcroft															17.51			
Adwick Jcn								17/20							17/53			
South Elmsall								17.26							17.59			
Hemsworth								17.33							18.06			
Fitzwilliam								17.37							18.10			
Hare Park Jcn								17/45							18/18			
Sandal								17/48							18.23			
WAKEFIELD (W)								17.51							18.27			
WAKEFIELD (W)		17.33						17.53	18.09						18.33			
Lofthouse		(To						17.59	(To						18.39			
Lofthouse N. Jcn		Brad		17/41				18/00	Brad				18/33		18/40			18/58
Ardsley		ford)		17.45				18.03	ford)				18.37		18.43			19.02
Ardsley				17.45				18.04					18.37		18.44			19.03
Wortley S. Jcn				17/53				18/12					18/45		18/52			19/10
BRADFORD			17.35		17.31	17.45				18.05		18.20		18.35				
Laisterdyke			17/41		17.38	17/51	17/55			18/11		18.27		18/41			18/47	
Stanningley			17.45		P	17.55	18.02			18.15		P		18/44			18/51	
Bramley					17.51					18.18		18.38						
Armley Moor					17.55					18.22		18.42						
Wortley W. Jcn			17/51		17/56	17/59	18/10			18/23		18/43		18/47			18/58	
Copley Hill CS	17.31										18.31							
Copley Hill Loco																18.50		
HOLBECK HL					17.58		18.12	18.14				18.45			18.54		19.00	
HOLBECK HL	17/35		17/53	17/55	17/58	18/01	18.14	18.16		18/25	18/35	18.45	18/47	18/49	18.56	18/57	19.04	19/12
Geldard Jcn																		
LEEDS	17.38		17.55	17.57	18.00	18.03	18.16	18.18		18.27	18.38	18.47	18.49	18.51	18.58	19.00	19.06	19.14
Platform	3	-	7	6	3	5	2	4	-	6	1	7	6	5	3	4	2	7
Train works	17.45		18.36	18.17	18.15	18.08	18.55	18.40		18.30	22.00	19.06	19.18	18.57	21.00		20.50	20.18
Engine works	17.47						18.55	18.45			20.42				19.20	19.42	19.30	

WORKING TIMETABLE : LEEDS CENTRAL - BRADFORD/DONCASTER (1957/8)

UP

Train				13.20		17.45			18.05				18.17		18.35			
From				KX		Bradford			Bradford				Bradford		Bradford			
Class	Pass	Light	Pass	ECS	XP	Pass	Pass	Pass	Light	Pass	Pass	ECS	Light	Pass	XP	XP	XP	Pcls
No.	1618	-	654	70	658	5566	1620	660		3185	668	3046	-	379	144	5568	680	035
Engine	N1	N1	4MTT	J50	DMU	DMU	DMU	DMU	A3	DMU	DMU	N1	B1	DMU	4MTT	DMU	DMU	A3
Diagram	CH72	AY3	LM15	CH74					DR14			CH75	DR84		LM11			DR14
Engine arr	16.20	17.31	15.52	13.30								16.58	18.18		18.16			
Stock arr	17.31		17.16	17.13	17.55	18.03	18.00	17.57		18.27	17.55	18.18		17.16		18.51	18.47	
Platform	4	4	2	5	7	5	7	6	-	6	7	4	4	-	2	5	7	-
LEEDS	17.50	17.52	17.55	17.58	18.06	18.08	18.15	18.17		18.30	18.36	18.40	18.45		18.55	18.57	19.06	
Geldard Jn						18/10									18/59			
HOLBECK HL	17.52							18.17							18.57			
HOLBECK HL	17.53	17/55	17/57	18/01	18/08		18.17	18/20		18/32	18/39	18/43	18/47		18.58		19/08	
Copley Hill Loco											18.27		18.50					
Copley Hill CS				18.05									18.47					
Wortley W. Jcn			17/59		18/10			18/21			18/41				19/01		19/10	
Armley Moor								18.22										
Bramley								18.27										
Stanningley			18.06		18/15			P			18.46				19/06		19/15	
Laisterdyke			18/10		18/19			18.38			18/50				19/10		19/19	
BRADFORD					18.23			18.43			18.55				19.23			
Wortley S. Jcn	17/55	17/58					18/19		18/28	18/34								
Ardsley	18.03						18.27											
Ardsley	18.04	18/07					18.27		18/33	18/39								
Lofthouse N. Jcn	18/07	18/12					18/29		18/35	18/41								
Lofthouse		18/15							18/36	18/42								
WAKEFIELD (W)		18.20							18.38	18.44					18.54			
WAKEFIELD (W)									18.45									19.20
Sandal									18.48									19.24
Hare Park Jcn									18/50									19/27
Fitzwilliam																		
Hemsworth																		
South Elmsall									18.57									19/40
Adwick Jcn									19/02									19/46
Carcroft																		
Bentley Crossing									19/05									19/50
DONCASTER									19.08									19.53
Destination	Castleford	Westgate	L. Moor			Harrogate	Castleford			Doncaster					Southport	Harrogate		KX
Route													Batley					

3DMU = 3-CAR Metro-Cammell diesel unit.. K = Routed via Wakefield Kirkgate. P = Routed via Pudsey Greenside. O/R = On rear (trailing) of ECS

The pleasant symmetry of the B1 4-6-0 is shown to advantage as (6)1296 of Bowling Junction backs down to platform 1 at Leeds Central. At the time of the photograph, 1950, parallel-boiler engines were deemed to be rather old-fashioned in appearance yet, thanks to some magic of aesthetics, the B1's never looked anything but thoroughly modern. The building behind the B1 is the goods depot of the ex-Lancashire & Yorkshire Railway which was served by LM trips from Copley Hill Yard. Access was from the Junction at Leeds B signalbox. (H.C. Casserley)

From their introduction in 1948 and until late 1951, Kings Cross had a batch of about a dozen A1 Pacifics which it used turn and turn about with A4's on its principal workings. The latter included several Leeds services and, since Copley Hill used A1's on its London services, there was for a time a want of variety on the main line expresses. In 1951, however, most of the Kings Cross A1's were deployed to Grantham which became an engine changing point for many East Coast expresses with A4 Pacifics taking over the London-based Leeds workings. During this early period, Kings Cross-based 60144 - named King's Courier in January 1951 - climbs the 1 in 100 bank out of Leeds Central and wheels a London express through Holbeck (High Level). (H.C. Casserley)

WORKING TIMETABLE : DONCASTER/BRADFORD - LEEDS CENTRAL (1957/8)

DOWN

Train		15.40	15.40				19.01	Turn	Turn	19.38	19.18	19.42			16.05	16.05		19.20
From		KX	KX				Harrogate	Turn	Turn	Harrogate	Doncaster	Castleford			KX	KX		Bradford
Route			Tingley	Batley												Tingley	Batley	
Class	Pass	XP	XP	Pass	XP	Pass	Light	Light	Pass	Pass	ECS	Pass	Pcls	XP	XP	XP	Pass	Pcls
No.	655	962	962	424	659	5567			5570	5569	964	431	651	663	102	102	420	651
Engine	DMU	A1	N1	DMU	DMU	DMU	B1	5MT	DMU	3DMU	DMU	DMU	B1	DMU	B1	B1	DMU	B1
Diagram	CH1	AY3					DR72	LM2					BJ77		CH25		AY4	BJ77
DONCASTER		18/28									19.18					19.28		
Bentley Crossing		18/30									19/21					19/31		
Carcroft																		
Adwick Jcn		18/35									19/25					19/37		
South Elmsall		18.38									19/29					19/40		
Hemsworth																		
Fitzwilliam																		
Hare Park Jcn		18/50									19/39					19/52		
Sandal		18.52									19/41					19/54		
WAKEFIELD (W)		18.55	(18.55)												19.57	(19.57)		
WAKEFIELD (W)		19.00	19.06	19.15							19.43				20.02	20.08		20.15
Lofthouse		19.05	19/11	(To							19/47				20/07	20/13		(To
Lofthouse N. Jcn		19.06	19/12	Brad							19/48	19/54			20/08	20/14		Brad
Ardsley				ford)								19.58						ford)
Ardsley		19/09	19/16								19/52	19.58			20/11	20/18		
Wortley S. Jcn		19/15	(To								20/01	20/04			20/17	(To		
BRADFORD	18.50		Brad		19.05				19.35				19.20	20.05		Brad		
Laisterdyke	18.57		ford)		19/11				19/41				19.34	20/11				
Stanningley	P				19/14				19.45				P	20/14				
Bramley	19.08												20.00					
Armley Moor	19.12												20.06					
Wortley W. Jcn	19/13		Brad		19/17		19.32	19.43	19/49				20.09	20/17		Brad		
Copley Hill CS																		
Copley Hill Loco																		
HOLBECK HL	19.15												20.11	20.19				(20.11)
HOLBECK HL	19.15	19/19		19/19	19/35	19/46	19/51			20/03	20/06	(20.27)	20/19	20.21				20.27
Geldard Jn						19/28				20/00								
LEEDS	19.17	19.19			19.21	19.30	19.38	19.50	19.53	20.02	20.04	20.08			20.21	20.24		20.29
Platform	5	4	-	-	7	5	2	2	6	7	6	6	4	7	5	-	-	4
Train works	19.24	19.42			19.47	19.38			19.57	20.06	20.30	22.28		21.18	20.42			22.00
Engine works		19.50					21.00	20.50							20.45			20.40

WORKING TIMETABLE : LEEDS CENTRAL - BRADFORD/DONCASTER (1957/8)

UP

Train					18.00	19.10		19.01				19.35	18.00	19.38				
From					Bradford	Bradford		Harrogate				Bradford	Bradford	Harrogate				
Class	Pass	Light	Pass	Light	Pcls	Pass		Pass	ECS	Pass	Light	Pass	Pcls	XP	Pass	Pass	Light	ECS
No.	1622		678		149	397	3203	5567	962	700	-	5570	149	5569	1624	706		102
Engine	3DMU	B1	DMU	5MT	BJ75		DMU	DMU	N1	DMU	A1	DMU	BJ75	3DMU	DMU	DMU	B1	J50
Diagram		DR72		LM2	B1				CH75		CH1		B1				BJ77	CH74
Engine arr		18.58		19.06					19.00		19.19					20.29		18.38
Stock arr	18.49		19.17			16.14		19.30	19.19	19.21		19.53		20.02	19.14	20.04		20.24
Platform	6	3	5	2	-	-	6	5	4	7	4	6	-	7	7	6	4	5
LEEDS	19.18	19.20	19.24	19.30		19.32		19.38	19.42	19.47	19.50	19.57		20.06	20.18	20.30	20.40	20.42
Geldard Jn												19/59						
HOLBECK HL						19.34			19.49						20.32			
HOLBECK HL	19/20	19/23	19/26	19/33		19/36		19/40	19/45	19.50	19/53			20/08	20/20	20.33	20/42	20/45
Copley Hill Loco											19.57							
Copley Hill CS									19.49									20.49
Wortley W. Jcn			19/28					19/42		19/52				20/10		20/35		
Armley Moor			19.29							19.54						20.37		
Bramley			19.34							19.58						20.41		
Stanningley			P					19.48		P				20/15		P		
Laisterdyke			19.45					19/52		20.09				20/19		20.52		
BRADFORD			19.50					19.57		20.14				20.23		20.57		
Wortley S. Jcn	19/22	19.26		19.35		19/38									20/22		20/44	
Ardsley	19.29					19/46									20.29			
Ardsley	19.29					19.47									20.29			
Lofthouse N. Jcn	19/31					19/50									20/31			
Lofthouse						19.52												
WAKEFIELD (W)					19.43	19.47	19.56					(19.43)						
WAKEFIELD (W)					(20.17)	20.02						20.17						
Sandal						K												
Hare Park Jcn						20/17												
Fitzwilliam						20.27												
Hemsworth						20.31												
South Elmsall						20.37												
Adwick Jcn						20/43												
Carcroft						20.45												
Bentley Crossing						20/49												
DONCASTER						20.52												
Destination	Castleford	Turn		Turn	Kirkgate		Doncaster					Ripon	Kirkgate		Castleford		Turn	
Route					Batley	Batley						Harrogate	Batley					

3DMU = 3-CAR Metro-Cammell diesel unit.   K = Routed via Wakefield Kirkgate.   P = Routed via Pudsey Greenside.   O/R = On rear (trailing) of ECS

WORKING TIMETABLE : DONCASTER/BRADFORD - LEEDS CENTRAL (1957/8)

DOWN

	667	–	5572	–	5571	1581	84	428	5507	987	675	3229	669	3066	681	5580	1583	88
Train		Light		Turn	20.35	20.37	17.20	20.40						20.45	19.48		21.45	18.20
From		City			Harrogate	Castleford	KX	Keighley						Doncaster	Manchester		Castleford	KX
Route								Batley										
Class	Pass	Light	XP	Light	Pass	Pass	Pullman	Pass	Pcls	Light	Pass	ECS	Pcls	Pass	Pass	Pass	Pass	XP
Engine	DMU	D49	3DMU	B1	DMU	3DMU	A4	DMU	4MTT	B1	DMU	J50	N1	DMU	5MT	DMU	DMU	A1
Diagram		NE	BJ77				KX38		NE	CH4		CH74	AY3		AG107				CH2
DONCASTER							20.25							20.45				21.24
Bentley Crossing							20/28							20.48				21/27
Carcroft														20.52				
Adwick Jcn							20/33							20/54				21/33
South Elmsall							20/37							21.00				21/36
Hemsworth														21.07				
Fitzwilliam														21.11				
Hare Park Jcn							20/49							21/19				21/48
Sandal							20/51							21/21				21/50
WAKEFIELD (W)							20.54							21.25				21.56
WAKEFIELD (W)							20.56	21.10						21.30				22.01
Lofthouse							21/01	(To						21.36				22/06
Lofthouse N. Jcn						20/49	21/02	Brad						21/37				22/07
Ardsley					20.53			ford						21.40				
Ardsley					20.53	21/05								21.41			21/57	22/10
Wortley S. Jcn					21/00	21/10								21/49			22/09	22/15
BRADFORD	20.20		20.35							21.05			21.09			21.35		
Laisterdyke	20.27		20/41							21.12			21.17		21.40	21.43		
Stanningley	P		20/44							21.17			21.28		21.45	P		
Bramley	20.38									21.20			21.32			21.54		
Armley Moor	20.42									21.24			21.37			21.58		
Wortley W. Jcn	20/43		20/48	20.50						21/25			21/38		21/52	21/59		
Copley Hill CS												21.35						
Copley Hill Loco											21.20							
HOLBECK HL	20.44									21.27			21.40		21.51	21.54	22.01	
HOLBECK HL	20.44		20.50	20.52		21.02	21.12			21.25	21.27	21/40	21.45	21.53	21.55	22.01	22.11	
Geldard Jn		20/48			21/00				21.22									22/17
LEEDS	20.46	20.50	20.52	20.54	21.02	21.04	21.14	–	21.26	21.27	21.29	21.45	21.47	21.55	21.57	22.03	22.13	22.19
Platform	6	M	5	M	5	6	4	–	M	1	7	4	3	7	2	6	7	5
Train works	21.36		20.57		21.06	21.26	21.22/4		22.00		22.47	22.35	01.05	22.52	22.45	22.06	23.28	23.12
Engine works		21.24		21.22			21.28	22.10		22.00		23.13	22.05		22.18			23.15

WORKING TIMETABLE : LEEDS CENTRAL - BRADFORD/DONCASTER (1957/8)

UP

	213	–	708	5572	3209	5571	1626	84	84	720	–	712	223	987	987	–	5580	–
Train	20.15			20.35		20.35		17.20	17.20				21.15	21.38				21.35
From	Bradford			Bradford		Harrogate		KX	KX				Bradford	Bradford				Bradford
Class	Pass	Light	Pass	XP	Pass	XP	Pass	Pullman	Pullman	Pass	Light	XP	Pass	XP	XP	Light	Pass	Light
Engine	DMU	B1	5MT	3DMU	B1	DMU	DMU	B1	D49	3DMU	A4	DMU	DMU	B1	B1	N1	DMU	4MTT
Diagram		CH25	LM2		DR72			BJ77	NE		KX38			AY1	CH4	AY3		NE
Engine arr		20.24	19.50		19.38			20.54	20.50		21.14			21.27	21.47			21.26
Stock arr			18.16	20.52	18.58	21.02	20.21	21.14	21.14	21.04	–	20.46		18.38			22.03	
Platform	–	5	2	5	3	5	7	4	4	6	4	6		1	3		6	M
LEEDS	20.45		20.50	20.57	21.00	21.06	21.18	21.22	21.24	21.26	21.28	21.36	22.00	22.05			22.06	22.10
Geldard Jn				20/59					21/26								22/08	22/12
HOLBECK HL			20.52											22.03				
HOLBECK HL		20/48	20.53		21/02	21/08	21/20	21/24		21/28	21.31	21/38		22.10	22/07			
Copley Hill Loco		20.52									21.35							
Copley Hill CS																		
Wortley W. Jcn			20/55			21/10		21/26		21/30		21/40						
Armley Moor										21.31								
Bramley										21.36								
Stanningley			21.02			21/15		21/31		P		21/45						
Laisterdyke			21.08			21/19		21/35		21/51		21/48						
BRADFORD						21.23		21.40		21.56		21.53						
Wortley S. Jcn				21/04	21/22											22/10	22/12	
Ardsley				21.15	21.28								22.04	22.20				
Ardsley				21.16	21.29								22.05	22/20		<u>22/20</u>		
Lofthouse N. Jcn				21/19	21/31								22/08	22/23				
Lofthouse				21.21									22/09					
WAKEFIELD (W)	20.53			21.25								21.53	22.13	22.27				
WAKEFIELD (W)				21.27									(22.36)	22.36				
Sandal				21/30										K				
Hare Park Jcn				21/33										22/52				
Fitzwilliam				21.43														
Hemsworth				21.47														
South Elmsall				21.53										23/06				
Adwick Jcn				21/59										23/12				
Carcroft				22.01														
Bentley Crossing				22.05										23/17				
DONCASTER				22.08										23.20				
Destination	M'ter		Harrogate	Doncaster	Castleford		Harrogate			Bradford			Combine	KX		Ardsley	Harrogate	City
Route													Batley	Tingley Kirkgate				

3DMU = 3-CAR Metro-Cammell diesel unit.. K = Routed via Wakefield Kirkgate. P = Routed via Pudsey Greenside. O/R = On rear (trailing) of ECS

WORKING TIMETABLE : DONCASTER/BRADFORD - LEEDS CENTRAL (1957/8)

DOWN

Train	18.20	21.48				Turn	21.20		22.20		22.50		23.10		20.30		20.25
From	KX	Harrogate					Ripon		Castleford		Harrogate			Castleford	Liverpool		Grimsby
Route	Tingley	Batley					Harrogate						Batley				Kirkgate
Class	XP	Pass	Pass	Pass	Light	Light	ECS	ECS	Pass	Pass	Pass	Pass	Pass	Pass	XP	Light	Fish
No.	88	432	5573	685	3229		5531	951	1585	687	5575	3068	440	437	699	-	1282
Engine	B1	DMU	DMU	3DMU	B1	5MT	DMU	N1	DMU	DMU	DMU	B1	DMU	3DMU	4MTT	J50	B1
Diagram	CH38				CH36	AG107		CH75				BJ75			LM20	CH74	CH26
DONCASTER												22.22					
Bentley Crossing												22.25					
Carcroft												22.29					
Adwick Jcn												22/31					22/36
South Elmsall												22.37					22.48
Hemsworth																	23/00
Fitzwilliam												22.46					
Hare Park Jcn												22/54					23/09
Sandal												22/56					K
WAKEFIELD (W)	(21.56)											23.00					23.32
WAKEFIELD (W)	22.07	22.20										23.03	23.08				23.43
Lofthouse	22.12	(To										23.08	(To				23/48
Lofthouse N. Jcn	22/13	Brad							22/32			23/09	Brad	23/22			23/49
Ardsley		ford)							22.36			23.12		23.25			23.55
Ardsley	22/17								22.36			23.13		23.26			(00.05)
Wortley S. Jcn	(To								22/42			23/21		23/31			
BRADFORD	Brad			22.05						22.45							
Laisterdyke	ford)			22/11						22.52					23/29		
Stanningley				22.15						P					23/34		
Bramley										23.03							
Armley Moor																	
Wortley W. Jcn				22/20		22.30				23.06					23/37		
Copley Hill CS								22.36									
Copley Hill Loco					22.21											23.35	
HOLBECK HL																	
HOLBECK HL				22/22	22/23	22/32		22/40	22/44	23/08		23/23		23/34	23/39	23/40	
Geldard Jn			22/19				22/36				23/16						
LEEDS			22.21	22.24	22.25	22.34	22.38	22.43	22.46	23.10	23.18	23.25		23.36	23.41	23.45	
Platform	-	-	1	1	4	2	M	3	7	6	1	5	-	7	2	M	
Train works		23.23	22.30				23.28	01.05/42	05.47	05.25	23.23	23.52		06.12	03.25		
Engine works					22.35	22.45		23.52				23.53			00.15	01.00	

WORKING TIMETABLE : LEEDS CENTRAL - BRADFORD/DONCASTER (1957/8)

UP

Train				22.15										Light
From				Bradford										-
Class	Light	Pass	Pass	Pass	Pass		Pass	Pass	ECS	Light	XP	ECS	ECS	Light
No.		724	1644	359	3229	722	5592	726			5575	734		
Engine	5MT	DMU	3DMU		B1	5MT	DMU	DMU	J50	A1	DMU	DMU	N1	B1
Diagram	AG107				CH36	AG107			CH74	CH2			CH75	BJ75
Engine arr	21.57				22.25	22.34			21.45	22.19				23.25
Stock arr		20.08	22.24		21.45	21.57	21.29	21.55	22.19		22.21/23.13	22.13/23.23	23.25	
Platform	M	6	1		4	2	7	7	5	5	1	M	5	5
LEEDS	22.18	22.28	22.30	22.35	22.45	22.47	22.52	23.12	23.15	23.23	23.28	23.52	23.53	
Geldard Jn						22/49								
HOLBECK HL				22.37	22.47		22.54							
HOLBECK HL	22/20	22/30	22/32	22/40	22/48		22/55	23/14	23/17	23/25	23/30	23/54	23/55	
Copley Hill Loco										23.20				
Copley Hill CS									23.19				23.57	
Wortley W. Jcn	22.22	22/32				22/50	22/57				23/27	23/32		23/57
Armley Moor							22.59							
Bramley							23.03							
Stanningley		22.38				22/58	P				23/32	23/37		00.05
Laisterdyke		22/42				23/02	23.14				23/36	23/44		00.08
BRADFORD		22.47				23/19	23.19				23.40	23.49		
Wortley S. Jcn			22/34		22/42									
Ardsley			22.41		22.50									
Ardsley			22.41		22.51									
Lofthouse N. Jcn			22/43		22/54									
Lofthouse					22/55									
WAKEFIELD (W)				22.52	22/59									
WAKEFIELD (W)					23.06									
Sandal					K									
Hare Park Jcn					23/24									
Fitzwilliam					23.34									
Hemsworth														
South Elmsall					23.42									
Adwick Jcn					23/48									
Carcroft					23.50									
Bentley Crossing					23/54									
DONCASTER					23.57									
Destination	Turn	Bradford	Castleford		Doncaster	Halifax	Harrogate	Bradford						Low Moor
Route		Stanningley	Batley		Kirkgate			Pudsey						

3DMU = 3-CAR Metro-Cammell diesel unit.   K = Routed via Wakefield Kirkgate.   P = Routed via Pudsey Greenside.   O/R = On rear (trailing) of ECS

The express turns between London and Leeds were distributed between Copley Hill, Doncaster and Kings Cross sheds; the London turns being instantly recognisable because streamlined A4 Pacifics were employed on all three duties.   The most prestigious of the Kings Cross workings was the down Yorkshire Pullman which left Kings Cross at 17.20 and conveyed sections for Hull, Leeds, Harrogate and Bradford.   The A4 booked to the duty spent the night on Copley Hill before returning the next day with the 10.00 Leeds to Kings Cross express.   The up Yorkshire Pullman. which left Leeds at 10.45, was a Copley Hill working, handled by an A1 Pacific.   60017 'Silver Fox' of Kings Cross pounds the down Yorkshire Pullman up the 1 in 200 climb through Greenwood circa 1948.

The Doncaster-based West Riding expresses were until the very late 1950's booked to be covered by A3 Pacifics although ex-works engines were often placed into the diagrams as a means of returning them to work.   This probably explains the use of Grantham A3 60056 'Centenary' which is seen pulling away from Doncaster with the 07.30 Leeds - Kings Cross.

Loco	Class	Aug-50	Sep-50	Oct-50	Nov-50	Dec-50	Jan-51	Feb-51	Mar-51	Apr-51	May-51	Jun-51	Jul-51
60114	8P: A1 4-6-2 (1948)												
60117	8P: A1 4-6-2 (1948)												
60118	8P: A1 4-6-2 (1948)												
60119	8P: A1 4-6-2 (1948)												
60120	8P: A1 4-6-2 (1948)												
60123	8P: A1 4-6-2 (1948)												
60125	8P: A1 4-6-2 (1948)												
60133	8P: A1 4-6-2 (1948)												
60134	8P: A1 4-6-2 (1948)												
60141	8P: A1 4-6-2 (1948)												
60044	7P: A3 4-6-2 (1922)												
60046	7P: A3 4-6-2 (1922)												
60056	7P: A3 4-6-2 (1922)												
60061	7P: A3 4-6-2 (1922)	X	X	X	Ex Doncaster				To Kings X	X	X	X	X
60062	7P: A3 4-6-2 (1922)												
60112	7P: A3 4-6-2 (1922)				To Doncaster	X	X	X	X	Ex Doncaster			
61029	5MT: B1 4-6-0 (1942)	X	Ex Ardsley					To Ardsley	X	X	X	X	X
61033	5MT: B1 4-6-0 (1942)	X	X	Ex Ardsley									
61295	5MT: B1 4-6-0 (1942)												
61310	5MT: B1 4-6-0 (1942)	X	X	X	X	X	X	Ex Ardsley					
68911	4F: J50 0-6-0T (1922)												
68913	4F: J50 0-6-0T (1922)												
68925	4F: J50 0-6-0T (1922)												
68937	4F: J50 0-6-0T (1922)												
68978	4F: J50 0-6-0T (1922)												
68984	4F: J50 0-6-0T (1922)												
68988	4F: J50 0-6-0T (1922)												
64173	3F: J6 0-6-0 (1911)												
64250	3F: J6 0-6-0 (1911)												
64260	3F: J6 0-6-0 (1911)												
69266	2P: N5 0-6-2T (1891)												
69271	2P: N5 0-6-2T (1891)							To Ardsley	X	X	X	X	X
69430	2P: N1 0-6-2T (1907)												
69436	2P: N1 0-6-2T (1907)												
69437	2P: N1 0-6-2T (1907)												
69440	2P: N1 0-6-2T (1907)												
69444	2P: N1 0-6-2T (1907)												
69446	2P: N1 0-6-2T (1907)												
69450	2P: N1 0-6-2T (1907)	X	X	X	X	X	X	X	X	X	X	Ex Hornsey	
69471	2P: N1 0-6-2T (1907)												
69472	2P: N1 0-6-2T (1907)									To Ardsley	X	X	X
69473	2P: N1 0-6-2T (1907)												
69483	2P: N1 0-6-2T (1907)	X	X	X	X	X	X	Ex Bradford					
67440	2P: C14 4-4-2T (1907)	X	X	X	X	X	X	X	Ex Ardsley			To Ardsley	X
67353	1P: C12 4-4-2T (1898)									To Ardsley	X	X	X
67372	1P: C12 4-4-2T (1898)												

Loco	Class	Aug-51	Sep-51	Oct-51	Nov-51	Dec-51	Jan-52	Feb-52	Mar-52	Apr-52	May-52	Jun-52	Jul-52
60114	8P: A1 4-6-2 (1948)												
60117	8P: A1 4-6-2 (1948)											To Grantham	X
60118	8P: A1 4-6-2 (1948)												
60119	8P: A1 4-6-2 (1948)												
60120	8P: A1 4-6-2 (1948)												
60123	8P: A1 4-6-2 (1948)		To Ardsley	X	X	X	X	X	X	X	X	X	X
60125	8P: A1 4-6-2 (1948)												
60133	8P: A1 4-6-2 (1948)												
60134	8P: A1 4-6-2 (1948)												
60141	8P: A1 4-6-2 (1948)												
60826	7P: V2 2-6-2 (1936)	X	Ex March										
60846	7P: V2 2-6-2 (1936)	X	Ex Doncaster										
60861	7P: V2 2-6-2 (1936)	X	Ex Doncaster										
60865	7P: V2 2-6-2 (1936)	X	Ex March										
60913	7P: V2 2-6-2 (1936)	X	Ex March										
60044	7P: A3 4-6-2 (1922)		To Doncaster	X	X	X	X	X	X	X	X	X	X
60046	7P: A3 4-6-2 (1922)		To Doncaster	X	X	X	X	X	X	X	X	X	X
60056	7P: A3 4-6-2 (1922)		To Doncaster	X	X	X	X	X	X	X	X	X	X
60062	7P: A3 4-6-2 (1922)		To Doncaster	X	X	X	X	X	X	X	X	X	X
60112	7P: A3 4-6-2 (1922)		To Doncaster	X	X	X	X	X	X	X	X	X	X
61033	5MT: B1 4-6-0 (1942)							To Ardsley	X	X	X	X	X
61129	5MT: B1 4-6-0 (1942)	X	X	X	X	X	X	X	X	X	X	X	Ex Ardsley
61295	5MT: B1 4-6-0 (1942)												
61309	5MT: B1 4-6-0 (1942)	Ex Ardsley											
61310	5MT: B1 4-6-0 (1942)							To Ardsley	X	X	X	X	X
61377	5MT: B1 4-6-0 (1942)	X	X	X	X	X	X	X	X	X	X	X	Ex Ardsley
61386	5MT: B1 4-6-0 (1942)	X	X	X	X	X	X	Ex Ardsley					
61387	5MT: B1 4-6-0 (1942)	X	X	X	X	X	X	Ex Ardsley					
68911	4F: J50 0-6-0T (1922)												
68913	4F: J50 0-6-0T (1922)												
68925	4F: J50 0-6-0T (1922)												
68937	4F: J50 0-6-0T (1922)												
68978	4F: J50 0-6-0T (1922)												
68984	4F: J50 0-6-0T (1922)												
68988	4F: J50 0-6-0T (1922)												
64173	3F: J6 0-6-0 (1911)												
64250	3F: J6 0-6-0 (1911)								To Boston	X	X	X	X
64260	3F: J6 0-6-0 (1911)								To Boston	X	X	X	X
64276	3F: J6 0-6-0 (1911)	X	X	X	X	X	X	X	Ex Boston				
64277	3F: J6 0-6-0 (1911)	X	X	X	X	X	X	X	Ex Boston				
69266	2P: N5 0-6-2T (1891)												
69430	2P: N1 0-6-2T (1907)												
69436	2P: N1 0-6-2T (1907)												
69437	2P: N1 0-6-2T (1907)												
69440	2P: N1 0-6-2T (1907)												
69444	2P: N1 0-6-2T (1907)												
69446	2P: N1 0-6-2T (1907)												
69450	2P: N1 0-6-2T (1907)												
69471	2P: N1 0-6-2T (1907)												
69473	2P: N1 0-6-2T (1907)												
69483	2P: N1 0-6-2T (1907)												
67353	1P: C12 4-4-2T (1898)	X	X	X	X	Ex Ardsley							
67372	1P: C12 4-4-2T (1898)												

Loco	Class	Aug-52	Sep-52	Oct-52	Nov-52	Dec-52	Jan-53	Feb-53	Mar-53	Apr-53	May-53	Jun-53	Jul-53
60114	8P: A1 4-6-2 (1948)							To Grantham	X	X	X	X	X
60117	8P: A1 4-6-2 (1948)	X	X	X	X	X	X	Ex Grantham					
60118	8P: A1 4-6-2 (1948)												
60119	8P: A1 4-6-2 (1948)												
60120	8P: A1 4-6-2 (1948)												
60125	8P: A1 4-6-2 (1948)							To Grantham	X	X	X	X	Ex Grantham
60131	8P: A1 4-6-2 (1948)	X	X	X	X	X	X	Ex Grantham					
60133	8P: A1 4-6-2 (1948)												
60134	8P: A1 4-6-2 (1948)												
60141	8P: A1 4-6-2 (1948)												
60158	8P: A1 4-6-2 (1948)	X	X	X	X	X	X	X	X	X	X	X	Ex Grantham
60826	7P: V2 2-6-2 (1936)												
60846	7P: V2 2-6-2 (1936)												To Ardsley
60861	7P: V2 2-6-2 (1936)												To Ardsley
60865	7P: V2 2-6-2 (1936)												
60913	7P: V2 2-6-2 (1936)												
61129	5MT: B1 4-6-0 (1942)												
61295	5MT: B1 4-6-0 (1942)												
61309	5MT: B1 4-6-0 (1942)												
61377	5MT: B1 4-6-0 (1942)												
61386	5MT: B1 4-6-0 (1942)												
61387	5MT: B1 4-6-0 (1942)												
61388	5MT: B1 4-6-0 (1942)	X	X	X	Ex Ardsley								
68911	4F: J50 0-6-0T (1922)												
68913	4F: J50 0-6-0T (1922)												
68925	4F: J50 0-6-0T (1922)												
68937	4F: J50 0-6-0T (1922)												
68978	4F: J50 0-6-0T (1922)												
68984	4F: J50 0-6-0T (1922)												
68988	4F: J50 0-6-0T (1922)												
64173	3F: J6 0-6-0 (1911)												
64276	3F: J6 0-6-0 (1911)												
64277	3F: J6 0-6-0 (1911)												
69266	2P: N5 0-6-2T (1891)		To Ardsley	X	X	X	X	X	X	X	X	X	X
69430	2P: N1 0-6-2T (1907)												
69436	2P: N1 0-6-2T (1907)												
69437	2P: N1 0-6-2T (1907)												
69440	2P: N1 0-6-2T (1907)												
69444	2P: N1 0-6-2T (1907)												
69446	2P: N1 0-6-2T (1907)											W/D	X
69450	2P: N1 0-6-2T (1907)												
69462	2P: N1 0-6-2T (1907)	X	X	X	X	X	X	X	X	X	X	X	Ex Hornsey
69468	2P: N1 0-6-2T (1907)	X	X	X	X	X	X	X	X	X	X	X	Ex Hornsey
69471	2P: N1 0-6-2T (1907)												
69473	2P: N1 0-6-2T (1907)		W/D	X	X	X	X	X	X	X	X	X	X
69477	2P: N1 0-6-2T (1907)	X	Ex Hornsey										
69483	2P: N1 0-6-2T (1907)												
67353	1P: C12 4-4-2T (1898)				To Ardsley	X	X	X	X	X	X	X	X
67372	1P: C12 4-4-2T (1898)										W/D	X	X

Loco	Class	Aug-53	Sep-53	Oct-53	Nov-53	Dec-53	Jan-54	Feb-54	Mar-54	Apr-54	May-54	Jun-54	Jul-54
60117	8P: A1 4-6-2 (1948)												
60118	8P: A1 4-6-2 (1948)												
60119	8P: A1 4-6-2 (1948)												
60120	8P: A1 4-6-2 (1948)												
60122	8P: A1 4-6-2 (1948)	X	X	X	Ex Grantham								
60125	8P: A1 4-6-2 (1948)										To Grantham	X	X
60131	8P: A1 4-6-2 (1948)												
60133	8P: A1 4-6-2 (1948)												
60134	8P: A1 4-6-2 (1948)												
60141	8P: A1 4-6-2 (1948)												
60148	8P: A1 4-6-2 (1948)	X	X	X	Ex Grantham						To Grantham	X	X
60158	8P: A1 4-6-2 (1948)										To Grantham	X	X
60826	7P: V2 2-6-2 (1936)				To Ardsley	X	X	X	X	X	X	X	X
60859	7P: V2 2-6-2 (1936)	X	X	X	X	X	Ex Woodford						
60865	7P: V2 2-6-2 (1936)												
60913	7P: V2 2-6-2 (1936)												
60051	7P: A3 4-6-2 (1922)	X	X	X	X	X	X	X	X	X	Ex Grantham		
60053	7P: A3 4-6-2 (1922)	X	X	X	X	X	X	X	X	X	Ex Grantham		
60058	7P: A3 4-6-2 (1922)	X	X	X	X	X	X	X	X	X	X	Ex Doncaster	
60106	7P: A3 4-6-2 (1922)	X	X	X	X	X	X	X	X	X	Ex Grantham		
61129	5MT: B1 4-6-0 (1942)												
61155	5MT: B1 4-6-0 (1942)	X	X	X	X	X	X	X	X	X	X	Ex Gorton	
61162	5MT: B1 4-6-0 (1942)	X	X	X	X	X	X	X	X	X	X	Ex Gorton	
61295	5MT: B1 4-6-0 (1942)				To Ardsley	X	X	X	X	X	X	X	X
61309	5MT: B1 4-6-0 (1942)												
61377	5MT: B1 4-6-0 (1942)								To Ardsley	X	X	X	X
61386	5MT: B1 4-6-0 (1942)												
61387	5MT: B1 4-6-0 (1942)												
61388	5MT: B1 4-6-0 (1942)												
64911	5F: J39 0-6-0 (1926)	X	X	X	X	X	X	X	X	X	Ex Ardsley		
68911	4F: J50 0-6-0T (1922)												
68913	4F: J50 0-6-0T (1922)												
68925	4F: J50 0-6-0T (1922)												
68937	4F: J50 0-6-0T (1922)												
68978	4F: J50 0-6-0T (1922)												
68984	4F: J50 0-6-0T (1922)												
68988	4F: J50 0-6-0T (1922)												
64173	3F: J6 0-6-0 (1911)												
64276	3F: J6 0-6-0 (1911)												
64277	3F: J6 0-6-0 (1911)												
69430	2P: N1 0-6-2T (1907)												
69436	2P: N1 0-6-2T (1907)												
69437	2P: N1 0-6-2T (1907)												W/D
69440	2P: N1 0-6-2T (1907)												
69444	2P: N1 0-6-2T (1907)												
69450	2P: N1 0-6-2T (1907)												
69462	2P: N1 0-6-2T (1907)												
69468	2P: N1 0-6-2T (1907)								W/D	X	X	X	X
69471	2P: N1 0-6-2T (1907)												
69477	2P: N1 0-6-2T (1907)												
69483	2P: N1 0-6-2T (1907)												

ALLOCATION AND TRANSFERS : LEEDS (COPLEY HILL) MPD

Loco	Class	Aug-54	Sep-54	Oct-54	Nov-54	Dec-54	Jan-55	Feb-55	Mar-55	Apr-55	May-55	Jun-55	Jul-55
60117	8P: A1 4-6-2 (1948)												
60118	8P: A1 4-6-2 (1948)												
60119	8P: A1 4-6-2 (1948)												
60120	8P: A1 4-6-2 (1948)												
60122	8P: A1 4-6-2 (1948)												
60131	8P: A1 4-6-2 (1948)												
60133	8P: A1 4-6-2 (1948)												
60134	8P: A1 4-6-2 (1948)												
60141	8P: A1 4-6-2 (1948)												
60859	7P: V2 2-6-2 (1936)												
60865	7P: V2 2-6-2 (1936)												
60913	7P: V2 2-6-2 (1936)												
60051	7P: A3 4-6-2 (1922)												
60053	7P: A3 4-6-2 (1922)												
60058	7P: A3 4-6-2 (1922)												
60106	7P: A3 4-6-2 (1922)												
61129	5MT: B1 4-6-0 (1942)												
61155	5MT: B1 4-6-0 (1942)					To Doncaster	X	X	X	X	X	X	X
61162	5MT: B1 4-6-0 (1942)				To Doncaster	X	X	X	X	X	X	X	X
61309	5MT: B1 4-6-0 (1942)												
61386	5MT: B1 4-6-0 (1942)												
61387	5MT: B1 4-6-0 (1942)												
61388	5MT: B1 4-6-0 (1942)												
64911	5F: J39 0-6-0 (1926)												
68911	4F: J50 0-6-0T (1922)												
68913	4F: J50 0-6-0T (1922)												
68925	4F: J50 0-6-0T (1922)												
68937	4F: J50 0-6-0T (1922)												
68978	4F: J50 0-6-0T (1922)												
68984	4F: J50 0-6-0T (1922)												
68988	4F: J50 0-6-0T (1922)												
69691	3P: N7 0-6-2T (1914)	X	X	Ex Ardsley									
69694	3P: N7 0-6-2T (1914)	X	X	Ex Ardsley									
69695	3P: N7 0-6-2T (1914)	X	X	Ex Ardsley									
69696	3P: N7 0-6-2T (1914)	X	X	Ex Ardsley									To Bradford
64173	3F: J6 0-6-0 (1911)												
64276	3F: J6 0-6-0 (1911)												
64277	3F: J6 0-6-0 (1911)												
69430	2P: N1 0-6-2T (1907)												
69436	2P: N1 0-6-2T (1907)	To Bradford	X	X	X	X	X	X	X	X	X	X	X
69440	2P: N1 0-6-2T (1907)					To Ardsley	X	X	X	X	X	X	X
69444	2P: N1 0-6-2T (1907)												
69450	2P: N1 0-6-2T (1907)												
69462	2P: N1 0-6-2T (1907)	To Kings X	X	X	X	X	X	X	X	X	X	X	X
69471	2P: N1 0-6-2T (1907)	To Bradford	X	X	X	X	X	X	X	X	X	X	X
69475	2P: N1 0-6-2T (1907)	X	X	X	X	X	X	X	Ex Hatfield	To Bradford	X	X	X
69477	2P: N1 0-6-2T (1907)	To Kings X	X	X	X	X	X	X	X	X	X	X	X
69483	2P: N1 0-6-2T (1907)								W/D	X	X	X	X
67438	2P: C13 4-4-2T (1903)	X	X	X	Ex Gorton								

ALLOCATION AND TRANSFERS : LEEDS (COPLEY HILL) MPD

Loco	Class	Aug-55	Sep-55	Oct-55	Nov-55	Dec-55	Jan-56	Feb-56	Mar-56	Apr-56	May-56	Jun-56	Jul-56
60117	8P: A1 4-6-2 (1948)												
60118	8P: A1 4-6-2 (1948)												
60119	8P: A1 4-6-2 (1948)					To Grantham	X	X	X	X	X	X	X
60120	8P: A1 4-6-2 (1948)												
60122	8P: A1 4-6-2 (1948)		To Grantham	X	X	X	X	X	X	X	X	X	X
60131	8P: A1 4-6-2 (1948)												
60133	8P: A1 4-6-2 (1948)												
60134	8P: A1 4-6-2 (1948)												
60141	8P: A1 4-6-2 (1948)												
60148	8P: A1 4-6-2 (1948)	X	Ex Grantham										
60841	7P: V2 2-6-2 (1936)	X	Ex New Eng										
60859	7P: V2 2-6-2 (1936)												
60865	7P: V2 2-6-2 (1936)												
60913	7P: V2 2-6-2 (1936)												
60051	7P: A3 4-6-2 (1922)												
60052	7P: A3 4-6-2 (1922)	X	Ex Leicester										
60053	7P: A3 4-6-2 (1922)												
60058	7P: A3 4-6-2 (1922)												
60106	7P: A3 4-6-2 (1922)		To Leicester	X	X	X	X	X	X	X	X	X	X
61129	5MT: B1 4-6-0 (1942)												
61309	5MT: B1 4-6-0 (1942)												
61386	5MT: B1 4-6-0 (1942)												
61387	5MT: B1 4-6-0 (1942)												
61388	5MT: B1 4-6-0 (1942)												
64911	5F: J39 0-6-0 (1926)												
68911	4F: J50 0-6-0T (1922)												
68913	4F: J50 0-6-0T (1922)												
68925	4F: J50 0-6-0T (1922)												
68937	4F: J50 0-6-0T (1922)												
68978	4F: J50 0-6-0T (1922)												
68984	4F: J50 0-6-0T (1922)												
68988	4F: J50 0-6-0T (1922)												
69691	3P: N7 0-6-2T (1914)					To Plaistow	X	X	X	X	X	X	X
69694	3P: N7 0-6-2T (1914)												
69695	3P: N7 0-6-2T (1914)					To Plaistow	X	X	X	X	X	X	X
69696	3P: N7 0-6-2T (1914)	X	X	X	X	X	X	X	X	Ex Bradford	X	X	X
64173	3F: J6 0-6-0 (1911)												
64276	3F: J6 0-6-0 (1911)												
64277	3F: J6 0-6-0 (1911)												
69430	2P: N1 0-6-2T (1907)												
69444	2P: N1 0-6-2T (1907)												
69450	2P: N1 0-6-2T (1907)												
67433	2P: C13 4-4-2T (1903)	X	X	X	X	X	Ex Ardsley						
67438	2P: C13 4-4-2T (1903)												

ALLOCATION AND TRANSFERS : LEEDS (COPLEY HILL) MPD

Loco	Class	Aug-56	Sep-56	Oct-56	Nov-56	Dec-56	Jan-57	Feb-57	Mar-57	Apr-57	May-57	Jun-57	Jul-57
60117	8P: A1 4-6-2 (1948)												
60118	8P: A1 4-6-2 (1948)												
60120	8P: A1 4-6-2 (1948)												
60131	8P: A1 4-6-2 (1948)												
60133	8P: A1 4-6-2 (1948)												
60134	8P: A1 4-6-2 (1948)												
60141	8P: A1 4-6-2 (1948)												
60148	8P: A1 4-6-2 (1948)												
60841	7P: V2 2-6-2 (1936)												
60859	7P: V2 2-6-2 (1936)												
60865	7P: V2 2-6-2 (1936)												
60885	7P: V2 2-6-2 (1936)	X	X	Ex Heaton									
60913	7P: V2 2-6-2 (1936)												
60051	7P: A3 4-6-2 (1922)												
60052	7P: A3 4-6-2 (1922)												
60053	7P: A3 4-6-2 (1922)												
60058	7P: A3 4-6-2 (1922)												
61129	5MT: B1 4-6-0 (1942)												
61214	5MT: B1 4-6-0 (1942)	X	X	Ex Stockton									
61309	5MT: B1 4-6-0 (1942)												
61386	5MT: B1 4-6-0 (1942)												
61387	5MT: B1 4-6-0 (1942)												
61388	5MT: B1 4-6-0 (1942)												
64911	5F: J39 0-6-0 (1926)												
68911	4F: J50 0-6-0T (1922)												
68913	4F: J50 0-6-0T (1922)												
68925	4F: J50 0-6-0T (1922)												
68937	4F: J50 0-6-0T (1922)												
68978	4F: J50 0-6-0T (1922)												
68984	4F: J50 0-6-0T (1922)												
68988	4F: J50 0-6-0T (1922)												
69694	3P: N7 0-6-2T (1914)				To Tilbury	X	X	X	X	X	X	X	X
69696	3P: N7 0-6-2T (1914)				To Yarmouth (ST	X	X	X	X	X	X	X	X
64173	3F: J6 0-6-0 (1911)												
64276	3F: J6 0-6-0 (1911)												
64277	3F: J6 0-6-0 (1911)												
69430	2P: N1 0-6-2T (1907)					W/D	X	X	X	X	X	X	X
69434	2P: N1 0-6-2T (1907)	X	X	X	X	X	X	Ex Bradford					
69444	2P: N1 0-6-2T (1907)			W/D	X	X	X	X	X	X	X	X	X
69450	2P: N1 0-6-2T (1907)												
69457	2P: N1 0-6-2T (1907)	X	X	X	X	X	X	X	Ex Bradford	W/D	X	X	X
69462	2P: N1 0-6-2T (1907)	X	X	X	X	X	X	X	X	X	X	Ex Hornsey	
69469	2P: N1 0-6-2T (1907)	X	X	X	Ex Ardsley					W/D	X	X	
69477	2P: N1 0-6-2T (1907)	X	X	X	X	X	X	X	X	X	X	Ex Hornsey	X
67433	2P: C13 4-4-2T (1903)								To Ardsley	X	X	X	X
67438	2P: C13 4-4-2T (1903)								To Ardsley	X	X	X	X
67246	1P: G5 0-4-4T (1894)	X	X	X	X	Ex Blaydon		To S'land	X	X	X	X	X
67280	1P: G5 0-4-4T (1894)	X	X	Ex Hull (BG)					To Hull (BG)	X	X	X	X
67311	1P: G5 0-4-4T (1894)	X	X	Ex Hull (BG)					To Hull (BG)	X	X	X	X
67329	1P: G5 0-4-4T (1894)	X	X	X	X	Ex Hexham		To S'land	X	X	X	X	X

ALLOCATION AND TRANSFERS : LEEDS (COPLEY HILL) MPD

Loco	Class	Aug-57	Sep-57	Oct-57	Nov-57	Dec-57	Jan-58	Feb-58	Mar-58	Apr-58	May-58	Jun-58	Jul-58
60117	8P: A1 4-6-2 (1948)												
60118	8P: A1 4-6-2 (1948)												
60120	8P: A1 4-6-2 (1948)												
60123	8P: A1 4-6-2 (1948)	X	Ex Ardsley										
60130	8P: A1 4-6-2 (1948)	X	Ex Ardsley										
60131	8P: A1 4-6-2 (1948)												
60133	8P: A1 4-6-2 (1948)												
60134	8P: A1 4-6-2 (1948)												
60141	8P: A1 4-6-2 (1948)												
60148	8P: A1 4-6-2 (1948)												
60841	7P: V2 2-6-2 (1936)												
60843	7P: V2 2-6-2 (1936)	X	X	X	X	X	X	X	X	X	X	Ex York	
60859	7P: V2 2-6-2 (1936)												
60865	7P: V2 2-6-2 (1936)												
60885	7P: V2 2-6-2 (1936)												
60913	7P: V2 2-6-2 (1936)												
60976	7P: V2 2-6-2 (1936)	X	X	X	X	X	X	X	X	X	X	Ex York	
60051	7P: A3 4-6-2 (1922)		To Heaton	X	X	X	X	X	X	X	X	X	X
60052	7P: A3 4-6-2 (1922)		To Heaton	X	X	X	X	X	X	X	X	X	X
60053	7P: A3 4-6-2 (1922)		To Gateshead	X	X	X	X	X	X	X	X	X	X
60058	7P: A3 4-6-2 (1922)		To Gateshead	X	X	X	X	X	X	X	X	X	X
61017	5MT: B1 4-6-0 (1942)	X	X	X	X	X	X	X	X	X	X	Ex York	
61115	5MT: B1 4-6-0 (1942)	X	X	X	X	X	X	X	X	X	X	Ex York	
61129	5MT: B1 4-6-0 (1942)												
61214	5MT: B1 4-6-0 (1942)												
61267	5MT: B1 4-6-0 (1942)	X	Ex Wakefield										
61309	5MT: B1 4-6-0 (1942)												
61320	5MT: B1 4-6-0 (1942)	X	Ex Wakefield										
61339	5MT: B1 4-6-0 (1942)	X	X	X	X	X	X	X	X	X	X	Ex York	
61386	5MT: B1 4-6-0 (1942)												
61387	5MT: B1 4-6-0 (1942)												
61388	5MT: B1 4-6-0 (1942)												
64911	5F: J39 0-6-0 (1926)								To Ardsley	X	X	X	X
68911	4F: J50 0-6-0T (1922)												
68913	4F: J50 0-6-0T (1922)												
68925	4F: J50 0-6-0T (1922)												
68937	4F: J50 0-6-0T (1922)		To Ardsley	X	X	X	X	X	X	X	X	X	X
68978	4F: J50 0-6-0T (1922)												
68984	4F: J50 0-6-0T (1922)												
68988	4F: J50 0-6-0T (1922)												
64173	3F: J6 0-6-0 (1911)												
64276	3F: J6 0-6-0 (1911)												
64277	3F: J6 0-6-0 (1911)												
69434	2P: N1 0-6-2T (1907)												
69450	2P: N1 0-6-2T (1907)												
69462	2P: N1 0-6-2T (1907)												
69477	2P: N1 0-6-2T (1907)												

ALLOCATION AND TRANSFERS : LEEDS (COPLEY HILL) MPD

Loco	Class	Aug-58	Sep-58	Oct-58	Nov-58	Dec-58	Jan-59	Feb-59	Mar-59	Apr-59	May-59	Jun-59	Jul-59
60117	8P: A1 4-6-2 (1948)												
60118	8P: A1 4-6-2 (1948)												
60120	8P: A1 4-6-2 (1948)												
60123	8P: A1 4-6-2 (1948)												
60130	8P: A1 4-6-2 (1948)												
60131	8P: A1 4-6-2 (1948)												
60133	8P: A1 4-6-2 (1948)												
60134	8P: A1 4-6-2 (1948)												
60141	8P: A1 4-6-2 (1948)												
60148	8P: A1 4-6-2 (1948)												
60837	7P: V2 2-6-2 (1936)	X	X	X	X	X	X	X	X	X	X	Ex York	
60841	7P: V2 2-6-2 (1936)												
60843	7P: V2 2-6-2 (1936)		To T'mouth	X	X	X	X	X	X	X	X	X	X
60859	7P: V2 2-6-2 (1936)												
60864	7P: V2 2-6-2 (1936)	X	X	X	X	X	X	X	X	X	X	Ex York	
60865	7P: V2 2-6-2 (1936)		To T'mouth	X	X	X	X	X	X	X	X	X	X
60877	7P: V2 2-6-2 (1936)	X	X	X	X	X	X	X	X	X	X	Ex York	
60885	7P: V2 2-6-2 (1936)												
60913	7P: V2 2-6-2 (1936)		To T'mouth	X	X	X	X	X	X	X	X	X	X
60939	7P: V2 2-6-2 (1936)	X	X	X	X	X	X	X	X	X	X	Ex York	
60976	7P: V2 2-6-2 (1936)		To Heaton	X	X	X	X	X	X	X	X	X	X
61017	5MT: B1 4-6-0 (1942)							To Wakefield	X	X	X	X	X
61115	5MT: B1 4-6-0 (1942)												
61129	5MT: B1 4-6-0 (1942)												
61189	5MT: B1 4-6-0 (1942)	X	X	X	X	X	X	X	X	Ex Ardsley			
61214	5MT: B1 4-6-0 (1942)												
61267	5MT: B1 4-6-0 (1942)		To H'pool	X	X	X	X	X	X	X	X	X	X
61309	5MT: B1 4-6-0 (1942)												
61320	5MT: B1 4-6-0 (1942)												
61339	5MT: B1 4-6-0 (1942)												
61386	5MT: B1 4-6-0 (1942)												
61387	5MT: B1 4-6-0 (1942)		To Darl'ton	X	X	X	X	X	X	X	X	X	X
61388	5MT: B1 4-6-0 (1942)												
64911	5F: J39 0-6-0 (1926)	X	Ex Ardsley										
43099	4MT 2-6-0 (1947)	X	X	X	X	X	X	X	X	X	X	Ex Selby	
43100	4MT 2-6-0 (1947)	X	X	X	X	X	X	X	X	X	X	Ex Selby	
68911	4F: J50 0-6-0T (1922)												
68913	4F: J50 0-6-0T (1922)												
68925	4F: J50 0-6-0T (1922)												
68978	4F: J50 0-6-0T (1922)				W/D	X	X	X	X	X	X	X	X
68984	4F: J50 0-6-0T (1922)												
68988	4F: J50 0-6-0T (1922)												
40074	3P 2-6-2T (1935)	X	X	X	X	X	Ex Manningham						
40112	3P 2-6-2T (1935)	X	X	X	X	X	Ex Manningham						
40114	3P 2-6-2T (1935)	X	X	X	X	X	Ex Manningham						
64173	3F: J6 0-6-0 (1911)												
64276	3F: J6 0-6-0 (1911)			W/D	X	X	X	X	X	X	X	X	X
64277	3F: J6 0-6-0 (1911)												
69434	2P: N1 0-6-2T (1907)								W/D	X	X	X	X
69450	2P: N1 0-6-2T (1907)								W/D	X	X	X	X
69462	2P: N1 0-6-2T (1907)									W/D	X	X	X
69477	2P: N1 0-6-2T (1907)									W/D	X	X	X

ALLOCATION AND TRANSFERS : LEEDS (COPLEY HILL) MPD

Loco	Class	Aug-59	Sep-59	Oct-59	Nov-59	Dec-59	Jan-60	Feb-60	Mar-60	Apr-60	May-60	Jun-60	Jul-60
60117	8P: A1 4-6-2 (1948)												
60118	8P: A1 4-6-2 (1948)												
60120	8P: A1 4-6-2 (1948)												
60123	8P: A1 4-6-2 (1948)												
60130	8P: A1 4-6-2 (1948)												
60131	8P: A1 4-6-2 (1948)												
60133	8P: A1 4-6-2 (1948)												
60134	8P: A1 4-6-2 (1948)												
60141	8P: A1 4-6-2 (1948)												
60148	8P: A1 4-6-2 (1948)												
60808	7P: V2 2-6-2 (1936)	X	X	X	X	X	X	X	X	X	X	X	Ex Heaton
60809	7P: V2 2-6-2 (1936)	X	X	X	X	X	X	X	X	X	X	X	Ex Heaton
60837	7P: V2 2-6-2 (1936)			To York	X	X	X	X	X	X	X	X	X
60841	7P: V2 2-6-2 (1936)											To Grantham	X
60859	7P: V2 2-6-2 (1936)												
60864	7P: V2 2-6-2 (1936)			To York	X	X	X	X	X	X	X	X	X
60877	7P: V2 2-6-2 (1936)			To York	X	X	X	X	X	X	X	X	X
60885	7P: V2 2-6-2 (1936)				To Thornaby	X	X	X	X	X	X	X	X
60939	7P: V2 2-6-2 (1936)			To York	X	X	X	X	X	X	X	X	X
60069	7P: A3 4-6-2 (1922)	X	X	X	X	X	X	X	X	X	X	X	Ex Tweedm'th
60070	7P: A3 4-6-2 (1922)	X	X	X	X	X	X	X	X	X	X	X	Ex Gateshead
60072	7P: A3 4-6-2 (1922)	X	X	X	X	X	X	X	X	X	X	X	Ex Tweedm'th
61115	5MT: B1 4-6-0 (1942)												
61129	5MT: B1 4-6-0 (1942)												
61189	5MT: B1 4-6-0 (1942)												
61214	5MT: B1 4-6-0 (1942)												
61309	5MT: B1 4-6-0 (1942)												
61320	5MT: B1 4-6-0 (1942)												
61339	5MT: B1 4-6-0 (1942)												
61386	5MT: B1 4-6-0 (1942)												
61388	5MT: B1 4-6-0 (1942)	To York	X	X	X	X	X	X	X	X	X	X	X
64911	5F: J39 0-6-0 (1926)												
42649	4MT 2-6-4T (1935)	X	X	X	Ex Low Moor						To Wakefield	X	X
42650	4MT 2-6-4T (1935)	X	X	X	Ex Low Moor						To Wakefield	X	X
43099	4MT 2-6-0 (1947)			To Ardsley	X	X	X	X	X	X	X	X	X
43100	4MT 2-6-0 (1947)			To Ardsley	X	X	X	X	X	X	X	X	X
68892	4F: J50 0-6-0T (1922)	X	X	X	X	X	X	X	X	X	X	Ex Ardsley	
68911	4F: J50 0-6-0T (1922)												
68913	4F: J50 0-6-0T (1922)												
68925	4F: J50 0-6-0T (1922)												
68984	4F: J50 0-6-0T (1922)												
68988	4F: J50 0-6-0T (1922)												
40074	3P 2-6-2T (1935)												
40112	3P 2-6-2T (1935)												
40114	3P 2-6-2T (1935)												
64173	3F: J6 0-6-0 (1911)												
64268	3F: J6 0-6-0 (1911)	X	Ex Ardsley										
64277	3F: J6 0-6-0 (1911)												

Booked to be worked by the Kings Cross A4 Pacific that worked down with the 08.00 Kings Cross to Leeds, there were times when Copley Hill had to fill the breach as in the above scene when 60117 'Bois Roussel' was seen leaving Grantham in 1953 with the 15.35 Leeds - Kings Cross 'White Rose'. In spite of having the raised status of a title, the up West Riding was in fact a semi-fast service which called at Wakefield, Doncaster, Retford, Newark, Grantham and Peterborough and took no less than four and a quarter hours to run from Leeds to London. The allocation of names to trains during the early BR years was sometimes done on a rather casual basis.

The West Riding expresses were regarded as being quite separate from the East Coast expresses - the carriage workings were even in different publications - and whilst many East Coast workings changed engines at either Peterborough or Grantham, Leeds trains did not and most Copley Hill engines not only worked through from Leeds to London but worked back the same day in order to amass the yardstick 400-miles per day. (To accrue the same mileage, Kings Cross engines on East Coast workings simply did two return trips a day between London and Grantham). A1 60114 'W.P. Allen' of Grantham lays a smoke screen upon leaving Grantham, having just taken over a London - Newcastle express in 1953.

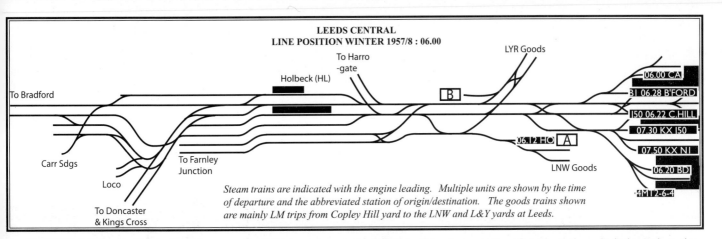

LEEDS CENTRAL
LINE POSITION WINTER 1957/8 : 06.00

Steam trains are indicated with the engine leading. Multiple units are shown by the time of departure and the abbreviated station of origin/destination. The goods trains shown are mainly LM trips from Copley Hill yard to the LNW and L&Y yards at Leeds.

STATION LOG: At Leeds Central as at most BR locations, the new day starts not at midnight but at six in the morning; the change being marked by thousands of railwaymen all over the country starting work some three hours earlier than the rest of the country.

At most stations the day's work is little different from that undertaken by generations of previous railwaymen but at Leeds there is a difference since it is one of the few locations to have had the new diesel multiple-units thrust upon it and the novelty has not yet worn off.

The diesels were initially employed on the intensively-worked nine-mile run to Bradford

Castleford services and a handful of Leeds - Doncaster services are now worked by multiple units.

The diesel invasion has been quite complete so far as local services are concerned and the only steam-worked services to Harrogate or Bradford are either through trains from London or parcels services. Castleford is left with only one steam service; an evening rush-hour train which is worked by an N1 0-6-2T

One of the steam-hauled parcels trains is sitting in platform 2, its B1 4-6-0 waiting to follow the 06.20 Bradford diesel. The parcels train calls at Holbeck to pick up Midland and

trains of stock are brought in by tank engines which steam heat until departure time.

Apart from the Castleford locals, the GN remains largely steam-hauled as well it might since the A1 Pacifics diagrammed to many trains are barely ten years old. In addition to the London expresses, there is a frequent service of stopping trains to Doncaster handled in the main by B1 4-6-0's which, like the A1's, are practically new. This, however, has not stopped diesel multiple-units from making an appearance on the main line and of the thirteen stopping trains between Leeds and Doncaster, three are worked by diesels. One of these is

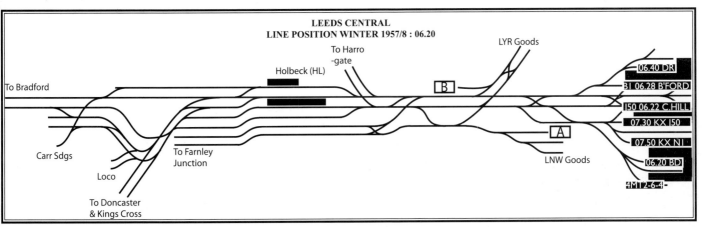

LEEDS CENTRAL
LINE POSITION WINTER 1957/8 : 06.20

Exchange but latterly their use has extended to the Castleford services and to Harrogate. The latter is an innovation since Harrogate services were traditionally operated by the North Eastern from Leeds City. Had the Harrogate workings been dieselised from Leeds City, they would have resulted in a separate diesel programme whilst transferring the trains to Leeds City not only allowed the diagrams to be integrated with the existing GN workings but saw the introduction of a near-hourly service of expresses between Harrogate and Bradford.

The diesels have also taken over the hourly

North Eastern transfer traffic before serving most stations to Bradford via Pudsey: strict punctuality being called for since its fifty-five minute schedule has to be squeezed in between successive Leeds - Bradford diesels.

It will be noticed that a fair proportion of the station's platform accommodation is occupied - seemingly unnecessarily - by the empty stock of the first two London trains. The reason is to ensure that the trains are platformed with an ample margin to cover problems that might cause delays and to give the restaurant car staff time to stock up and generally get ready. Both

the 06.40 departure in platform 1 which calls at eight local stations and connects at Doncaster with the 07.30 Leeds - Kings Cross. Cynics waste no time in pointing out that the service is now three minutes slower than it had been behind a steam engine.

In the opposite direction a Copley Hill B1 4-6-0 approaches Holbeck with the 04.20 ex Sheffield, a six-vehicle train (two non-corridor coaches and four parcels vehicles) which is the Leeds extension of the 21.40 Swindon - York express. The engine will later work the 15.40 local to Doncaster.

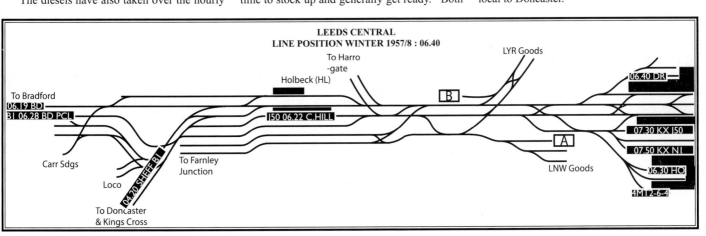

LEEDS CENTRAL
LINE POSITION WINTER 1957/8 : 06.40

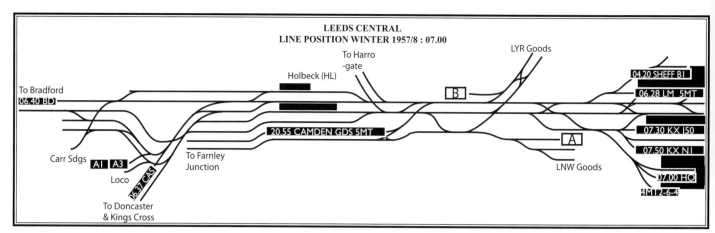

STATION LOG: The importance of Leeds is no better demonstrated than by the fact that within the space of twenty minutes it commands no less than two express services to London.

The engines for both workings can be seen ringing off Copley Hill loco; the engine for the 07.30 being closely followed by the locomotive for the 07.50; a Doncaster A3 and a Copley Hill A1 respectively.

It might be expected that one of the trains would run fast with the other calling at the more important intermediate points yet in fact both trains are of near-equal status since both run non-stop between Doncaster and Kings Cross. One might also have expected that if two trains

Leeds to Holbeck, the banking of departing trains is only allowed under the most stringent of conditions and not only must it be limited to the length of the platform but the Traffic Inspector must ride on the footplate to supervise the operation. Both the 07.30 and 07.50 departures are started in this way.

The Great Northern expresses are not the only express services to use the station and the first of the Lancashire & Yorkshire workings can be seen in platform 2. Like most of the L&Y services from Leeds, it is formed of a 3-coach LMS corridor set (Brake Third, Composite and Brake Third) which will combine at Low Moor with an identical set from Bradford.

slightly greater than those of the LNWR, the L&Y has the combined handicaps of having to merge trains at Low Moor plus an overall distance fourteen miles greater than the LNW.

On the other hand the L&Y trains tend to be light, usually no more than six vehicles, over gradients that are far less severe than those of the LNW. In all, fifteen three-coach sets are employed in the service but, alas, no catering vehicles.

Arriving as the 06.28 from Low Moor, the train arrives in platform two where the engine is uncoupled and released either to turn on Wortley angle or, if it has arrived tender-first, to be coupled up to the other end of the train.

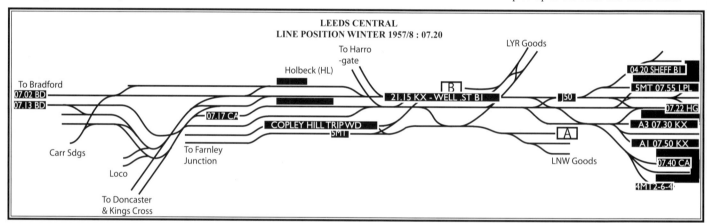

had to leave the West Riding at the same time, one might start from Bradford and the other Leeds yet, here again, both trains have very similar compositions and consist of six coaches from Leeds with five vehicles from Bradford being attached at Wakefield Westgate.

The principal difference between the pair is the running time, for whilst the 07.30 'West Riding' is allowed only 213 minutes including 18 minutes recovery time, the 07.50 is allowed 233 and 25 respectively.

Although the line climbs at 1 in 100 from

Generally the Leeds portions of these trains are worked by 2-6-4T's as far as Low Moor but the 07.55 is one of the exceptions to the rule; the Bradford section being the subordinate section. The Leeds engine - a Southport Black 5 4-6-0 - will work through to Liverpool Exchange.

With the LNW service from Leeds City via Huddersfield, there are fifteen daily expresses between Leeds and Liverpool; seven of which run via Low Moor and Sowerby Bridge. The latter route is extremely smartly run and although the running times to Liverpool are

At around the same time a J50 arrives from Copley Hill loco to take the stock of the 04.20 ex Sheffield to the carriage sidings. The B1 which brought the train in will be prepared by Copley Hill for the 15.40 to Doncaster.

As the White Rose and its J50 banker blast away from the station, they are passed by the 06.20 from Doncaster, the stock - four non-corridor coaches - of which forms the 08.22 back to Doncaster. The engine is released through the centre road to take the gas tanks and any other loose vehicles to Copley Hill.

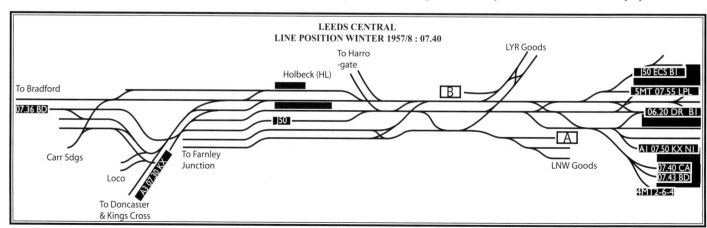

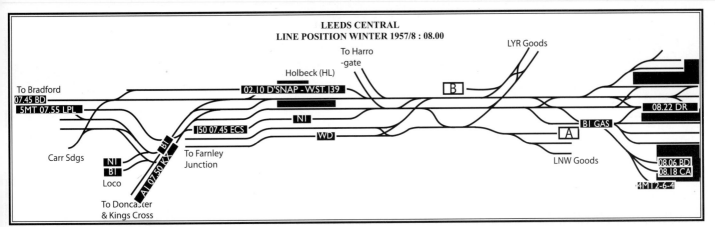

LEEDS CENTRAL
LINE POSITION WINTER 1957/8 : 08.00

STATION LOG: The rush hour in the West Riding is a curious thing and although the greater part of the traffic heads for Leeds, significant numbers travel out to Bradford and Wakefield. Thus arriving trains have to be turned round very quickly to form outward services as opposed to being taken empty to the carriage sidings.

The 07.45 ex-Bradford provides a fairly good example since it arrives in Leeds at 08.09 and then returns to Bradford with another complement of season-ticket holders only six minutes later. This intensive working is made

satisfaction in dealing with complex movements and the general feeling, especially amongst signalmen, is that multiple-unit operation has caused a rather interesting job to become rather dull.

Perhaps the worst aspect of diesel working is remembering that the first train into a terminal platform has to be the last out. The workings do not always reflect this seemingly obvious maxim and there are many times when departures from platforms 6 and 7 are blocked in by subsequent arrivals. To avoid this problem one has to keep several steps ahead and when necessary shunt

shuttle to and fro. The usual method is for the fireman of each engine to advise the signalman of the train the engine is booked to work, the information being passed from box to box but if any doubt or confusion arises then the Controller, who has the engine workings at his fingertips, has to be consulted.

A B1 4-6-0 comes off shed to work the 08.22 Doncaster slow from platform 3 and is followed by an N1 0-6-2T to work the empties of the 04.00 from Kings Cross to Copley Hill.

A second B1 - the engine that arrived with the 06.20 from Doncaster - ambles tender-first

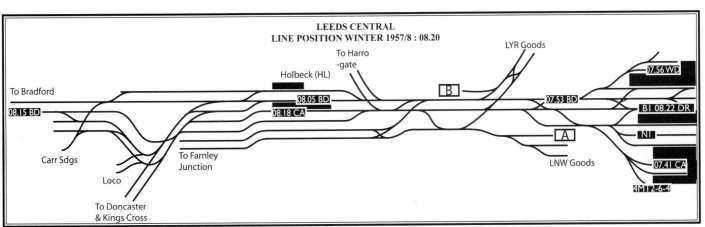

LEEDS CENTRAL
LINE POSITION WINTER 1957/8 : 08.20

possible by the use of diesel multiple units where the reversal in platform 2 requires nothing more involved than the driver walking from one end of the train to the other. With a steam working one has to dispose of the inward engine, find an outward engine (and somewhere to put it until the time comes for it to back onto its train) whilst very often the station pilot is employed to release the inward locomotive.

One might have thought that this simplification of matters would be welcomed by most operating staff but in fact the converse applies. Most railwaymen take considerable

units into the siding at A box or the siding roads in the station to create a little breathing space. The alternative - essential when the service is running badly - is to ignore the booked diesel workings and turn trains around on the basis of the last in is the first out. Since diesels are regarded as carriages rather than engines, their diagrams are sometimes more of a guide than a fixed rule.

Steam and its associated challenges still make up the greater part of a day's work and not the least of these are the problems associated with identifying the various light engines that

to Copley Hill with the spent gas tanks (used for the dining cars) whilst a third arrives with the 07.33 from Doncaster and, after being released, runs light to Copley Hill to be readied for an afternoon turn to Doncaster.

The LM 2-6-4T that has been simmering in the loco yard for some hours comes to life and backs onto the 08.12 ex Sowerby Bridge which forms the 08.55 to Low Moor and Liverpool Exchange. The inward engine, when released, releases in turn the engine of the 07.33 ex Doncaster. Simply keeping watch on engine movements is almost a full time job.

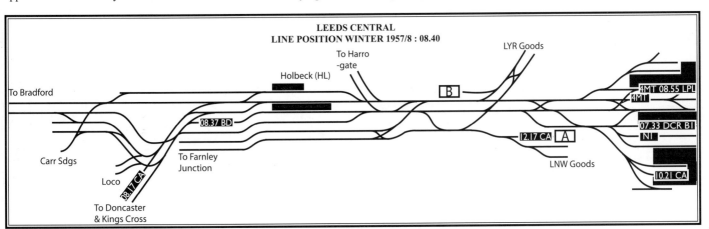

LEEDS CENTRAL
LINE POSITION WINTER 1957/8 : 08.40

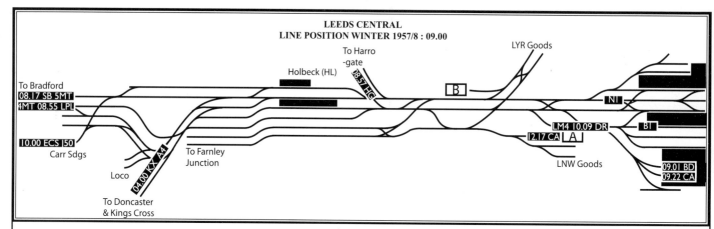

LEEDS CENTRAL
LINE POSITION WINTER 1957/8 : 09.00

STATION LOG: It is a curious fact that Leeds has never been selected as a base for any A4 Pacifics: the only sheds to have an allocation being Kings Cross, Grantham, Gateshead and Haymarket. When Copley Hill joined the ranks of sheds that ran London expresses through to Kings Cross, it was deemed preferable to provide brand-new A1 Pacifics instead of engines that had been at work for a decade and a half.

A4 Pacifics, however, are far from being strangers at Leeds since the London workings are shared between Copley Hill, Doncaster and Kings Cross and the last-mentioned diagrams the class to cover all three of its Leeds workings.

miles in 118 minutes - but in practice the fifteen minutes recovery time added to the schedule means that the engine can steam easily for much of the journey and still reach London on time.

The A4 used for the 10.00 has spent all night at Leeds, having arrived in the area with the previous night's Yorkshire Pullman from London. After reaching Kings Cross it will complete its day's work with an evening Kings Cross - Edinburgh express as far as Grantham, returning to London with a fish train from Aberdeen.

The A4 which arrives with the 04.00 newspaper express from London will be

train will return to Bradford in the 12.22 parcels train from Leeds.

On the Midland side, the 08.55 to Liverpool has departed behind a 4MT 2-6-4T; its place being taken by the 08.17 ex Sowerby Bridge, a train that would be unremarkable were it not for the fact it is worked by one of only two Newton Heath 4-6-0's normally to be seen in Leeds Central. (The other is the 5XP which works the 03.25 Leeds - Manchester).

The 08.17 does not have a return working and the stock is taken empty to Low Moor at 09.45 by the 2-6-4T that arrived with the 08.12 from Low Moor. The Newton Heath Black Five

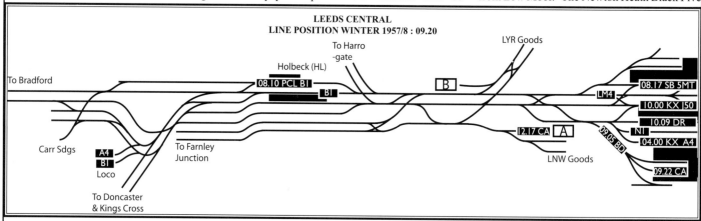

LEEDS CENTRAL
LINE POSITION WINTER 1957/8 : 09.20

At this time of day two A4 Pacifics can be seen next to each other as one of the class runs in with the 04.00 express from Kings Cross whilst another backs down from Copley Hill loco to work the 10.00 to London.

The 10.00 runs as an alternative to the Yorkshire Pullman - there is some resistance to the supplement - which leaves Leeds three-quarters of an hour later. It is a fast train and after collecting the Halifax (via Bradford) portion at Wakefield, calls only at Retford and Newark. In theory, it has a mile-a-minute booking from Newark to Kings Cross - 120

serviced at Copley Hill and will return south with the 12.30 Leeds to Kings Cross.

As well as A4 Pacifics - very much regarded as the creme-de-la-creme - runaday B1 4-6-0's are much in evidence. One is passing Holbeck on its way to work the 10.09 Leeds to Doncaster stopping train whilst another - the engine off the 07.33 from Doncaster - arrives on Copley Hill loco to be prepared for the 15.40 Leeds to Doncaster. A third B1 stops at Holbeck with a parcels train from Bradford and is overtaken by the 09.05 Bradford - Leeds diesel whilst it unloads parcels. Most of the vehicles in the

goes onto Copley Hill Loco before bringing in the empty stock for the 12.55 Leeds - Liverpool, the only LM train dealt with by Copley Hill. The 4-6-0 then runs light to Farnley Junction shed where it remains until working the 22.00 Leeds City - Birmingham as far as Stockport.

Since the J50 0-6-0T covering the station pilot is hemmed in behind the 10.00 London, before leaving with the 09.45 Low Moor empties, the LM 2-6-4T is used to pull out the Bradford parcels stock from platform 1 in order to release the B1 so that it can run back to Copley Hill.

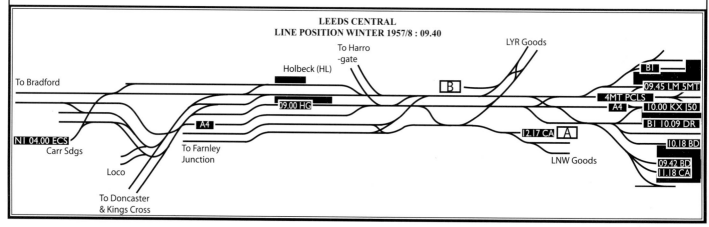

LEEDS CENTRAL
LINE POSITION WINTER 1957/8 : 09.40

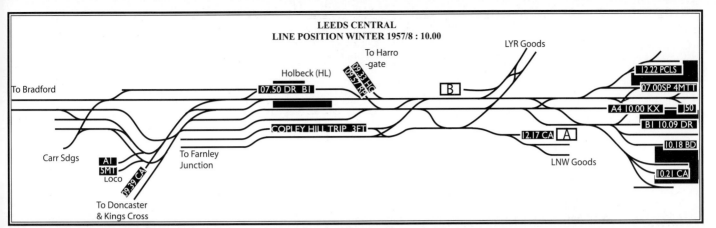

LEEDS CENTRAL
LINE POSITION WINTER 1957/8 : 10.00

STATION LOG: The coming hour sees two expresses leave for London in fairly close succession: the first being the 10.00 from Leeds which pulls out behind the Kings Cross A4 that brought in the previous night's Yorkshire Pullman whilst the second is the 10.45 up Pullman, worked by a Copley Hill A1.

Both convey Bradford sections but whilst the 10.00 collects its portion in the conventional way at Wakefield Westgate, the Bradford section of the Pullman runs into Leeds behind a B1 4-6-0 where it combines with the five Harrogate coaches which are brought in by a BR 4MT 2-6-4T. Thirteen minutes are allowed

but it also occupies a unique spot in the Railway industry since the loco crew who man the train perform the extraordinary feat of working to London and back in one shift - a performance that probably makes the turn the most arduous of any on British Railways.

The crew return with the 15.40 ex Kings Cross - notable for its non-stop run to Wakefield - using the A1 that worked up with the 07.50 from Leeds.

Because of the nature of the turn, the crew sign on at Leeds Central and their engine is brought light from Copley Hill by the crew of the J50 carriage sidings pilot.

the engine and coaches continue forward as the 08.12 to Bradford and Leeds after a pause of eleven minutes.   This saves a good deal of empty stock and light engine movements although it complicates the carriage workings since the stock has to spend several days working between Leeds and Liverpool before finding its way back to Southport.

In the midst of all the passenger activity, parcels traffic continues to be active with the 07.50 ex-Doncaster - the last of the night's parcels trains - transferring traffic at Holbeck before reaching Leeds at 10.15.   Although consisting of no more than three vehicles -

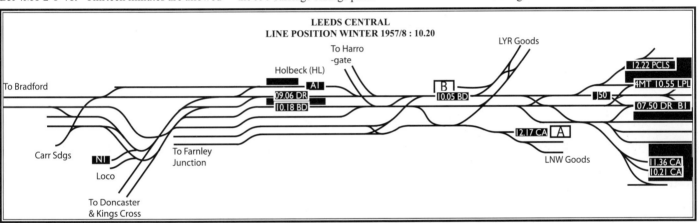

LEEDS CENTRAL
LINE POSITION WINTER 1957/8 : 10.20

for putting the train together, the A1 backing onto the Bradford vehicles in platform 4 and then attaching them to the Harrogate coaches in platform 5.   The J50 pilot then takes the BCK that provided the brake accommodation for the Bradford portion and attaches it to the 12.22 Parcels, releasing the Bradford B1 which can then turn on the Wortley angle in readiness for the Bradford section of the 08.00 ex Kings Cross. The 2-6-4T that brought in the Harrogate sections returns light to Leeds City.

From the perspective of the public the Pullman is a distinctive train for obvious reasons

On the Midland side of the station, a Low Moor 2-6-4T arrives with the 07.00 from Southport at 09.58; the engine running round the stock to form the 10.55 to Liverpool.

One is accustomed to trains arriving in Leeds from Manchester and Liverpool but Southport seems rather a strange starting point for a long-distance service.   The reason is that Southport is a popular dormitory resort for a large number of Manchester's season ticket holders for whom a 07.00 express from Chapel Street is run each morning and rather than complicate the work of Manchester Victoria at an extremely busy time,

most of its traffic is removed at Wakefield for Bradford - it is of interest since one of its vehicles left Kings Cross at 22.55 whilst another left Marylebone a couple of hours earlier to follow an unusual routing by leaving the GC main line at Kirkby South Junction to travel via Mansfield and the LDEC to join the GN main line at Tuxford.   The third vehicle started from Peterborough with traffic from East Anglia. The empties are taken to Copley Hill by the N1 0-6-2T seen leaving Copley Hill loco whilst the B1 train engine will take the empty stock of the 08.32 from Liverpool to the carriage sidings.

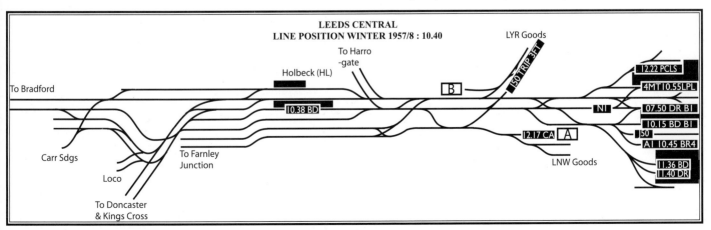

LEEDS CENTRAL
LINE POSITION WINTER 1957/8 : 10.40

Next stop Leeds. A1 60119 'Patrick Stirling' of Copley Hill starts the 11.50 Queen of Scots Pullman from platform 10, Kings Cross in 1950. Although appearing to be some twenty minutes slower that it had been before the war, the post-war timings were padded out with no less than twenty-two minutes of recovery time which, in fact, meant that the train was slightly faster - and two coaches heavier - than it had been in 1939. The Queen of Scots was unique in running to Glasgow (Queen Street) via Leeds, Harrogate and Edinburgh and enjoyed a remarkable array of motive power. A Copley Hill A1 worked the service to Leeds and was relieved by a Neville Hill A3 which worked as far as Newcastle. A Heaton A1 took over for the Newcastle to Edinburgh leg whilst the final 47 miles to Glasgow were handled by a B1 4-6-0.

PRINCIPAL PARCELS TRAIN FORMATIONS

01.05 LEEDS - MARCH

Vehicle	Attached at	From	To	Destination
Engine (B1 4-6-0)				
PMV	Leeds	Leeds	Doncaster	March
B	Leeds	Bradford	March	Norwich
Vanfit	Leeds	Leeds	Doncaster	Grimsby
Vanfit	Leeds	Leeds	Doncaster	
Vanfit	Wakefield (W)	Bradford (18.00)	March	Colchester
BG	Wakefield (K)	Burscough Bridge (17.54)	March	Colchester
BG	Wakefield (K)	Mytholmroyd (21.59)	March	Colchester
BG	Wakefield (K)	Burscough Bridge (17.54)	Doncaster	
SK	Doncaster	Doncaster	March	
BG	Doncaster	Newcastle (20.10)	March	
BG	Doncaster	York (00.54)	March	Ipswich
PMV	Doncaster	York (00.54)	March	Norwich
BZ	Lincoln	Sheffield (V) (02.10)	March	
BZ	Lincoln	Manchester (Mayfield) (22.15)	March	
BG	Lincoln	Manchester (Mayfield) (22.15)	March	Norwich

01.42 LEEDS - DONCASTER - SHEFFIELD

Vehicle	Attached at	From	To	Destination
Engine (B1 4-6-0)				
BS (N/Corr)	Leeds	Leeds	Sheffield (V)	Sheffield (V)
CL (N/Corr)	Leeds	Leeds	Sheffield (V)	Sheffield (V)
BG	Leeds	Leeds	Sheffield (V)	Sheffield (V)
BG	Leeds	Leeds	Sheffield (V)	Sheffield (V)
BG	Leeds	Leeds	Sheffield (V)	Nottingham
BZ	Leeds	Leeds	Sheffield (V)	Leicester
B	Leeds	Leeds	Doncaster	Kings Cross

22.35 LEEDS - DONCASTER

Vehicle	Attached at	From	To	Destination
Engine (B1 4-6-0)				
Pass section (5)	Leeds	Leeds	Doncaster	
Vanfit	Leeds	Leeds	Doncaster	Peterborough
B	Leeds	Leeds	Wakefield (K)	Leeds City

The above table gives some idea of the scope and complexity of parcels traffic operations. The trains shown are the principal parcels services to and from Leeds

07.50 DONCASTER - LEEDS

Vehicle	Attached at	From	To	Destination
Engine (B1 4-6-0)				
BG	Doncaster	Doncaster	Wakefield (K)	Mytholmroyd
TSO (ECS)	Doncaster	Doncaster	Wakefield (W)	Bradford
BCK (ECS)	Doncaster	Doncaster	Wakefield (W)	Bradford
BG	Doncaster	Kings Cross (22.55)	Wakefield (W)	Bradford
BG	Doncaster	Peterborough (02.45)	Leeds	Leeds
PMV	Doncaster	Marylebone (20.50)	Leeds	Leeds
BG	Doncaster	Kings Cross (22.55)	Leeds	Leeds

18.00 BRADFORD - DONCASTER

Vehicle	Attached at	From	To	Destination
Engine (B1 4-6-0)				
Vanfit	Bradford	Bradford	Wakefield (W)	Colchester
B	Bradford	Bradford	Doncaster	Norwich
B	Bradford	Bradford	Doncaster	Kings Cross

02.58 DONCASTER - LEEDS

Vehicle	Attached at	From	To	Destination
Engine (B1 4-6-0)				
PMV	Doncaster	Lowestoft (13.15)	Leeds	Leeds
B	Doncaster	Doncaster	Leeds	Leeds
B	Doncaster	Kings Cross (12.25)	Leeds	Leeds
BG	Doncaster	Kings Cross (18.32)	Leeds	Leeds
Vanfit	Doncaster	Doncaster	Wakefield (K)	Bradford
B	Doncaster	Marylebone (20.50)	Wakefield (K)	Bradford
B	Doncaster	Whitemoor (20.50)	Wakefield (K)	Bradford
BG	Doncaster	Kings Cross (12.25)	Wakefield (K)	Bradford
BG	Doncaster	Kings Cross (18.32)	Wakefield (K)	Bradford

04.20 SHEFFIELD (V) - DONCASTER - LEEDS

Vehicle	Attached at	From	To	Destination
Engine (B1 4-6-0)				
CL (N/Corr	Sheffield (V)	Sheffield (V)	Leeds	Leeds
BS (N/Corr)	Sheffield (V)	Sheffield (V)	Leeds	Leeds
BG	Sheffield (V)	Sheffield (V)	Leeds	Leeds
BG	Sheffield (V)	Sheffield (V)	Leeds	Leeds
BZ	Sheffield (V)	Leicester (01.11)	Leeds	Leeds
BG	Doncaster	Nottingham (00.27)	Leeds	Leeds
BG	Sheffield (V)	Manchester Mayfield (22.15)	Doncaster	Hull
PMV	Sheffield (V)	Wigan (19.38)	Doncaster	Doncaster
BZ (Stores)	Sheffield (V)	Gorton Works (17.00)	Doncaster	March
B	Sheffield (V)	Sheffield (V)	Rotherham	Sheffield (B. Rd)

In spite of the activity that went took place in Leeds Central, goods traffic was very much more important than passenger and there was no shortage of goods termini and marshalling yards in the Leeds area. The situation apropos goods traffic at Leeds Central was made more interesting by the fact that the two goods depots which straddled the largely ex-LNER passenger station were both ex-LMS and served by trip workings from the marshalling yard at Copley Hill. The latter was completely unrelated to its Great Northern namesake and was located on a branch of the Leeds (City) - Huddersfield - Manchester main line. This branch drew parallel with the Great Northern at Holbeck and ran side by side as far as Leeds B box at Leeds Central. Standard 'Austin 7' LMS 7F 0-8-0 49537 (Farnley Junction) passes Holbeck (High Level) with a trip working from Leeds LNW goods to Copley Hill Yard circa 1949. (H.C. Casserley)

Neither the grouping nor nationalisation made much difference to methods of operation and the goods lines that ran parallel to the GN main line between Holbeck (HL) and Leeds Central remained operationally separate for many years after nationalisation. Most of the traffic was conveyed by trip workings between Leeds and Copley Hill Yard although one through service from London (Camden) was operated. Motive power for the trips was provided either by 3F 0-6-0T's from Farnley Junction shed or by main line engines as a prelude or finale to a main line working: hence the appearance of 7F 0-8-0 49523 of Aintree, seen running tender-first past Holbeck for a Leeds - Copley Hill service. The 7F 0-8-0's were replaced at Farnley Junction during the late 1940's by Austerity 2-8-0's. The maximum loads that could be taken were 60 wagons of goods between Leeds and Copley Hill and 35 in the opposite direction. Both were within the capacity of a standard LMS 3F 0-6-0T. (H.C. Casserley)

Very few GN trains turned round in Leeds Central and most were run empty to and from Copley Hill carriage sidings between workings. N1 0-6-2T's and J50 0-6-0T's were used for most workings although main line engines were booked to some of the workings. J50 69888 of Copley Hill takes the up goods line at Holbeck High Level with a train of empty stock for Copley Hill; the valves lifting as the engine is eased off. Capable of very high outputs for short periods of time, the J50 0-6-0's were well suited to the Leeds Central ECS duties (H.C. Casserley)

Several ex- Great Central C14 4-4-2T's were allocated to Ardsley for working the Leeds - Castleford passenger service. (6)7440 pauses at Holbeck (High Level) with a Castleford - Leeds Central local whilst an LMS 7F 0-8-0 reverses towards the LNW goods yard prior to working a trip service to Copley Hill. The trailing junction ahead of 7440 is the route from Harrogate. (H.C. Casserley)

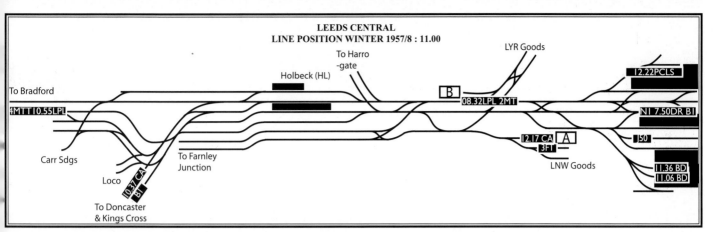

STATION LOG: It is not often that a class 2 engine can be seen on an express passenger turn but the 08.32 Liverpool - Leeds is an exception; the three-coach Leeds section being worked from Low Moor by one of the very efficient LMS 2MT 2-6-2T's. Most of the work done by this engine covers services between Bradford, Huddersfield and Penistone but in between it puts in this brief appearance at Leeds, running back light to Low Moor as soon as it has been released.

In contrast to the usual arrangement whereby L&Y trains turn round in the station, the three vehicles of the Liverpool are taken empty to

years past the principal morning express from London was the 10.20 ex Kings Cross, the view being that the majority of passengers wanted to leave London at around ten in the morning. As a concession to the minority, a West Riding section was combined with the 07.25 Kings Cross to Edinburgh but latterly the service has expanded into a train in its own right, running - somewhat unusually - to Bradford via Leeds.

The service, the 08.00 ex Kings Cross, arrives in Leeds at 11.44 and although three and three-quarter hours is not a bad speed for an express, memories of the pre-war West Riding with its two hours and forty-three minutes timing

It is interesting to note that of the three Kings Cross A4's booked to run to Leeds, only one - the down Yorkshire Pullman - is worked by London men. The 04.00 ex Kings Cross is brought in by a set of Grantham men whilst the 08.00 is worked by the Copley Hill crew that took the 07.30 as far as Doncaster. (This last, which contains less than two hours driving in an eight hour turn of duty, can scarcely be described as the most productive of turns).

The Doncaster B1 that brought in the Doncaster parcels takes the stock of the 08.32 from Liverpool to Copley Hill sidings and releases the 2MT 2-6-2T which hurries away to

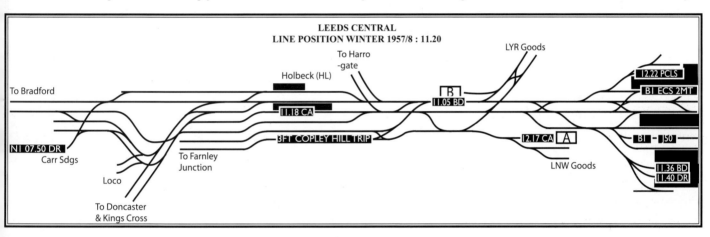

Copley Hill by the B1 which brought in the 07.50 Doncaster parcels. After cleaning, they return to form the 12.55 to Liverpool.

The activity surrounding the Liverpool service contrasts strongly with that of the 11.40 slow train to Doncaster which not so long ago was the return working of the 04.00 ex Kings Cross but is now a very unimpressive two-coach diesel railcar tucked away in platform 7.

A postwar development in express services has been the greater importance accorded to early morning services from London. For many

rankle more than a little. Many believe that the twenty three minutes recovery time given to the train is excessive, to say the least.

Waiting in attendance are a B1 and a J50 to deal with the service when it runs in. The B1, which arrived with the Pullman from Bradford and has turned on Wortley angle in the meantime, will work the Bradford section of the 08.00 forward whilst the J50 will take the remaining coaches to Copley Hill sidings. The A4 will be serviced at Copley Hill loco and made ready for the 15.35 'White Rose' to Kings Cross.

Low Moor shed where it will be made ready for the 14.55 Bradford - Penistone.

As one N1 0-6-2T enters the carriage sidings with the empties of the Doncaster parcels, another runs light from the loco to take the empty stock of the morning Cleethorpes express, due at 12.03, to Copley Hill. Another light engine, an Ardsley B1 4-6-0, approaches from Bradford to work the 12.22 Parcels. This is the engine that earlier worked the Bradford section of the 07.50 Doncaster parcels from Wakefield Westgate via Batley.

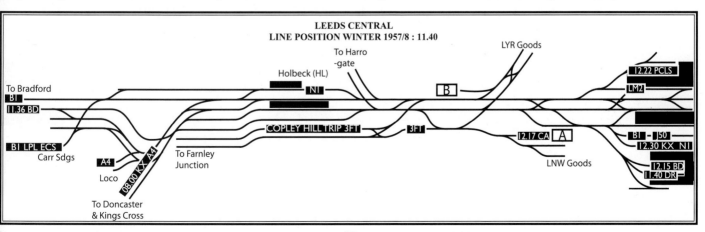

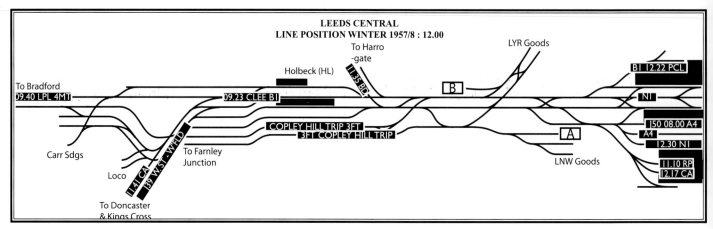

LEEDS CENTRAL
LINE POSITION WINTER 1957/8 : 12.00

STATION LOG: For the second time this morning, two A4's can be seen together at Leeds, one having arrived with the 08.00 from Kings Cross whilst the other waits to take over the 11.45 Harrogate - London.

Other than the fact the West Riding seems to favour Cleethorpes above all other holiday resorts, there is no obvious connection between Leeds and Humberside yet a through express is operated between Cleethorpes and Leeds; the only booked passenger working to use the Stainforth - Adwick Junction connection that overmuch.

An interesting element of the working is the fact that the train has to turn round very rapidly in order to clear the platform for the 11.15 stopping service from Doncaster and to facilitate this, the B1 is permitted to run to Copley Hill attached to the rear of the empty stock. Running trains with engines at both ends is not normally allowed but an exception is made for ECS trains in both directions between Leeds and Copley Hill. The trailing engine, however, is not allowed to assist in any way but must allow itself to be hauled.

Peterborough, it is quite a good train although if the twenty-four minutes of recovery time were excised, it would be a good deal better.

On the Midland side of affairs, the 09.40 from Liverpool has arrived in platform 2; hauled from Low Moor by one of the familiar 2-6-4T's. The return working of the coaches is the 13.55 to Liverpool but the engine works back with the 12.55 Liverpool, the stock of which runs in empty from Copley Hill at 12.35. The engine for the 13.55, another 2-6-4T, is sent light from Low Moor loco.

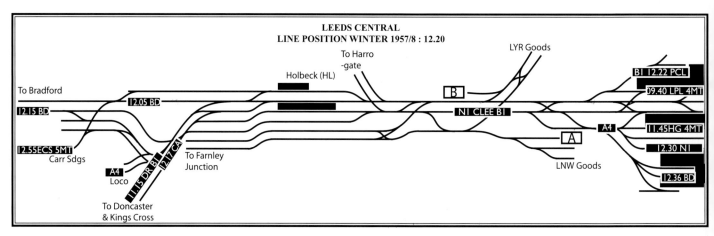

LEEDS CENTRAL
LINE POSITION WINTER 1957/8 : 12.20

links the Doncaster - Leeds and Doncaster - Cleethorpes routes. Made up of only six coaches - until recently it was only four - it is not a heavy train and, on the very level route involved, no test of strength for the Immingham B1 4-6-0 booked to the train.

The stock works back to Cleethorpes with the 16.10 from Leeds whilst the engine performs one of the most wasteful rituals imaginable by running light for the entire 72 miles to Immingham loco.

Needless to say, if the Controller at Wakefield can devise a reason to keep the engine at Leeds, he will do so without troubling his conscience

As the Cleethorpes stock prepares to leave from platform 3, the adjacent platform is occupied by a stranger from the North Eastern in the shape of a BR Standard 2-6-4T; a number of the type having lately taken over from the once-familiar D49 4-4-0's. The train is the 11.45 from Harrogate which is quickly picked up by the waiting A4 and shunted across to the dining portion in platform 5. Fifteen minutes is allowed for the operation.

Worked to London by the A4 which came down with the 04.00 from Kings Cross and due at 16.25 after stops at Wakefield, Doncaster and

The engine that brings in the stock of the 12.55 Liverpool is the Newton Heath Black Five that arrived in the area with the 08.17 from Sowerby Bridge. When it is released at 12.55 it will run light to Farnley Junction shed where it will remain until ringing off to work the 22.00 parcels from Leeds City to Stockport. It will finish the day with the 03.55 Stockport to Manchester Victoria parcels.

At 12.32 the 11.15 slow from Doncaster arrives, its empties being taken empty to Copley Hill by the N1 that brought in the ECS of the 12.30 to Kings Cross. The B1 train engine will return to Doncaster with the 17.16 ex Leeds.

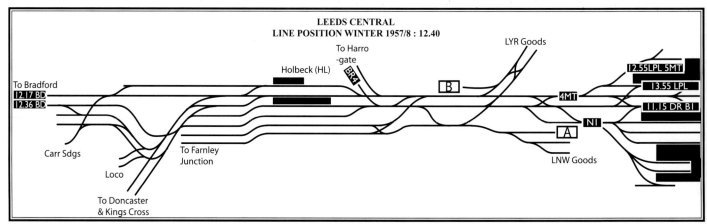

LEEDS CENTRAL
LINE POSITION WINTER 1957/8 : 12.40

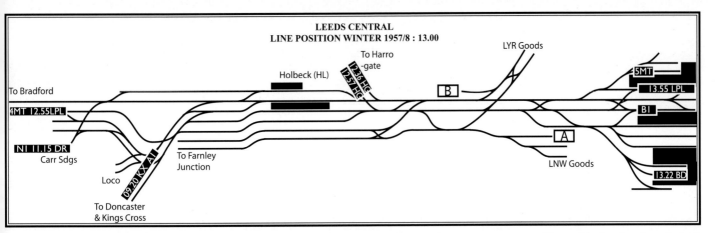

LEEDS CENTRAL
LINE POSITION WINTER 1957/8 : 13.00

STATION LOG: As one o'clock strikes the station falls uncharacteristically quiet with only the 13.22 Bradford diesel plying for trade. The stock of the 13.55 to Liverpool sits in No.2 waiting for its engine to arrive from Low Moor whilst a pair of light engines wait for their respective roads to Farnley Junction and Copley Hill respectively. The silence is little more than momentary and after a few minutes of quiet, the smell and noise of diesel units, which their horribly raucous departures, returns and remains.

The principal event of the moment is the arrival of the 09.20 'White Rose' from Kings

Cross, which is something of a crack train since it runs non-stop between London and Doncaster and maintains the same running times as the 10.00 Flying Scotsman. A considerable effort has been made in recent years to accelerate the more important Great Northern expresses and no less than fifteen and a half minutes has been pared from the London - Doncaster running times during the last six years. Unfortunately this benefit is not immediately apparent since the saving in time has been balanced out by very liberal injections of recovery time. In 1952, for example, the service ran from London

to Doncaster in 169 minutes plus 7 minutes recovery time whereas now the train is allowed 152 minutes with 18 minutes recovery. Thus the perceived improvement of six minutes rather hides the gains that have actually been achieved.

The White Rose is one of two Copley Hill lodging turns and is the return working of yesterday's up Queen of Scots Pullman. Compared with the Yorkshire Pullman turn where the crew work to London and back in the same shift, the White Rose can scarcely be described as an arduous duty since the men sign on at 07.50 and are relieved on arrival in Leeds

after a day of just over five hours.

The stock is not taken to Copley Hill but remains in the station until returning to London as the 15.35 Leeds - Kings Cross. The engine, however, has to be released and to facilitate this, the stock is shunted into No.2 siding by the J50 0-6-0T that brought in the empties of the 14.04 Leeds to Doncaster.

During this time a LMS 2-6-4T arrives light from Low Moor loco and is coupled up to the 13.55 Liverpool express in platform 2.

Close behind this engine is the empty stock of the 08.00 Kings Cross - Bradford which has

no return working and is therefore brought back to Leeds, together with the postal vehicles of the 22.45 ex Kings Cross.

A train of ECS approaches from Bradford and this is the stock of the 08.00 Kings Cross plus a few postal vehicles. Worked by the B1 4-6-0 that covered the up Pullman and the 08.00 ex Kings Cross, the train will be brought into No.1 siding where another B1 - the engine that arrived with the 11.15 from Doncaster and is now ringing off Copley Hill loco - will take it to the carriage sidings. The B1 that works in from Bradford will return light to Low Moor loco, its day over.

The three-coach 14.04 to Doncaster is a more interesting train than appearances suggest since it is based in distant East Anglia and starts the day with the 06.27 March to Doncaster via Spalding, Sleaford and Lincoln, calling at most stations on the Joint line. It then forms the 11.15 Doncaster - Leeds and the 14.04 Leeds - Doncaster before making its way back to the fens with the 16.35 Doncaster to March. Occasionally, when things are running badly at Doncaster, the 06.27 engine is used to work the 11.15 which brings to Leeds the rare sight of a March V2 2-6-2.

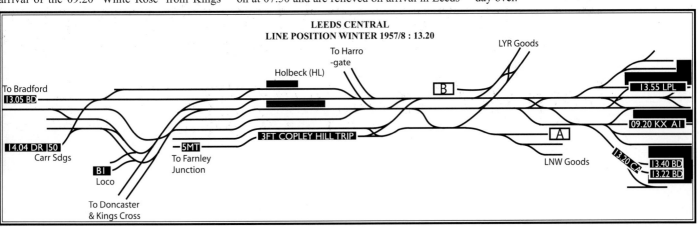

LEEDS CENTRAL
LINE POSITION WINTER 1957/8 : 13.20

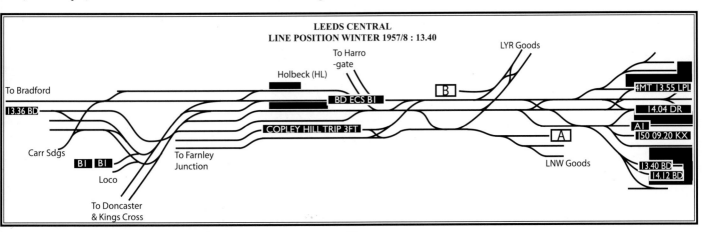

LEEDS CENTRAL
LINE POSITION WINTER 1957/8 : 13.40

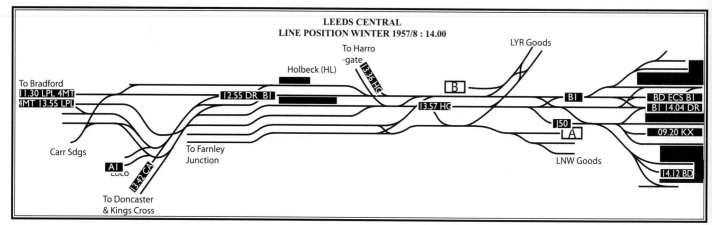

LEEDS CENTRAL
LINE POSITION WINTER 1957/8 : 14.00

STATION LOG: Stopping trains do not normally arouse much interest but the 12.55 Doncaster - Leeds, due at 14.06, has some interesting features. The combined return working of the 08.22 and 10.09 Leeds - Doncaster trains, the 12.55 is made up of no less than nine coaches which is three times the norm for a stopping train and has to be divided on arrival at Leeds with the rear section being added to the Bradford - Copley Hill stock - known as the 'odd-stock' - in No.1 siding whilst the leading four coaches remain in the station to form the 15.40 back to Doncaster.

After the rear vehicles have been disposed

Wortley West the train, now facing Leeds, runs to the carriage sidings in the normal way.

The B1 that brought the train from Bradford to Leeds runs light to Low Moor loco for disposal.

Whilst this shuffling of stock takes place, the 11.30 from Liverpool arrives in platform 2 behind a Low Moor 2-6-4T. As soon as the odd stock has cleared No.1 siding, the 2-6-4T runs round its train; both engine and coaches forming the 15.55 to Low Moor and Liverpool. The three-coach set follows quite an intensive diagram since it started the day with the 07.55 Leeds - Liverpool and will later work the 20.30

On the topic of foreign visitors, some live in hopes of seeing 60700, the W1 4-6-4, at Leeds but although there is no bar to its running over the main line between Leeds and Doncaster, it is prohibited between Hare Park and Wakefield via Kirkgate and since several stopping trains use this route, not to mention diverted expresses, it is not the most welcome of visitors. Since its booked duty is the 10.06 Doncaster - Kings Cross and the 15.52 return, the opportunities for 60700 to visit the West Riding do not normally arise.

Like the 09.20 from Kings Cross, the 10.20 does not repair to Copley Hill but remains in the

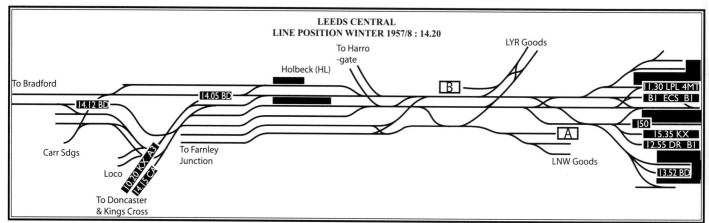

LEEDS CENTRAL
LINE POSITION WINTER 1957/8 : 14.20

of, the J50 pilot releases the train engine by pulling the coaches out and propelling them back in; the B1 running light to Copley Hill to be made ready for the 17.45 to Doncaster.

After the five Doncaster coaches have been added, the ECS train in No.1 siding is ready to depart but all concerned have to be reminded that the working does not go direct to Copley Hill but, since it includes TPO vehicles that require turning, has to run to Wortley South Junction and then reverse to Wortley West Junction, the B1 propelling under special regulations. From

Liverpool - Bradford.

One cannot complain that the London trains lack motive power variety since the three services that have arrived so far have produced two A4's and an A1. The 10.20 from Kings Cross, due in Leeds at 14.28 - extends the range by producing one of the older A3 Pacifics. Since the 10.20 is a Doncaster diagram, it is often used by Kings Cross as a means of getting engines to Doncaster works and there is therefore a fair chance of the train turning up behind an A2 - a class not normally seen at Leeds - or a V2.

station to form the 17.33 to Kings Cross. The stock will be shunted into No.2 siding by the pilot until the time for departure approaches.

The return working of the A3 which works the 10.20 is the 16.43 Doncaster stopping train.

The new A1 Pacifics have made the A3's a much less familiar sight than was once the case although two can be seen together at Leeds at this time of day, the second engine being the Pacific which arrives light from Neville Hill loco in readiness to take over the down Queen of Scots Pullman.

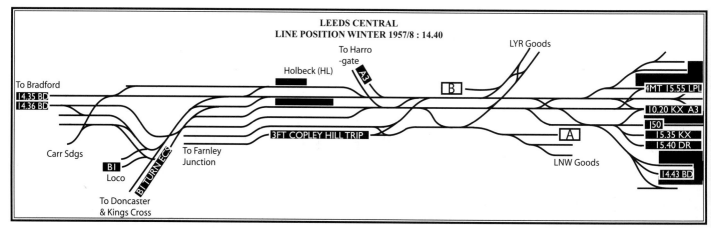

LEEDS CENTRAL
LINE POSITION WINTER 1957/8 : 14.40

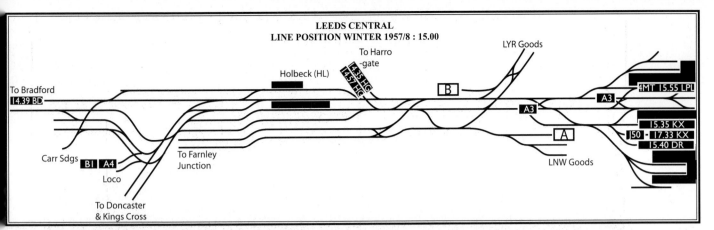

LEEDS CENTRAL
LINE POSITION WINTER 1957/8 : 15.00

STATION LOG: The attraction of the hour is the down Queen of Scots Pullman, the 11.50 Kings Cross to Glasgow (Queen Street). Worked to Leeds by a Copley Hill A1, the train is the only one of the day to run non-stop from London; a feature that on its own makes the service something special. The running time of three hours and thirty-one minutes is nominally twenty minutes slower than in 1939 but since the postwar train has eighteen minutes recovery time - there was none before the war - and is three vehicles heavier, it is fair to say that the working is rather more exacting than it was in

will take the train forward from Newcastle, giving way at Edinburgh to a B1 4-6-0 for the last 47 miles to Glasgow.

As the Neville Hill A3 positions itself (being passed in the process by the A3 that brought in the 10.20 from London) for the arrival of its train, an A4 and a B1 ring off Copley Hill shed to work the 15.35 'White Rose' to Kings Cross and the 15.40 local to Doncaster. The shed has also sent a pair of B1 4-6-0's to the carriage sidings; one of the engines hauling the empty stock of the 16.13 Leeds - Cleethorpes whilst the other - the train engine - trails in the

Where local trains were provided, running, of course, from Leeds City, they tended to call at all stations with a timing of forty-five minutes for the eighteen miles.

Nowadays, the picture is quite different and not only is there a regular service of local trains but the number of intermediate calls is limited to two or three whilst several run non-stop. The 27 minute timing of the latter means that the former service has been cut by almost twenty minutes. By contrast the very much heavier Queen of Scots is booked to take thirty minutes to Harrogate.

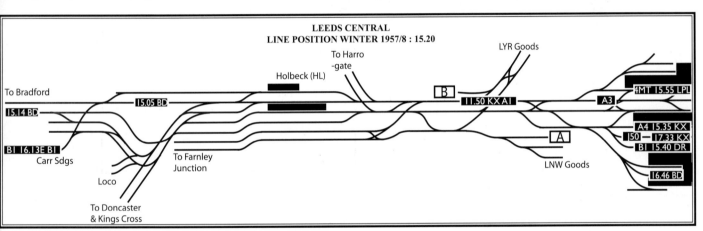

LEEDS CENTRAL
LINE POSITION WINTER 1957/8 : 15.20

LNER days.

During the eight minutes turn-round in Leeds, the A1 and the leading pair of Pullman coaches is uncoupled whilst a Neville Hill A3 is attached at the far end for the leg to Newcastle via Harrogate and Northallerton. After the train has departed, the J50 pilot will shunt the two Pullmans into No.2 siding to wait for the up train and leave the way clear for the A1 to reverse and make its way to Copley Hill.

The train sees quite a selection of motive power and in addition to the A1 and A3 already mentioned, another A1 - from Heaton depot -

rear. The leading engine will work the 17.16 Doncaster stopping service and both, of course, work the Cleethorpes stock tender-first.

Thanks to the diesel workings and the new Bradford - Harrogate service, travel between Leeds Central and Harrogate is not the novelty it once was and even diehard traditionalists have to conceded that in many respects the new service is a considerable improvement on the old.

In fact stopping trains between Leeds and Harrogate were rather a scarcity in the pre-diesel order and for much of the day passengers had to depend upon the handful of through expresses.

The diesel service to Harrogate looks very well on paper but the reality is marred to some extent by the noise, vibration and smell of the multiple-units.

Cynics maintain that an equally good service - without the rough edges - could have been given by a handful of V3 2-6-2T's and a couple of sets of LNER coaches: an initiative that would have allowed the very high capital cost of multiple units and their specialised depots to be used elsewhere. Who knows, they may be right but the politics of the day insists upon modernisation, whatever the cost.

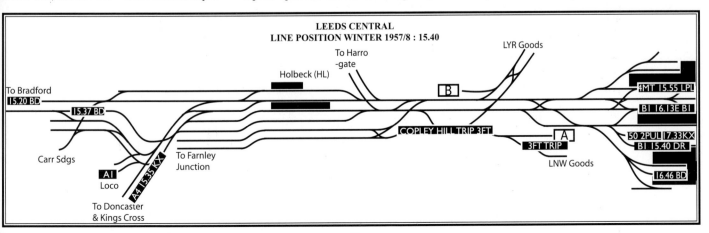

LEEDS CENTRAL
LINE POSITION WINTER 1957/8 : 15.40

Taken in 1949 just after it had been delivered and whilst it was still a Doncaster engine, A1 60144 overtakes B1 4-6-0 1296 as it reverses out of Leeds Central for Copley Hill depot. (H.C. Casserley)

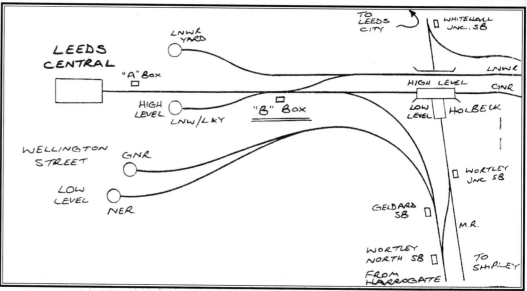

Maps of the Leeds area tend to be rather incomprehensible because of the close intertwining of the several companies that served the area. The maps on this page therefore show only those lines associated with Leeds Central and clarify, hopefully, the position of the lines in its vicinity.

Attention is drawn to the goods arrangements whereby the ex-LMS trains ran in a straightforward manner from Copley Hill Yard to the depots adjacent to Leeds Central whilst ex-LNER goods services from Doncaster and Kings Cross, etc, had to reverse at Leeds B and again at Geldard in order to gain entry to Wellington Street terminal. Through goods trains running from Geldard to Leeds B had to be hauled by the Wellington Street pilot as far as Leeds B with the train engine assisting in rear. In the opposite direction and in clear weather, trains were permitted to propel from Leeds B to Geldard before entering Wellington Street. (Maps by courtesy of Mr R. Pulleyn.)

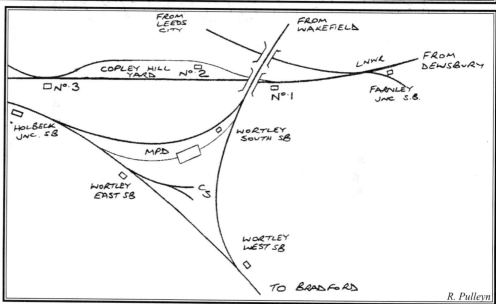

R. Pulleyn

38

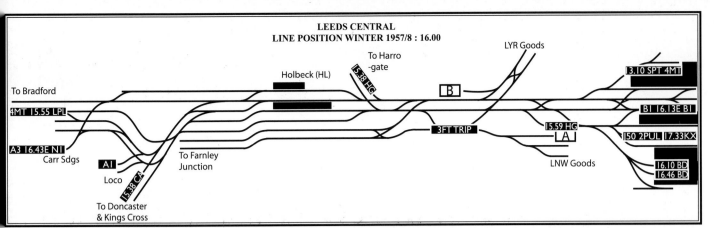

LEEDS CENTRAL
LINE POSITION WINTER 1957/8 : 16.00

STATION LOG: Rarely quiet at any time of day, during the evening peak service Leeds Central is especially busy with departures leaving at a rate of a train every six minutes between 16.00 and 19.00. The actual number of departures is twenty-nine and is a considerable increase on the service of a few years ago when only twenty-two departures were scheduled in the same period.

The reason for the increase lies in the diesel service which has no light engine or empty stock movements; trains turning round, when necessary, in three or four minutes. Destinations served during the peak period are: Bradford:

engine, a Neville Hill A3, will back out and run light to its home station.

As with the down train, the up Queen of Scots hides its light under something of a bushel since although it is advertised as being twenty minutes slower than it was before the war, no less than twenty three minutes of today's 210 minutes are recovery time. Thus in real terms, the train is both heavier and faster than it was in 1939.

To ease line occupation, advantage is taken of the concession which allows empty stock trains to run with an engine at either end between Copley Hill and Leeds. The coaches

that may come in useful is the B1 which brought in the stock of the 16.13 to Cleethorpes. This stands spare until working the 17.16 Doncaster and may be useful in any emergency during the first hour of the rush hour. Copley Hill is one of the few major sheds not to provide a stand-by pilot.

London Midland trains play only a minor role in the rush hour. The 17.11 to Manchester and Liverpool provides a direct service to Halifax and in recognition of the number of season-ticket holders, marries up with the main portion from Bradford at Halifax instead of Low Moor. In addition to the 17.11, there is a 17.55

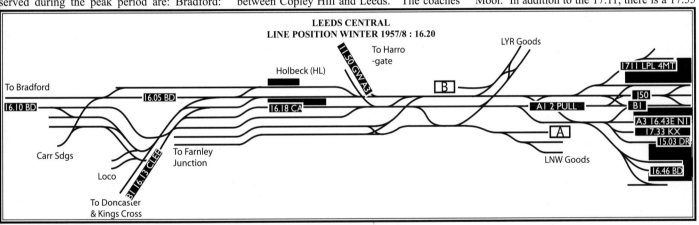

LEEDS CENTRAL
LINE POSITION WINTER 1957/8 : 16.20

12 trains (10), Doncaster/Cleethorpes: 5 (3), Castleford: 4 (4), London: 2 (3), Manchester/ Liverpool: 2 (1) and Harrogate: 4 (1). The figures in brackets show the number of departures in 1953, before the arrival of diesels.

The complexity of the suburban service is not helped by the arrival of the up Queen of Scots at 16.25. Eleven minutes are allowed for its reversal which involves the relieving engine, a Copley Hill A1, collecting the two Pullman cars from No.2 siding and backing them onto the train after its arrival in platform 2. After the service has pulled out for London, the inward

for the 16.13 to Cleethorpes are worked in with a B1 4-6-0 at each end whilst the empties for the 16.43 to Doncaster are brought in by an N1 0-6-2T with an A3 Pacific at the trailing end.

The reliability of diesel railcars has not proved to be as high as that of steam and the incidence of failure is such that a unit is kept spare at the station, ready to plug any gap that may occur. The unit in question works in with the 15.03 stopping train from Doncaster and then remains spare until forming the 19.32 back to Doncaster. It is normally stabled in the siding just beyond A box. Another resource

local train which runs only as far as Low Moor.

The stock of the 17.11 arrives with the 13.10 from Southport; the inward engine - a 2-6-4T - working the 17.55 to Low Moor. The working of the 17.11 engine is an interesting since it brings a Bank Hall Black 5 into Leeds. This particular example works the 12.30 Liverpool - Bradford stopping train as far as Low Moor - where it is relieved by a 2MT 2-6-2T - before turning and running light to Leeds to work home with the 17.11. Surprisingly, given the number of Liverpool trains, Merseyside engines are quite rare at Leeds Central.

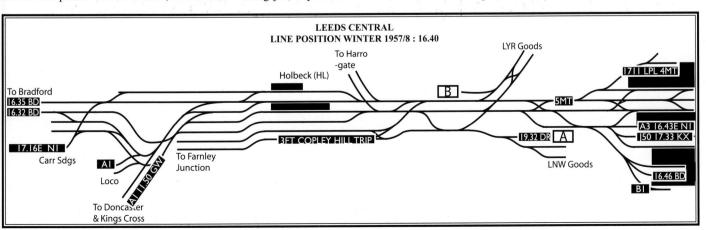

LEEDS CENTRAL
LINE POSITION WINTER 1957/8 : 16.40

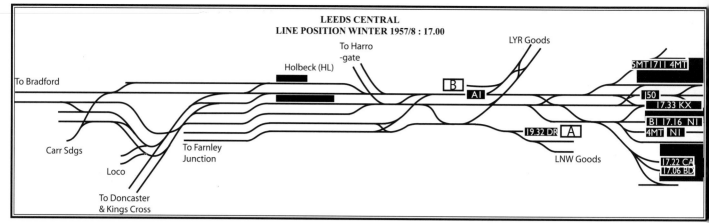

STATION LOG: For a brief hour the station regains something of its pre-diesel atmosphere as J50 0-6-0T's and N1 0-6-2T's congregate in numbers that remind one of the old days. One of the J50's is the station pilot which is waiting to take the stock of the 13.20 ex Kings Cross to Copley Hill whilst another of the same class has its spell as pilot in Wellington Street goods interrupted in order to bring in the empty coaches of the 17.45 for Doncaster.

With the sharp gradient between Leeds and Copley Hill, the powerful J50's - class 4 - are well suited to slogging up the bank with trains of empty coaching stock and given their reluctance to maintain boiler pressure for sustained periods, in many ways it is ideal work for them.

Three Great Northern N1's will make an appearance: two bringing in the empties of the 16.43 and 17.16 Doncaster trains whilst a third - a comparative stranger from Ardsley - will arrive with the 17.00 local from Wakefield Kirkgate.

Of the other engines present, one is the LM 2-6-4T that brought in the 13.10 from Southport and which, when released by the departure of the 17.11 to Liverpool, will drop onto the stock of the 14.30 ex Liverpool and work it out as the 17.55 local to Low Moor. Another 2-6-4T - one

of the BR Standard type - arrives in the station to work out the Harrogate section of the 13.20 from Kings Cross.

Two Great Northern trains occupy platforms three and four; the latter dealing with the 17.16 stopping train to Doncaster which is made up of five non-corridor coaches worked by a Doncaster B1 4-6-0. Platform 3 is dealing with the last train of the day to Kings Cross, the stock having been positioned by the station pilot prior to the arrival of its Copley Hill A1 Pacific from the loco.

Even though it takes all but four hours to reach London, the 17.33 is a very popular train and calls only at Wakefield, where the Bradford section is attached, Peterborough and Hitchin. In common with other east coast trains, the 17.33's schedule has been liberally peppered with recovery time, so much so that if the A1 runs at normal speeds, it will have to sit in Peterborough for no less than eighteen minutes waiting for the booked departure time.

Altogether recovery time - an aberration devised by the very remote timing office at Liverpool Street - amounts to twenty-six minutes which is both an absurdity and an admission that the railway cannot run its trains to time.

The 14.30 from Liverpool - formed of

four coaches rather than the usual three - runs in at 17.16 and no time is wasted in releasing the Low Moor Black 5 which has brought the train in and which has to run light back to Low Moor to take over the 16.30 Liverpool - Leeds. During this time the 2-6-4T that worked in with the 13.10 from Southport, backs onto the far end of the Liverpool train which becomes the 17.55 Leeds - Liverpool.

The 13.20 Kings Cross - Harrogate arrives at 17.13 and divides into two sections: one for Harrogate and the other, the dining section, for Copley Hill sidings. The engine that has brought the express from London is the Doncaster A3 that took out the 07.30 to Kings Cross this morning and although it has done well in excess of the four-hundred mile daily yardstick for Pacifics, its day is not over yet and it still has work to do. When it has been coaled and watered at Copley Hill, it will be taken light to Wakefield for the 19.20 London Parcels.

One of the few local workings that is not railcar-worked runs in at 17.31 behind an Ardsley N1 0-6-2T and leaves at 17.50 for Castleford behind another of the same class. Consisting of three non-corridors and worked entirely by Great Northern engines, it is a pleasing reminder of days past.

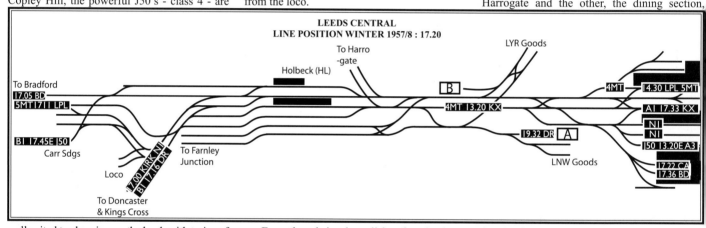

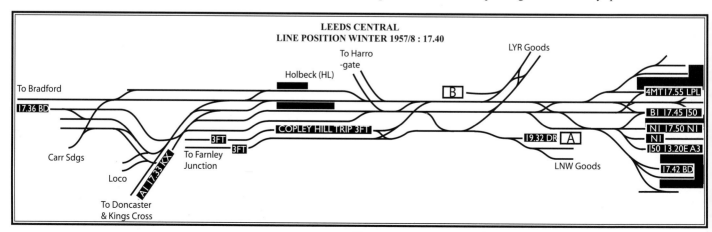

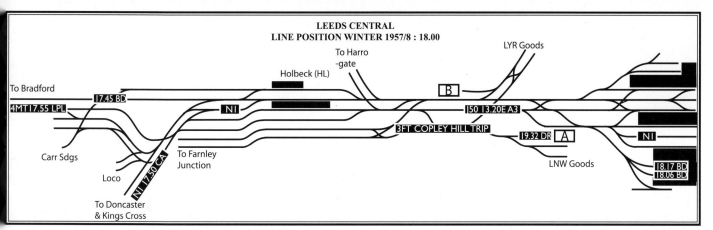

LEEDS CENTRAL
LINE POSITION WINTER 1957/8 : 18.00

STATION LOG: Now you see them, now you don't! A short time ago there were so many trains in the station that you could hardly move for them but now, as the rush-hour dies down and a J50 0-6-0T takes away the empties of the 13.20 ex-Kings Cross, there are just a handful of diesel railcars and an N1 0-6-2T, the latter waiting to work the empties of the 17.13 ex Doncaster to Copley Hill.

The peace is broken at 18.16 with the arrival of the 15.30 from Liverpool Exchange and, a

box, uncouple and shunt clear leaving the stock to run into the platform by gravity and under the control of the guard or a shunter. It is an unusual concession and one that it not available at the majority of locations).

The N1 0-6-2T pilot drops onto the rear of the Doncaster arrival and works it to Copley Hill. The train engine, a Doncaster B1 4-6-0, follows a minute or two later to be turned, coaled and prepared for the 20.05 London goods from Wellington Street goods station.

Doncaster. The diesels may be horribly noisy and uncomfortable when accelerating but when cruising at maximum speed, travelling in them is not an unpleasant sensation especially as the large windows give the impression of travelling at a higher speed than the train is actually doing. If only something could be done about the bus-type seating arrangements..............

It is rather sobering that on Fridays when the service is extended to Kings Cross and the diesel replaced by a Copley Hill A1, no less than eight

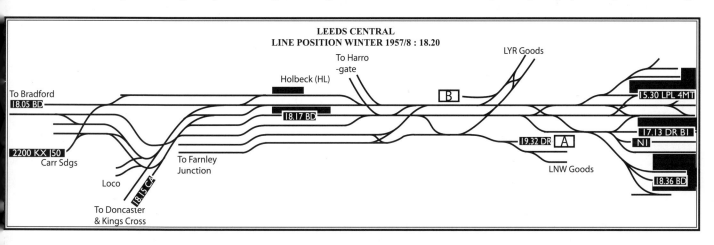

LEEDS CENTRAL
LINE POSITION WINTER 1957/8 : 18.20

couple of minutes later, by the 17.13 stopping train from Doncaster.

Since the Liverpool arrival only has thirty-nine minutes in which to turn round and form the 18.55 to Southport, some smart work is required of the station staff, not only in sweeping and cleaning the three vehicles but in releasing the 2-6-4T and allowing it to run round. It goes without saying that the inadvertent stabling of stock in the centre road - which happens - is a pitfall to watch out for. (When it proves impossible to run an engine through No.1 siding, there is a concession at Leeds which allows a train to be shunted without running the engine round. The engine can propel the stock out to A

The 18.05 diesel from Bradford is an interesting service since it breaks the mould of local services by running through to Doncaster after a three minute turn-round in Leeds.

Calling only at Wakefield after leaving Leeds, it is something of a high speed service; its purpose being to provide a late-evening service to London by connecting at Doncaster with the 17.05 Newcastle - Kings Cross, due at 22.10.

Although conveying only a limited payload and lacking any refreshment facilities, it is hardly to be compared with the TEE railcars operating on the continent yet there is something undeniably impressive about holding 70 mph for mile after mile between Wakefield and

extra minutes (plus two recovery) have to be inserted into the schedule. Of course a railcar has nothing like the capacity of an express but when a local train is able to better an express in even one respect, times are not what they were!

Although the evening is young and the peak service still has some distance to run, the first of the night trains is drawn into the station: a J50 arriving with the stock of the 22.00 to Kings Cross. The early arrival is because of the very large quantities of mails and parcels traffic that the train conveys and once the J50 has run-round the stock and shunted it into platform 1, loading will be a continuous process until the time for departure arrives.

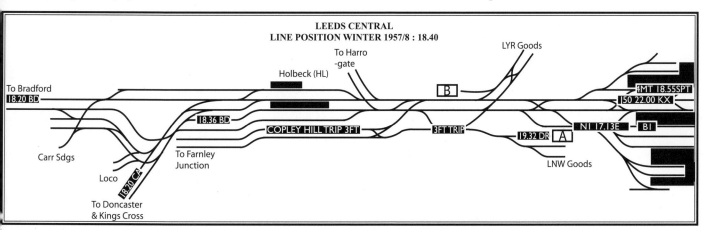

LEEDS CENTRAL
LINE POSITION WINTER 1957/8 : 18.40

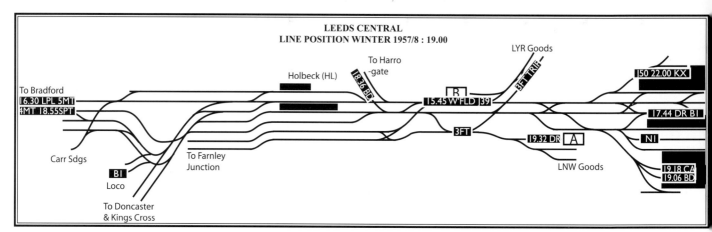

STATION LOG: Night travel between the West Riding and London is not the Great Northern's strong suit and the passenger is far better catered for by the Midland which runs several trains - and a sleeping car service - from Leeds City. None of these trains make unreasonable demands on the passenger's stamina in the way that the Great Northern does with interminable stops at every major point on the route and ejection from the train at four in the morning.

The sole overnight train from Leeds to Kings Cross, the 22.00 runs primarily for mail

the 16.30 ex Liverpool and the 15.40 from Kings Cross arrive in close succession. The Liverpool arrival is notable because it is worked from Liverpool to Low Moor by a Southport 4-6-0 with the Bradford section being taken forward by another Southport Black 5. The Leeds portion is worked forward by the same 4-6-0 that earlier worked the Leeds section of the 14.30 from Liverpool.

Both engine and coaches form the 20.50 stopping train to Manchester (Victoria), the engine being released to turn on Wortley Angle, keeping close quarter with the B1 4-6-0 that has

the A1 they bring down from London is the engine that worked up with the 07.50 from Leeds. The same engine may be put into the same turn tomorrow although there is no tradition at Copley Hill of keeping engines in the same diagram for long periods.

The N1 0-6-2T pilot backs onto the stock and works it to the carriage sidings, the A1 following a few minutes later.

The West Riding - often referred to as the Leeds Flyer - is quite a *cause celebre* in East Coast circles with its intensive roster and modern A1 Pacific. The old guard derive

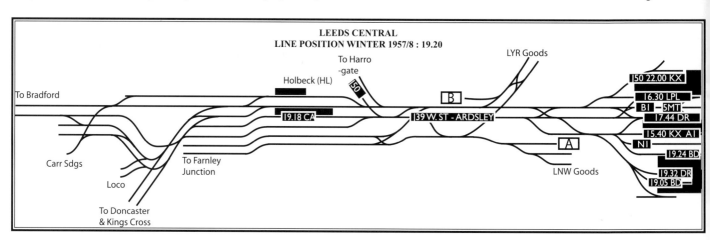

purposes and so sensitive is the railway to complaints by the Post Office that the normally generous allowance of recovery time is expanded to thirty minutes, eleven of which are in the last two and a half miles of the journey. Thus, if the train leaves Peterborough on time and gets a clear run thereafter, the passenger will be even further inconvenienced by having to alight at three forty-five. A travelling Post Office is included in the formation and mail is collected at speed by the lineside apparatus at Huntingdon and Cadwell.

As loading of the London train commences,

arrived with the 17.44 Doncaster stopping train and returns, with its coaches, at 21.00.

The Kings Cross arrival - the West Riding - is something of a celebrity for not only is it the fastest service from London after the Queen of Scots but its crew have completed was is probably the hardest turn of duty of British Railways: working to Kings Cross with the 10.45 ex-Leeds and turning round after only sixty-three minutes in London. It is pretty certain that no-one on the train is more relieved to tread the soil of Leeds than the fireman.

The crew do not keep the same engine and

some satisfaction from noting that its Bradford portion, detached at Wakefield, is still worked by an N1 0-6-2T. Lesser trains have one of the multitudinous B1 4-6-0's!

During the evening unscheduled shunting movements have to be planned with care since the situation regarding station pilots becomes somewhat fluid. The J50, presently heating the 22.00 London, disappears with the ECS of the 16.05 ex-Kings Cross and cover after that is rather sporadic with a worrying gap between 20.42 and 21.27 when no pilot is available at all.

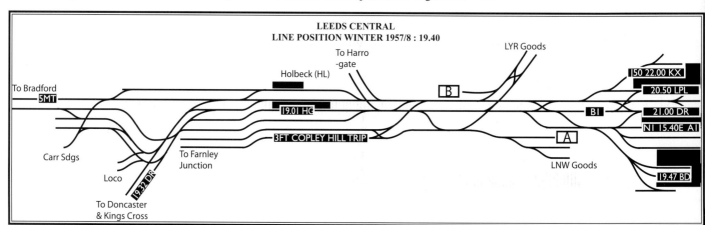

The view looking towards Holbeck from platform 3 showing quite clearly the track layout as far as B box which is visible in the middle distance. The signals have been cleared for an up train out of platform 3 whilst an up train has been cleared into platform 3. A 3-car diesel multiple-unit has been stabled in the siding to the north of A box whilst 4MT 2-6-4T 42145 waits to leave platform 2 with a train of empty stock for Copley Hill. (KRM/J. Marshall)

Shortly after the view at the top of the page was taken, 4MT 2-6-4T 42145 was given the road and was photographed approaching B box with its train of stock. (KRM/J. Marshall)

A panoramic view of Leeds Central at a fairly quiet time. At one side of the station a diesel unit stands in platform 7 whilst on the other side a 2-6-4T prepares to pull away from platform 2 with a train of empty stock. Another set of empty stock which will form an express for Kings Cross occupies platform 5. In adition to all seven platforms, the two confusingly named centre roads can be clearly seen. The one between platforms 2 and 3 was referred to as No.2 siding and used as an engine release road. No.3 siding was the road between platforms 4 and 5 and, since neither platform had an engine release facility, was used to stable stock and parcels vehicles. No.1 siding ran parallel to platform 1. (KRM/J. Marshall)

A1 Pacific 60117 'Bois Roussel' stands in platform 3 at the head of a local train to Doncaster on 24th September 1960. (KRM/J. Marshall)

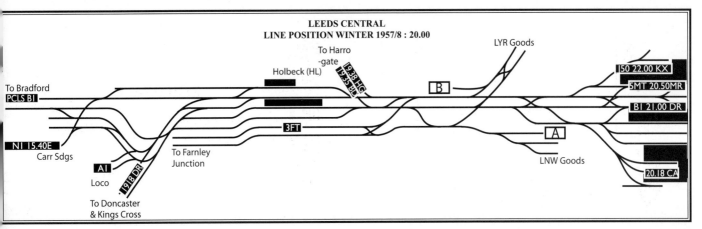

LEEDS CENTRAL
LINE POSITION WINTER 1957/8 : 20.00

STATION LOG: With its very large fleet of Pacifics, it is not easy to find a Great Northern express that is hauled by anything else but the Wakefield District can produce two examples; both of which can be seen at Leeds on any evening.

The first of these provides a remarkable example of historical continuity since the train concerned employs precisely the same engine for much of its run as it did before the war. The service in question is the 16.05 from Kings Cross which during the 1930's was a combined express for the West Riding and Tyneside and

however, is the engine and the booked engine is still the W1, now numbered 60700.

The 4-6-4 does not remain with the train throughout but is relieved at Doncaster where the train is divided into York and West Riding sections, each being taken forward by a B1 4-6-0.

The engine of the Leeds portion is completing the second half of a diagram that commenced with the 01.40 Leeds - Sheffield and continued with the 15.40 Leeds - Doncaster stopping train.

A two-minute stop is made at Holbeck to

is a Brake Composite coach which provided the guard's and local accommodation for the Pullman and this is left in No.2 siding by the pilot when it shunts the remainder of the train to No.1 platform.

The B1 that worked in with the 16.05 from Kings Cross goes light to Copley Hill, its nineteen-hour day over.

The second London express to be B1-hauled in the 22.00 overnight service which is diagrammed to a Copley Hill 4-6-0. The B1 only works as far as Doncaster however where it is replaced by a Pacific. The Copley Hill engine

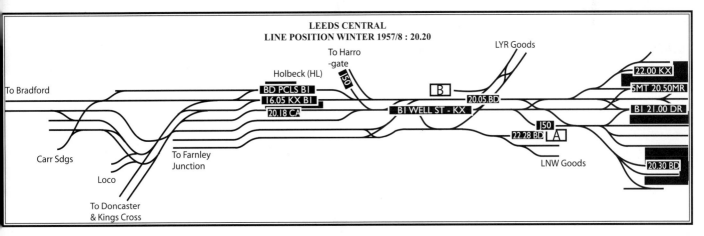

LEEDS CENTRAL
LINE POSITION WINTER 1957/8 : 20.20

was notable for running neck and neck with the Coronation streamliner as far as Finsbury Park, the Leeds train using the slow line. The regular engine as far as Doncaster was the rebuild of the rather disappointing watertube compound of 1927, W1 4-6-4 10000.

Twenty years on, the train still exists although much of its traffic has been abstracted by the 15.40 White Rose. The interesting parallel running out of London has been dispensed with; the train being retarded by five minutes and sandwiched between the 16.00 Edinburgh and the 16.15 Cleethorpes. What has not changed,

connect with the 20.21 Leeds City - Ilkley, the B1 drawing level with another of the same class on a parcels service from Bradford.

The arrival of this pair of trains means some fast work for the J50 pilot at Leeds which has to attach the Bradford vehicles to the 22.00 Kings Cross before leaving with the empty stock of the 16.05 from Kings Cross at 20.42. The B1 that brought in the Bradford train runs light to turn on the Wortley Angle; its next duty being the Bradford portion of the down Yorkshire Pullman.

The leading vehicle of the Bradford parcels

works back to Leeds with the 21.15 goods from Kings Cross Goods to Leeds, Wellington Street.

The service to Lancashire finishes rather early since apart from a late-night train to Halifax, the 20.50 stopping train to Manchester is the last L&Y train to leave the station until 03.25.

As the stock of the 16.05 Kings Cross pulls away for Copley Hill, the station is left without any means of shunting until the arrival of the engine to work the 22.00 which is booked in early in case last minute attachment are needed.

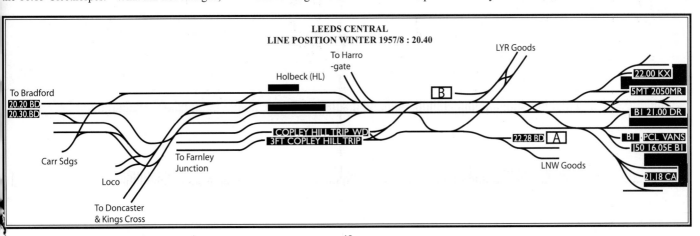

LEEDS CENTRAL
LINE POSITION WINTER 1957/8 : 20.40

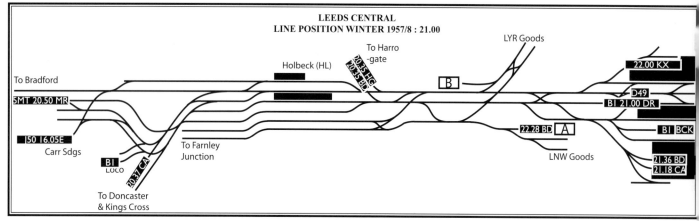

LEEDS CENTRAL
LINE POSITION WINTER 1957/8 : 21.00

STATION LOG: As the 20.50 Manchester pulls out, followed by the ECS of the 16.05 from Kings Cross, its B1 4-6-0 and the 21.00 Doncaster stopping train, the station prepares for the reception of what might well be regarded as the day's principal services: the Yorkshire Pullman from Kings Cross.

Worked from London by a Kings Cross A4, the train is divided in two sections upon arrival with two vehicles for Bradford and five for Harrogate.   Since neither of the two Bradford vehicles - usually 1st class *Eunice* and 3rd class

The Harrogate section is worked forward by a Starbeck D49 4-4-0 - a type never too common on the ex-Great Northern and now becoming even rarer through withdrawals - which arrives light from Leeds City. Unlike the Bradford section, the Harrogate portion remains all-Pullman throughout and local passengers who do not wish to pay the supplement for half-an-hour's travel have a choice of the 20.57 or 22.06 diesel trains.

After the two sections have departed, the A4 reverses out of the station for Copley Hill

as the Pullman is concerned, in fact it is only four minutes slower than its pre-war counterpart. In common with the other London - Leeds trains, the position is skewed by the addition of twenty-two minutes recovery time.

Two more parcels trains enter the station, one - the 20.40 from Keighley - being a transfer service, recently introduced, from the Midland which brings vans for the 22.00 and the 22.35 whilst the other is the 21.09 from Bradford and conveys a Norwich van which will form part of the 01.05 to March.

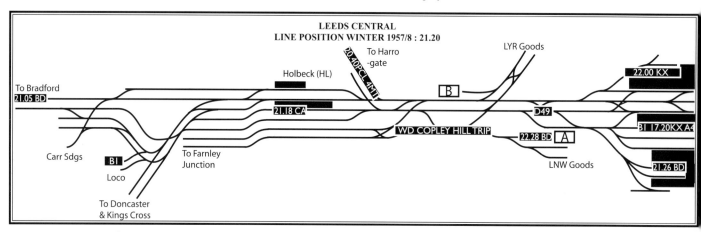

LEEDS CENTRAL
LINE POSITION WINTER 1957/8 : 21.20

No. 67 - have brake compartments, the B1 which works them forward, back down with an LNER Brake Composite which not only accommodates the guard but takes care of local passengers, few of whom appreciate having to part with the two-shilling - the price of a paperback book or a decent dinner - supplement. In a sensible world someone at Liverpool Street might waken to the fact that the Pullman is followed by a diesel after an interval of only four minutes and might just as well be excluded from the local timetable. In the meantime the practiced haughtiness of the Pullman staff as they direct local passengers to the non-Pullman coach is pure theatre.

loco where it will remain until working back to London with the 10.00 Leeds to Kings Cross.

Running to a schedule of three hours and fifty-four minutes, the Pullman is often criticised for being significantly slower than it had been in 1939 when it had a timing of three hours and twenty-eight minutes. Reference is also made to the lack of a really fast post-war evening service, memories of the two hour and forty-three minute running of the pre-war West Riding Limited still being fresh.

The lack of interest shown by British Railways in restoring some of the high points of pre-war running is difficult to explain but so far

The usual arrangement is for the Keighley train to run into No.1 siding and for its London van to be picked up by the B1 4-6-0 of the 22.00 and attached to the train in No.1 platform. The 2-6-4T then attaches its other van to the 22.35 Doncaster before returning light to the Midland.

The Bradford train runs into platform 3, its N1 0-6-2T running round and, when it is clear to do so, leaving the van in No.3 platform until the rest of the 01.05 stock arrives at 22.43.

It has to be remembered that Parcels traffic can fluctuate considerably from one day to the next and trains can double in size quite easily.

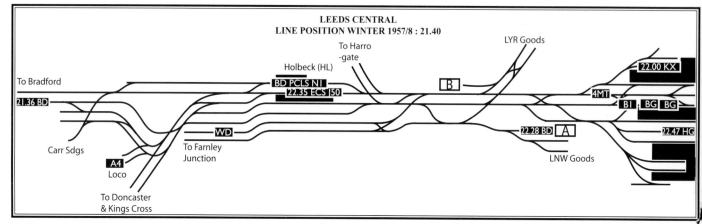

LEEDS CENTRAL
LINE POSITION WINTER 1957/8 : 21.40

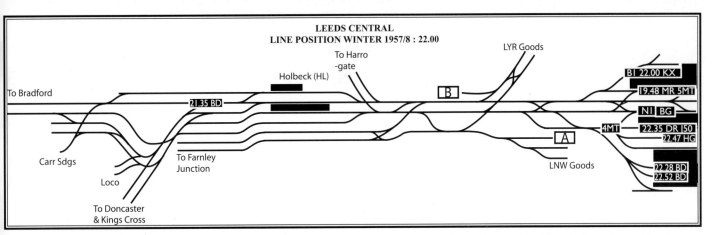

LEEDS CENTRAL
LINE POSITION WINTER 1957/8 : 22.00

STATION LOG: The departure of the 22.00 to Kings Cross leaves only one main line GN service to go: the 22.35 Doncaster slow which serves most of the local stations and runs via Wakefield Kirkgate. Serving both the pub trade and the home-going late turn from the many collieries on the line, the 22.35 is a well filled train and consists of five coaches (an articulated BSK-SK, CK, SK and BSK) plus a vanfit for Doncaster and a parcels brake for Wakefield Kirkgate. The latter arrives with the Keighley parcels and is transferred at Wakefield

17.13 Doncaster to Leeds. Thus the coaches that work the 22.35 on Monday do not find their way back into the train until the following Thursday.

The Ardsley N1 that arrived with the Bradford Parcels shunts its parcels van to the end of No.3 platform and follows the 22.00 London, running light to its home station whilst the 4MTT off the Keighley parcels runs back to Leeds City leaving the station without a pilot for the time being.

At 21.57, the 19.48 slow train from

those who object both to the supplement and to the perception that taking dinner on the Pullman is obligatory. (In fact dining on the Pullman is quite optional although the Kings Cross reservation staff make a point of stating otherwise).

Calling only at Peterborough, Doncaster and Wakefield, the 18.20 takes only five minutes more to reach Leeds than the Pullman and in addition has a Halifax portion which is removed at Wakefield. The booked engine is the Copley Hill A1 that worked out with the up Yorkshire

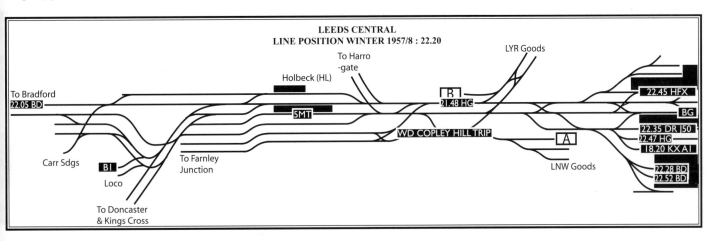

LEEDS CENTRAL
LINE POSITION WINTER 1957/8 : 22.20

to the 21.40 Congleton - Leeds City, thus inscribing a rather interesting circular journey. The vanfit goes forward to Peterborough from Doncaster in the 00.45 (a rather humble train in spite of its exalted reporting number: No.1) York - Peterborough parcels.

The cycle followed by the five passenger coaches in the 22.35 is not without interest since on reaching Doncaster the set forms the Hull connection with the 20.20 Kings Cross - Edinburgh. It then stables until the evening when it works an evening Hull - Sheffield service It returns to the West Riding the following day with the 14.35 Sheffield to Doncaster and the

Manchester (Victoria) arrives; a service made interesting by the fact it is diagrammed for a 5MT 4-6-0 from Agecroft which is not a location strongly represented at Leeds Central. The 4-6-0 does not spend long in Leeds however but is therefore hurriedly released to turn on the Wortley angle before taking its coaches out as the 22,45 local service to Halifax. The engine makes its way back to Manchester with a Mytholmroyd - Oldham Road goods.

The last train of the day from Kings Cross, the 18.20, runs in at 22.19 and although a popular train in its own right, is regarded as an alternative to the Yorkshire Pullman by

Pullman whilst the Halifax coaches are worked from Wakefield to Bradford by a Copley Hill B1 4-6-0 and from Bradford by a Sowerby Bridge 2-6-4T. The ECS of the main part of the train is taken to Copley Hill by the J50 that brought in the empties of the 22.35.

At 22.21 the B1 4-6-0 for the 22.35 Doncaster rings off Copley Hill loco and backs down to the station at about the same time as the Agecroft Black 5 for the 22.45 Halifax arrives back from turning.

As the 22.35 pauses at Holbeck to pick up traffic, it is passed by an N1 0-6-2T with the empty stock for the 01.05 and 01.35 departures.

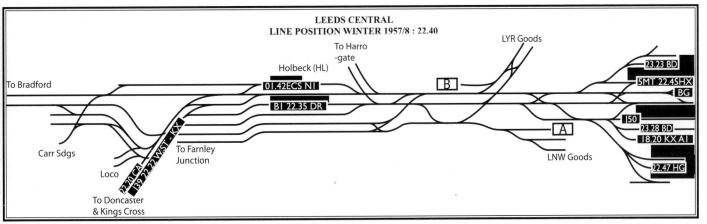

LEEDS CENTRAL
LINE POSITION WINTER 1957/8 : 22.40

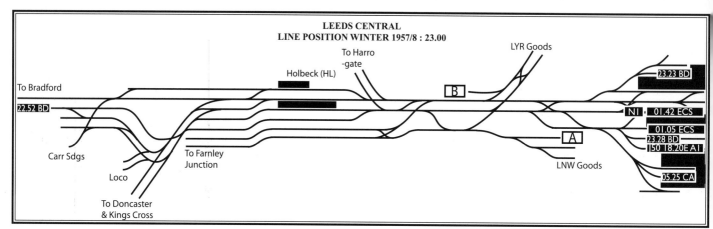

LEEDS CENTRAL
LINE POSITION WINTER 1957/8 : 23.00

STATION LOG: The method by which the empty stock for the 01.05 and the 01.42 Sheffield - brought in as a combined train from Copley Hill - reaches its platforms varies according to the amount of traffic being handled and the whim of the foreman shunter. The N1 0-6-2T can leave the train at A box, letting the stock gravitate into one of the sidings; the N1 then shunting the train into its respective parts - not forgetting the van that was earlier brought in from Keighley. Alternatively the stock can run straight into platform 3 where the engine can run round and carry on with the shunting.

The main line departures have finished for

completes its diagram by running light from Leeds to Low Moor. (Although all Bradford steam has been concentrated at Low Moor, the tendency to refer to the GN workings as belonging to Bowling Junction remains).

The last London Midland arrival is the 20.30 Liverpool - Bradford which is worked from Low Moor by one of the shed's LMS 2-6-4T's. Even though it is late in the day this is the first appearance of this particular engine in Leeds even though it has been in traffic since six this morning. The day has been spent on passenger trains between Bradford Exchange and Huddersfield but as a final touch to the

and Bradford respectively whilst a pair of units - a useful resource when things are running awry - run empty to Bradford at 23.28.

The last inward locals arrive at 23.10 (Bradford), 23.18 (Harrogate) and 23.36 (Castleford) and all that remains is for the three units that start tomorrow's service from Leeds to be put in their respective places.

This is not always as easy as it sounds and very often the Controller will want them taken out of their booked workings because of maintenance requirements. The simplest way around this is to place one unit each in platforms 6,7 and the siding at A box which means that

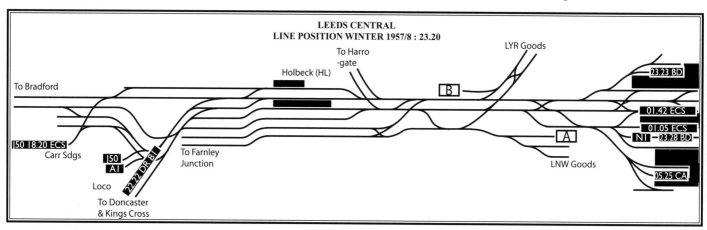

LEEDS CENTRAL
LINE POSITION WINTER 1957/8 : 23.20

the day but there are still a couple of arrivals to deal with, one each from the LM and GN. The latter is the first to arrive and is the 22.22 from Doncaster, a slow service that connects with nothing in particular on the East Coast but is nevertheless made up of eight coaches which is quite a good load for a stopping train. The engine is a B1 4-6-0 and is the only Bowling Junction engine to be seen at Doncaster in the normal course of events. The outward working is the 18.00 Bradford - Doncaster parcels via Dewsbury and Wakefield and the engine

diagram, the engine has been booked to work the last L&Y service into Leeds. Like the B1 4-6-0 that works in with the 22.22 from Doncaster, the 2-6-4T will conclude its day by running light back to Low Moor.

The three coaches of the 20.30 Liverpool will remain in the station to form the 03.25 to Manchester.

The diesel service which has been intensive for the last 18 hours suddenly dies as though a switch was thrown. The last local trains leave at 22.30, 22.47 and 23.23 for Castleford, Harrogate

they can come and go without interfering with anything. If, instead, two units are stabled in one of the platforms, then it is almost certain that in the middle of the night the Controller will want the rearmost set be changed over with another which means a great deal of shunting and an additional driver.

The J50 pilot which worked away the empties of the 18.20 Kings Cross returns at 23.45, relieving the N1 which brought in the parcels empties and is now required to work away the empties of the 22.22 ex-Doncaster.

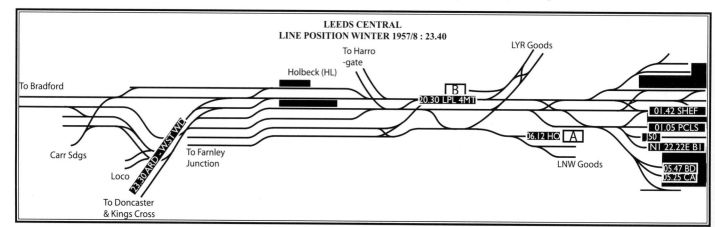

LEEDS CENTRAL
LINE POSITION WINTER 1957/8 : 23.40

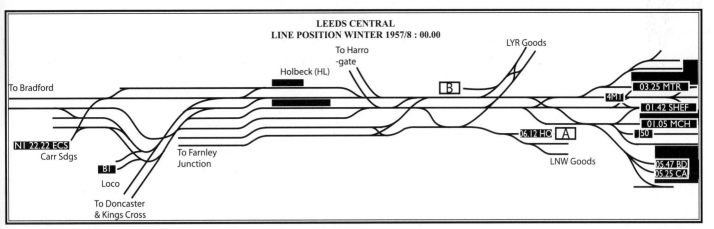

LEEDS CENTRAL
LINE POSITION WINTER 1957/8 : 00.00

STATION LOG : In a station that plays host to ex-L&Y and ex-Great Northern services, it is an interesting irony that the first arrival of the day should be neither but instead an ex-LNW working from Leeds City.

The train is the 00.02 from Leeds City South - the LNW section of the Leeds City complex - which brings in a van for the 03.25 to Manchester and another with loose traffic for East Anglia.

After being loaded with loose transfers for the LNW and collecting a pair of fish vanfits for Bradford Forster Square and Harrogate, the service returns to Leeds City at 00.48. The

J50 - does not commence work until 04.25.

Being a passenger station, goods traffic is not generally dealt with at Leeds Central and the only exception is the 20.25 Grimsby fish which arrives at 00.25 behind the B1 4-6-0 that worked out with the 16.13 Leeds - Cleethorpes express. It usually arrives with four vanfits one which is unloaded in the station and one each for Halifax, Bradford Forster Square and Harrogate. The last two are picked up by the Farnley Junction 2-6-2T and worked away in the 00.48 to Leeds City which the Halifax van is added to the 03.25 by the station pilot. The Leeds van is unloaded in the platform and then shunted into the dock or

has to remember - it is surprising how these obvious points are easy to overlook - to turn the engine on Wortley Angle. (It also pays to get someone to peer round the tender. Having adjusted the engine diagram, turned the engine and advised everyone who needs to know, the last thing you want is for the fireman to arrive ten minutes before departure time to announce that he can see the tender floor).

At 00.50 the B1 for the 01.05 March parcels arrives from Copley Hill loco and is coupled up. Although it leaves Leeds with only four vehicles - vans for March, Norwich, Grimsby and Doncaster - the 01.05 is something of a

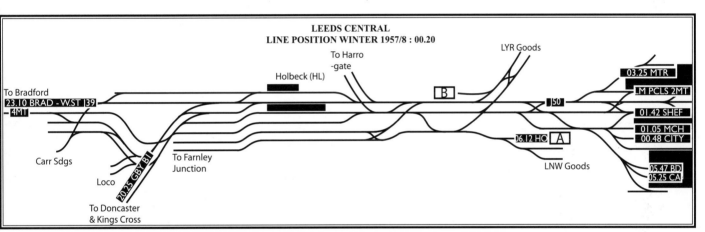

LEEDS CENTRAL
LINE POSITION WINTER 1957/8 : 00.20

engine used is a Farnley Junction 2-6-2T.

The stock of the 03.25 to Manchester - a standard LMS three-coach corridor set - arrived at 23.41 as the 20.30 from Liverpool Exchange and has been shunted from platform 2 to platform 1 by the J50 station pilot. The same engine collects the Manchester van from the Leeds City trip when it arrives and attaches it to the front of the 03.25.

The pilot is not on continuous duty but finishes at 01.00 by which time all shunting has to be completed since the next pilot - another

No.1 siding when empty.

It should be mentioned that the train consists of much more than four vans when it starts from Cleethorpes and most of its load is removed at Wakefield Kirkgate, Westgate and Spring Lane, Ardsley. After reaching Leeds and being relieved of its train, the B1 remains in the station, steam heating the 01.42 Sheffield until the booked engine arrives at 01.32.

On days when engine shortage reaches crisis point, it is not unknown for the Fish engine to be used to work the 01.42 in which case someone

heavyweight and for part of its journey conveys quite a respectable load. Some of the vehicles included have an interesting ring - Mytholmroyd to Colchester, Manchester (Mayfield) to Norwich and Burscough Bridge to Doncaster, for example - and suggest that the planning for parcels trains is a great deal more intricate than that of passenger trains. The B1 works only as far as Doncaster and returns with the 04.20 from Sheffield, due into Leeds at 06.53. The entire working is a complex one and requires the engine to be in steam for over 21 hours.

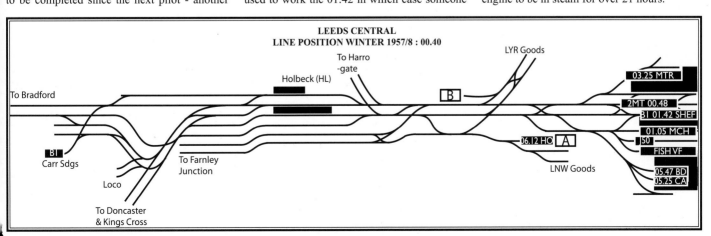

LEEDS CENTRAL
LINE POSITION WINTER 1957/8 : 00.40

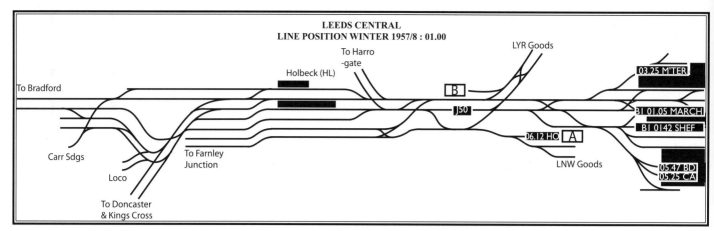

LEEDS CENTRAL
LINE POSITION WINTER 1957/8 : 01.00

STATION LOG: With the parcels trains marshalled and platformed, there is nothing left for the pilot to do and the J50 is released from duty to make its way light to Copley Hill loco, leaving the station without a pilot for the next three and a half hours. In extremis, the B1 which arrived with the Grimsby fish and is steam heating the 01.42 Sheffield tender-first could be used although it should not be necessary.

In the meantime the fireman of the 01.05 uses the last few minutes of station time to get his B1 good and hot. Whistles are blown, the last items of goods are heaved on board as doors are slammed shut and the train is given the right away. With only four vehicles behind the engine,

uphill track than the much more powerful Pacifics which work the principal expresses. Fortunately the latter are generally formed of no more than six or seven vehicles between Leeds and Wakefield, where the Bradford coaches are attached, and the relatively light loads generally allow the sometimes uncertain Pacifics to scale the heights of Ardsley without trouble.

The greatest concern is the up Queen of Scots Pullman which can load up to ten Pullman cars. The incoming engine can give assistance for the platform length but after that the train engine - an A1 Pacific - is on its own. It is a time when driving skill and experience count for more than usual.

morning).

The three sets in question form the 05.25 Castleford, the 05.47 Bradford and the 06.12 empty cars to Horsforth respectively, the last of the trio usually being stationed in the A-box siding from where it can run straight to Horsforth. The Bradford and Castleford sets are both two-coach Leyland units whilst the Horsforth empties is formed by a three car Metro-Cammell set.

These units have had a mixed reception. Drivers like them for their comfort but are unhappy at the fact that they do not require firemen whilst first-class passengers enjoy the novelty of the driver's eye view but complain

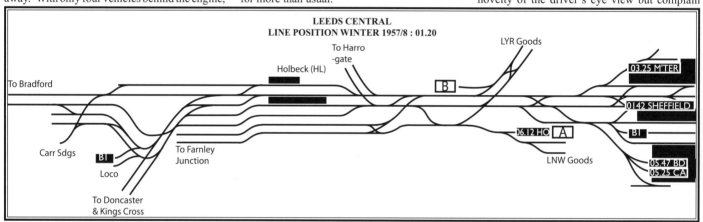

LEEDS CENTRAL
LINE POSITION WINTER 1957/8 : 01.20

nothing should go wrong but nonetheless on wet nights the departure is watched with some concern since there is no station pilot available to give the B1 a hand should it slip to a stand on the 1 in 100 climb to Holbeck. If the worst happens the steam heat engine can be taken off the 01.42 and be used to give assistance but on most occasions fears proved groundless and the B1 bashes its way past Holbeck and up the five-mile bank to Ardsley, much of which is also inclined at around 1 in 100.

The B1 4-6-0's are only moderately powered engines yet they are a great deal steadier on

Hidden away in the local platforms, six and seven, are the diesel multiple-units which are positioned - provided the powers-that-be don't want to change them over with something else - in readiness for the morning's local services. Although the diesels are technically motive power items, they are actually treated as coaching stock for operating purposes and stable between workings in exactly the same way as conventional carriage stock. (The main difference is that conventional coaches do not suffer immobility through flat batteries when the time comes to resume duties on a frosty

that the units are excessively noisy and vibrate a great deal.

The B1 4-6-0 for the 01.42 Sheffield rings off shed and backs down to the station. This is a double-shifted engine, the first set of men taking the engine through to Sheffield Victoria and back whilst the second sign on at 14.22 and work the 15.40 stopping train to Doncaster, returning with the 19.28 Doncaster - Leeds. This last is something of a novelty since it is the West Riding section of the 16.05 ex Kings Cross and provides one of the few instances of a B1 4-6-0 working a London - Leeds express.

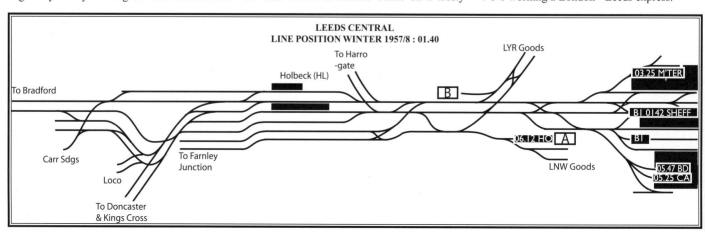

LEEDS CENTRAL
LINE POSITION WINTER 1957/8 : 01.40

A1 Pacific 60134 'Foxhunter' waits for the road to Copley Hill Loco at the end of platform 4 after having arrived with an express from Kings Cross. Although less well liked than the Gresley Pacifics - the A1's could be rough riding - they were the first (and as it turned out, the last) large express passenger engines to be allocated in numbers to Copley Hill and the shed obtained very good results from them. It is probably true to say that by the mid-1950's something like 65% of all express work south of Grantham was handled by the A1's although they never personified the east coast in the way that the A4 and A3 Pacifics did. (KRM/J.Marshall)

Less than a mile out of Bradford, B1 4-6-0 61386 passes through St Dunstans with an express for Wakefield and Kings Cross. After the Leeds local services had been taken over by diesel units, only enough full-time work for three B1's remained at Bradford; work generally limited to parcels trains to and from Leeds and the Kings Cross service which was worked only as far as Wakefield Westgate, where the trains were combined with Leeds - London workings. The large fleet of N1 0-6-2T's which had been the mainstay of the Bradford - Leeds suburban service also found itself unemployed and in 1958 the Bradford's Great Northern locomotive shed closed to become a dmu depot with the remaining steam being transferred to the L&Y shed at Low Moor.

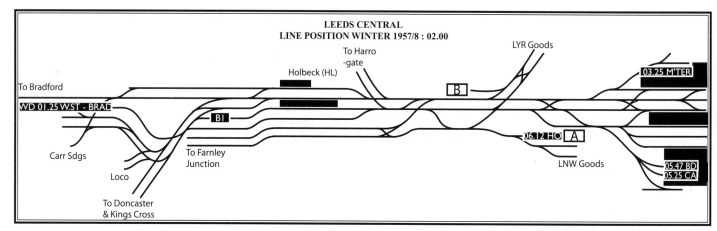

STATION LOG: After the departure of the 01.42 to Sheffield, the station enters its quietest period with nothing departing until the 03.25 passenger and parcels train leaves for Manchester Victoria via Halifax and Hebden Bridge.

The 03.25 runs as a complete train to Manchester and is therefore an exception to the general rule governing the operation of L&Y trains from Leeds Central which are usually subsidiary sections of Bradford - Liverpool expresses, taken the ten miles to Low Moor by a local LMS 2-6-4 tank. The main sections of these trains are invariably worked by LMS

fact - the train being which is the return working of the 00.20 Manchester Exchange to Leeds City via Diggle Junction and Huddersfield. It is the only instance of an engine running from Manchester to Leeds via Huddersfield and returning via Hebden Bridge; the L&Y and the LNW continuing to work as though the other did not exist.

With its pair of vans and three coaches the 03.25 is not much of a challenge for a 5XP and it comes as a surprise to note that the L&Y's principal night train, the 00.12 Manchester Exchange to Newcastle News, is granted nothing bigger than a Newton Heath 5MT 4-6-0.

It is also curious that the LNER has no equivalent to this rather hybrid type of engine since their locomotive fleet lacks an intermediate passenger engine between the class 5 B1 4-6-0 and the class 7 V2 2-6-2 or A3 Pacific.

The LMS preferred to build a wide range of engines for every conceivable load of train whilst the LNER opted to 'play safe' by producing very large engines for almost all main line work. The result of this policy has been to make it rather difficult to travel over much of the east coast main line behind anything smaller than a Green Arrow 2-6-2.

The West Riding main line is not quite so

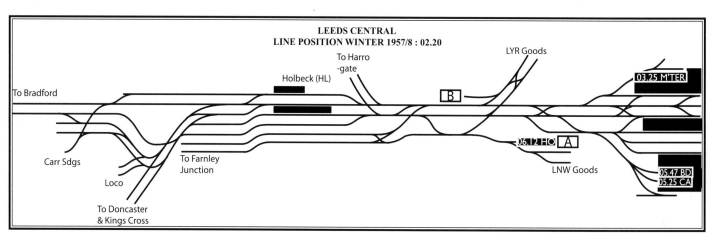

Black 5 4-6-0's whilst the stock consists of two three-coach LMS corridor sets: one from Bradford and the other from Leeds.

Engines larger than a Black Five are uncommon on the Lancashire and Yorkshire and the most notable exception to the rule is the daily Liverpool - Newcastle express which is worked as far as York by a Liverpool (Bank Hall) 5XP 'Jubilee' 4-6-0.

The other appearance of a 5XP is on the 03.25 Leeds Central to Manchester - not that there are many people around to witness the

The Newton Heath 5XP 4-6-0's work a varied set of duties. One pair of engines alternates between the 09.30 Manchester - Glasgow and the 10.50 Glasgow - Manchester expresses whilst a third engine works a business express from Manchester to Blackpool before spending the rest of the day shuttling between Manchester and Leeds on a series of all-stations workings. It is strange that an engine should be at the head of a major west coast express on one day yet the next is relegated to the slowest trains between Leeds City and Manchester.

generously equipped with Pacifics or Green Arrows and B1 4-6-0's cover many of the local trains between Leeds and Doncaster whilst a variety of Pacifics - except for the A2's - work the expresses. The chances, however, of seeing an unusual visitor at Leeds Central are high since ex-works engines from Doncaster often return to work on a Doncaster - Leeds local.

Whilst these and other thoughts divert our attention, the Newton Heath Jubilee 5XP 4-6-0 reverses over the Geldard branch and backs into the station, ready to work out the 03.25.

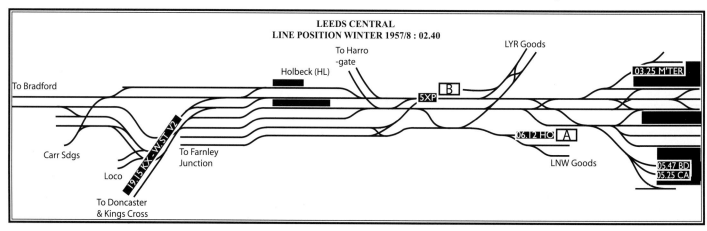

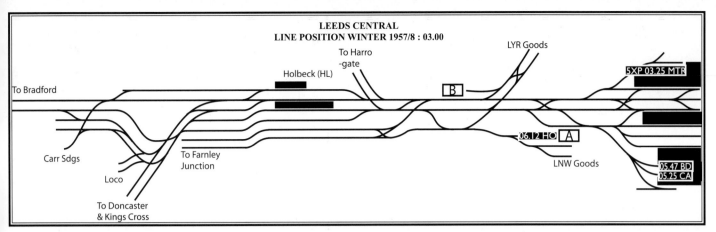

STATION LOG: There are no night trains between Kings Cross and Leeds in the sense that they operate to Newcastle, Edinburgh and Aberdeen and experienced passengers who want a comfortable night's travel between London and the West Riding use the Midland which has both sleeping cars and civilised arrival times in Leeds.

The nearest the Great Northern comes to offering an overnight service is the 22.45 from Kings Cross; a combined Leeds and Newcastle service, the sole attraction of which

recovery time which means that much of the journey is spent waiting at signals for the 22.35 Kings Cross - Edinburgh to clear the section ahead.

The extravagant pathing - a lamentable feature of latter-day GN scheduling - does not finish at Doncaster and with four more minutes recovery plus a ten minute stop at Wakefield - a setting down stop which means that train can leave as soon as the staff have finished with it - the train generally reaches Holbeck about a quarter of an hour before time where, after

Cross and the 13.20 Kings Cross to Leeds expresses; a working that allows only two and a quarter hours in London. The concluding element of the diagram is the 19.20 Wakefield (Westgate) - Kings Cross parcels train which the engine works as far as Doncaster.

In spite of such demanding diagramming there are those who still maintain that the A3's have had their day!

Most London to Bradford trains divide at Wakefield with the Bradford portion running via Ardsley and Morley Top but the 22.45 runs via

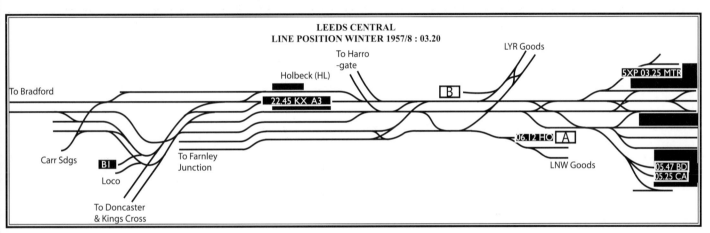

is an agreeable variety of motive power: a Kings Cross A4 to Grantham, a Grantham A2 to York and a Doncaster-based A3 taking the West Riding section from Doncaster to Leeds. To round things off, a Copley Hill B1 4-6-0 is used to work the Bradford section from Leeds Central.

However, if one is interested purely in creature comforts then the 22.45 is a train to avoid since it is the 'cheap fare' service and is invariably crowded to the limit with returning London day-trippers.

To add to its shortcomings, its schedule contains no less than twenty-three minutes of

it has unloaded exchange mails for the 03.25 Leeds Central to Manchester, it sits for about fifteen minutes whilst passengers reflect on the fact they could walk the remaining distance to Leeds in less than five minutes.

The engine working is perhaps the most interesting aspect of the train since the Doncaster A3 that works the West Riding section is following a highly intensive diagram of four hundred and thirty-five miles: almost the equivalent of a through run from Kings Cross to Glasgow Queen Street.

After reaching Leeds, the engine is serviced at Copley Hill for the 07.30 Leeds to Kings

Leeds; the B1 4-6-0 booked to work it forward, leaving Copley Hill loco at 03.20 and following the train into Leeds.

This engine also has a varied day albeit one less strenuous than that of the A3. After reaching Bradford it returns light to Leeds to shunt and work the 06.28 Leeds - Bradford parcels train, finishing the morning's work with the 08.10 Bradford - Leeds parcels. The rest of the morning is spent on Copley Hill loco where the engine is prepared for the afternoon Leeds - Cleethorpes express. The 4-6-0's final working is on the 20.25 Grimsby - Leeds fish, due in Leeds just after midnight.

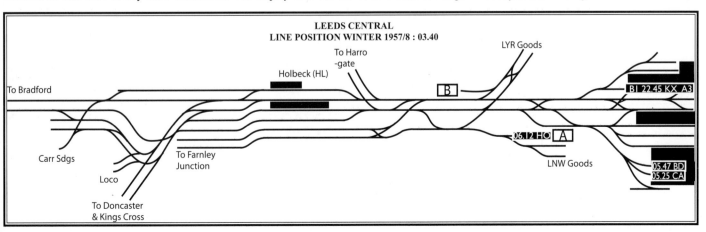

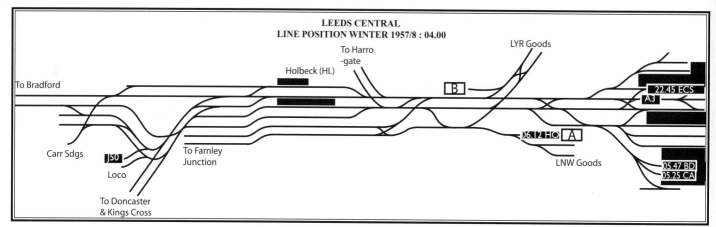

LEEDS CENTRAL
LINE POSITION WINTER 1957/8 : 04.00

STATION LOG: The A3 that brought the 22.45 Kings Cross - Bradford from Doncaster backs out of the station and heads slowly for Copley Hill loco where it will be prepared for the 07.30 express to London.

At about the same time a J50 0-6-0T rings out from Copley Hill to work the station pilot. As has been noted elsewhere, this particular duty is less flexible than it is at many locations and instead of being at the Inspector's beck and call throughout its turn of duty, it disappears for lengthy periods on ECS duties to and from Copley Hill sidings, during which times the

its traffic is for Bradford and is removed at Wakefield Kirkgate to be worked forward by an Ardsley B1 4-6-0 in the 04.10 Wakefield Kirkgate - Bradford via Ardsley and Wortley curve. Of the four vehicles that are brought into Leeds, one is from Lowestoft whilst two of the others are from Kings Cross; one leaving at 12.25 and the other at 18.35. The earlier of the two London vehicles picks up traffic from almost every station between Kings Cross and Doncaster whilst the other leaves London as part of the 18.35 express. The fourth vehicle starts from Doncaster and conveys miscellaneous

As a passenger station, Holbeck has an extremely decrepit air and has probably not seen more than ten shillings-worth of paint since the Kaiser's war. Parcels, however, care nothing for appearances and at certain times of the day the station is extremely busy with them.

The B1 and its train pulls away at 04.35 and is immediately replaced by the 03.15 Sowerby Bridge - Leeds parcels train which is allowed ten minutes to unload. This service has an interesting motive power arrangement since it runs the first four miles to Halifax behind a Sowerby Bridge 2-6-4T before exchanging

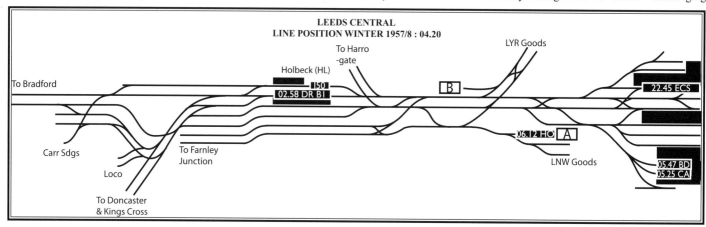

LEEDS CENTRAL
LINE POSITION WINTER 1957/8 : 04.20

pilot duties are covered by other engines. In all some thirteen changes of engine are made during the day whilst there are times when the station has no pilot assistance at all. It is a very unusual state of affairs given the level of business conducted at Leeds.

The first task of the J50 will be to release the engine of the 02.58 parcels from Doncaster and then, when unloading has been completed, to marry the vehicles with those of the 03.15 ex Sowerby bridge and take them to Copley Hill at 06.22.

Although the 02.58 ex Doncaster started out with eleven vehicles, the greater part of

exchange traffic.

The engine is a Doncaster B1 4-6-0 which after being released and turned, works the 08.22 Leeds - Doncaster stopping train.

The 02.58 makes a sixteen-minute call at Holbeck and draws attention to the fact that Holbeck's status as a parcels exchange point is of greater importance than its role as a passenger station.

The Great Northern platforms are directly above those of the Midland and North Eastern lines and the link is a useful and speedy alterative to man-handling barrows between the two Leeds stations.

it for a Low Moor version of the same class. Sowerby Bridge engines tend to work on the main line to Wakefield and Normanton and are actually rather uncommon in Leeds.

While the Sowerby Bridge train unloads in Holbeck, the B1 4-6-0 that earlier worked the Bradford portion of the 22.45 ex Kings Cross passes through light on its return from Bradford to shunt and work the 06.28 Leeds - Bradford parcels.

The first train of the day to leave Copley Hill carriage sidings - the empty stock for the 07.30 to Kings Cross - prepares, with a J50 0-6-0T at each end, to get under way.

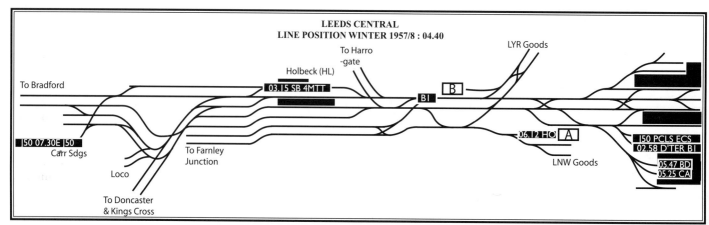

LEEDS CENTRAL
LINE POSITION WINTER 1957/8 : 04.40

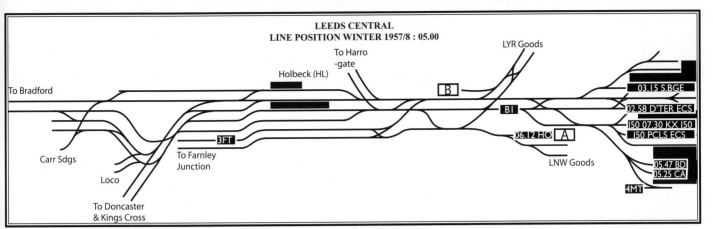

STATION LOG: The stock of the London trains is usually brought into the platforms early in order to allow the dining car staff as much time as possible to stock and prepare their vehicles and no chances are taken with the first two London expresses which are each booked into the station more than two hours before departure.

Even greater precautions are taken with the empties for the 07.30 since it is the first train for some time to leave Copley Hill sidings and to eliminate the risk of delay by greasy or wet rails, two J50 0-6-0T's are provided; one at each end of the train. This is a highly unusual

of vigorous shunting the dozen-odd parcels vehicles on hand in the station and forming them into the 05.30, 06.22 and 06.28 departures. The B1 4-6-0 that arrived light from Bradford after working the 22.45 from Kings Cross backs onto the 06.28 vehicles whilst the J50 0-6-0T which trailed in on the rear of the Kings Cross ECS shunts across to the 05.30 Copley Hill vans. On completing its spell of shunting the pilot attaches itself to the train of vans booked to leave for Copley Hill sidings at 06.22.

Whilst this activity is taking place, a driver arrives to start the three multiple units that have been stabled overnight; the first of which

diesels, the smooth running of the railway owes more to the skill and patience of fitters than at any time since George Stephenson. Such problems happen a little too regularly for comfort and it is little wonder that most traffic railwaymen regard diesels as being more trouble than they are worth.

One advantage they do possess is the ability to line up in a platform - most platforms will take several sets - and this is most useful at a station such as Leeds Central where trains sometimes threaten to outnumber platforms.

The last major movement of the night shift is that of the empty stock for the 07.50 Kings

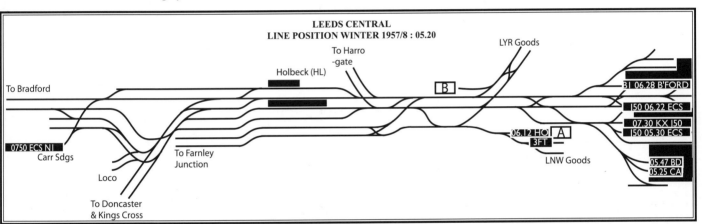

arrangement but one that is permitted between Copley Hill and Leeds. To reduce the incidence of light engine movements, some of the empty trains from Copley Hill to Leeds are hauled by a local engine with the train engine trailing. The trailing engine, however, is not permitted to assist the train but must limit itself to being hauled unless assistance is specifically asked for.

As the clock moves into the last hour of the night shift, the pace of activity quickens. The J50 station pilot moves onto the rear of the Sowerby Bridge arrival and starts a round

is booked to depart with the 05.25 local to Castleford. This, to say the least, is an anxious time especially on a cold winter's morning when one can almost guarantee a set of flat batteries. Since the driver signs on at 05.01, has ten minutes to read his notices and will take a similar period of time to decide whether or not the unit is working properly, time is not on the operators side.

If one should be declared a failure, all one can do is to call for a fitter and then step the units up until the defective diesel can be coaxed into life. It is no exaggeration to state that with

Cross which leaves Copley Hill behind an N1 0-6-2T. Like the J50 which earlier brought in the stock of the 07.30, the N1 will steam heat until departure time and then bank the train for the length of the platform.

The local services springs into life as the 05.25 to Castleford accelerates raucously and in as haze of fumes out of the station whilst two diesels - one empty - arrive from Bradford. In keeping with the arrangements at most British railway stations, one set of staff finish their eight-hour stretch of duty whilst another takes over. A new day starts at Leeds Central.

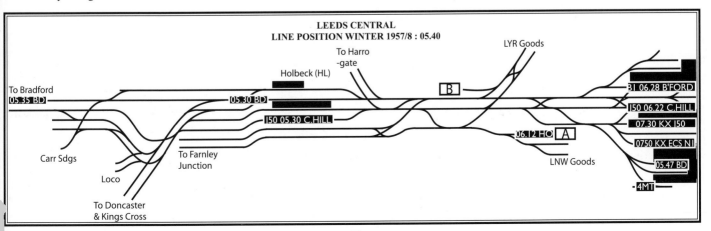

A1 60119 'Patrick Stirling' slows for the 20 mph speed restriction as it passes through Peterborough North with a Kings Cross - Leeds express in July 1960

LOCAL GN CARRIAGE WORKINGS : 1958

44 (3: BSK, CK, TSO)

	Working		Additional Vehicles	Comments
	Doncaster	09.05		
10.18	Lincoln	10.26	1: PMV	
12.47	Peterborough	02.41		2310 KX - York Pcls
03.30	Grantham	06.55		
07.16	Newark	07.41		
08.02	Grantham	08.26	5: BSK, SK, CK, SK, BSK	07.32 Nottingham - KX
10.55	Kings Cross	(04.00)		

45 (3: BSK, CK, TSO)

	Working		Additional Vehicles
	Holloway CS	02.20	11: BSO: CK, BSO, CK, TSO, BG, BG, BG, BG, B, BG
02.39	Kings Cross	04.00	11: BSO: CK, BSO, CK, TSO, BG, BG, BG, BG, BG
04.41	Hitchin	04.46	10: BSO: CK, BSO, CK, TSO, BG, BG, BG, BG, B
05.35	Peterborough	05.43	12: BSO: CK, BSO, CK, TSO, BG, BG, BG, BG, B, BZ, PMV
07.19	Retford	07.26	11: BSO: CK, BSO, CK, TSO, BG, BG, BG, BG, B, BZ
08.39	Wakefield (W)	08.44	5: BSO, CK, TSO, BG,B
09.06	Leeds	09.30	5: BSO, CK, TSO, BG,B
09.40	Copley Hill	16.13	1: BG
16.20	Leeds	16.43	1: BG
17.59	Doncaster	(09.05)	

53 Non Corr (4:BS, CL, S, BS)

	Working		Additional Vehicles	
	Doncaster	06.20		
07.33	Leeds	08.22		
09.45	Doncaster	12.55	5: BSK-SK, CK, SK, BSK	Rear Portion
14.06	Leeds	17.45	2: BG, BG	
18.46	Doncaster	(06.20)		

55 Non-Corr (5: BS, CL, S,S, BS)

	Working		Additional Vehicles
	Copley Hill	16.51	
16.58	Leeds	17.16	
18.11	Doncaster	22.22	3: CK, BSO, TSO
23.25	Leeds	23.52	3: CK, BSO, TSO
23.57	Copley Hill	(16.51)	

58 (3: BSK, CK, SK)

	Working		Additional Vehicles
	March	06.27	
10.12	Doncaster	11.15	
12.32	Leeds	12.46	
12.55	Copley Hill	13.23	
13.30	Leeds	14.04	
15.21	Doncaster	16.35	3: BZ, PMV, PMV
17.56	Lincoln	18.34	3: BZ, PMV, PMV
20.49	March	(06.27)	

88 (6: BSO-SO, CK, SK, SO-BSO)

	Working		Additional Vehicles	Comments
	Cleethorpes	09.23		
12.03	Leeds	12.19		
12.26	Copley Hill	15.32		
15.39	Leeds	16.13		
19.23	Cleethorpes	(09.23)		

135 (5: BSK-SK, CK, SK, BSK)

	Working		Additional Vehicles
	Sheffield	14.35	1: PMV
15.02	Mexborough	15.05	
15.20	Doncaster	17.13	1: POT
18.18	Leeds	18.40	1: POT
18.47	Copley Hill	21.35	2: B, VF
21.45	Leeds	22.35	2: B, VF
23.09	Wakefield (K)	23.17	1: VF
23.57	Doncaster	(01.22)	

136 (5: BSK-SK, CK, SK, BSK)

	Working		Additional Vehicles	
	Doncaster	07.33	1: SK	
08.41	Leeds	10.09	1: SK	
11.01	Doncaster	12.55	4: BS, CL, S, BS	Front Portion
14.06	Leeds	15.40		
16.48	Doncaster	17.44	1: PMV	
18.58	Leeds	21.00		
22.08	Doncaster	(07.33)		

137 (5: BSK-SK, CK, SK, BSK)

	Working		Additional Vehicles
	Doncaster	01.22	
02.33	Hull	19.00	2: S.S.
20.37	Doncaster	21.00	1: BZ
21.25	Sheffield	(14.35)	

140 Non Corr (2: BS, CL)

	Working		Additional Vehicles
	Copley Hill	22.36	
22.43	Leeds	01.42	5: BG, BG, BG, B, BZ
02.30	Doncaster	02.36	4: BG, BG, BG, BZ
03.31	Sheffield	04.20	7: BG, BG, PMV, BZ, BZ, BZ, B
04.31	Rotherham	04.36	6: BG, BG, PMV, BZ, BZ, BZ
05.03	Doncaster	05.25	4: BG, BG, BZ, BG
06.53	Leeds	07.45	4: BG, BG, BZ, BG
07.52	Copley Hill	(22.36)	4: BG, BG, BZ, BG

There was an impressive service of stopping trains between Leeds and Doncaster which was supported by an equally impressive array of carriage workings - there was no question of placing three or four coaches behind a B1 4-6-0 and letting them shuttle up and down the line all day!   The tables above show the basic formations of the stopping trains - some of which were integrated with main line services - together with the additional vehicles conveyed from time to time.   Many of the trains conveyed very respectable loads: the 04.00 KX - Leeds being made up of fifteen vehicles at one point in its journey whilst the 12.55 Doncaster - Leeds consisted of five corridor coaches and 4 non-corridor.

The N1 0-6-2T's had been a fixture in the West Riding since Edwardian times and worked the intensive Leeds and Bradford suburban services until diesel multiple units commenced operations in 1954.   The class did not disappear immediately but remained active on empty stock workings at Leeds Central and a number of miscellaneous duties around Bradford and Wakefield.   69450 runs light outside Leeds Central on 22 June 1957.   (KRM/V. Webster)

LMS THREE-COACH SETS (BTK, CK, BTK)

Set No.1

Arr	Location	Dep	
	Southport	07.00	RP
09.22	Low Moor	09.35	
09.33	**Bradford**	13.15	
13.22	Low Moor	13.28	FP
15.32	**Liverpool**	16.30	RP
18.31	Low Moor	18.41	
19.06	**Leeds**	20.50	
23.11	**Manchester**	(09.00)	

Set No.2

Arr	Location	Dep	
	Manchester	09.00	RP
10.11	**Southport**	13.10	FP
15.19	Low Moor	15.24	
15.30	**Bradford**	16.15	
16.22	Low Moor	16.28	FP
18.19	**Liverpool**	20.30	RP
23.13	Low Moor	23.23	
23.41	**Leeds**	(03.25)	

Set No.3

Arr	Location	Dep	
	Leeds	03.25	
05.11	**Manchester**	09.00	FP
10.11	**Southport**	13.10	RP
15.19	Low Moor	15.29	
15.52	**Leeds**	17.11	
17.41	Low Moor	17.47	FP
19.32	**Liverpool**	(08.32)	

Set No.4

Arr	Location	Dep	
	Liverpool	08.32	RP
10.31	Low Moor	10.41	10.41
11.01	**Leeds**	11.33	ECS
11.40	Copley Hill	12.28	ECS
12.35	**Leeds**	12.55	
13.15	Low Moor	13.28	RP
15.32	**Liverpool**	16.30	FP
18.31	Low Moor	18.36	
18.42	**Bradford**	(08.15)	

Set No.5

Arr	Location	Dep	
	Bradford	08.15	
08.22	Low Moor	08.28	RP
10.21	**Liverpool**	11.30	FP
13.37	Low Moor	13.42	
13.48	**Bradford**	17.15	
17.33	Halifax	17.47	RP
19.32	**Liverpool**	(08.32)	

Set No.6

Arr	Location	Dep	
	Liverpool	08.32	FP
10.31	Low Moor	10.36	
10.42	**Bradford**	14.15	
14.22	Low Moor	14.28	FP
16.22	**Liverpool**	17.22	RP
18.09	**Wigan**	(08.25)	

Set No.7

Arr	Location	Dep	
	Wigan	08.20	FP
09.07	**Liverpool**	09.40	RP
11.39	Low Moor	11.49	
12.06	**Leeds**	13.55	
14.17	Low Moor	14.28	RP
16.22	**Liverpool**	17.22	FP
18.09	**Wigan**	(08.25)	

Set No.8

Arr	Location	Dep	
	Wigan	08.20	RP
09.07	**Liverpool**	09.40	FP
11.39	Low Moor	11.44	
11.50	**Bradford**	12.55	ECS
13.05	Low Moor		

Set No.9

Arr	Location	Dep	
	Low Moor	06.28	
06.51	**Leeds**	07.55	
08.17	Low Moor	08.28	FP
10.21	**Liverpool**	11.30	RP
13.37	Low Moor	13.47	
14.08	**Leeds**	15.55	
16.16	Low Moor	16.28	RP
18.19	**Liverpool**	20.30	FP
23.13	Low Moor	23.18	
23.24	**Bradford**	(06.32)	

Set No.10

Arr	Location	Dep	
	Bradford	06.32	
09.28	**Liverpool**	12.30	
15.05	**Bradford**	(09.15)	

Set No.11

Arr	Location	Dep	
	Bradford	09.15	
09.22	Low Moor	09.28	FP
11.22	**Liverpool**	14.30	RP
16.41	Low Moor	16.46	
17.16	**Leeds**	17.55	
18.16	Low Moor	(06.28)	

Set No.12

Arr	Location	Dep	
	Low Moor	08.12	
08.34	**Leeds**	08.55	
09.15	Low Moor	09.28	RP
11.22	**Liverpool**	14.30	FP
16.41	Low Moor	16.46	
16.52	**Bradford**	(08.30)	

Set No.13

Arr	Location	Dep	
	Bradford	08.30	
	Blackpool		
	Manchester	15.42	
16.04	**Halifax**	16.42	
18.19	**Manchester**	18.48	
21.57	**Leeds**	22.45	
23.20	**Halifax**	23.35	ECS
23.41	**Sowerby Bge**	(05.58)	

Set No.14

Arr	Location	Dep	
	Sowerby Bge	05.58	
06.28	**Bradford**	11.15	
11.22	Low Moor	11.28	FP
13.32	**Liverpool**	15.30	RP
17.36	Low Moor	17.48	
18.16	**Leeds**	18.55	
19.17	Low Moor	19.29	RP
21.57	**Southport**	(07.00)	

Set No.15

Arr	Location	Dep	
	Southport	07.00	FP
09.22	Low Moor	09.35	
09.58	**Leeds**	10.55	
11.16	Low Moor	11.28	RP
13.32	**Liverpool**	15.30	FP
17.36	Low Moor	17.41	
17.48	**Bradford**	19.15	
19.22	Low Moor	19.29	FP
21.57	**Southport**	(07.00)	

STRENGTHENING VEHICLES

Set No.10A
Composite Corridor

Arr	Location	Dep
	Bradford	06.32
09.28	**Liverpool**	12.30
15.05	**Bradford**	(06.32)

Set No.10B
2 Non-Corr Thirds

Arr	Location	Dep
	Bradford	06.32
09.28	**Liverpool**	12.30
15.05	**Bradford**	(06.32)

Set No.11A
Composite Corridor

Arr	Location	Dep	
	Bradford	09.15	
09.22	Low Moor	09.28	FP
11.22	**Liverpool**	14.30	RP
16.41	Low Moor	16.46	
17.16	**Leeds**	17.55	
18.16	Low Moor	(08.12)	

Set No.12A
Composite Corridor

Arr	Location	Dep	
	Low Moor	08.12	
08.34	**Leeds**	08.55	
09.15	Low Moor	09.28	RP
11.22	**Liverpool**	14.30	FP
16.41	Low Moor	16.46	
16.52	**Bradford**	(08.30)	

Loco	Class	Aug-50	Sep-50	Oct-50	Nov-50	Dec-50	Jan-51	Feb-51	Mar-51	Apr-51	May-51	Jun-51	Jul-51
61031	5MT: B1 4-6-0 (1942)	X	X	X	X	X	X	X	X	X	Ex Ardsley		
61229	5MT: B1 4-6-0 (1942)												
61230	5MT: B1 4-6-0 (1942)												
61267	5MT: B1 4-6-0 (1942)												
61268	5MT: B1 4-6-0 (1942)												
61294	5MT: B1 4-6-0 (1942)												
61296	5MT: B1 4-6-0 (1942)												
68892	4F: J50 0-6-0T (1922)												
68895	4F: J50 0-6-0T (1922)												
68897	4F: J50 0-6-0T (1922)												
68898	4F: J50 0-6-0T (1922)												
68902	4F: J50 0-6-0T (1922)												
68906	4F: J50 0-6-0T (1922)												
68908	4F: J50 0-6-0T (1922)												
68912	4F: J50 0-6-0T (1922)												
68922	4F: J50 0-6-0T (1922)												
68923	4F: J50 0-6-0T (1922)												
68932	4F: J50 0-6-0T (1922)												
68933	4F: J50 0-6-0T (1922)												
68934	4F: J50 0-6-0T (1922)												
68940	4F: J50 0-6-0T (1922)												
68941	4F: J50 0-6-0T (1922)												
68942	4F: J50 0-6-0T (1922)												
68943	4F: J50 0-6-0T (1922)												
68944	4F: J50 0-6-0T (1922)												
68959	4F: J50 0-6-0T (1922)												
68969	4F: J50 0-6-0T (1922)												
64170	3F: J6 0-6-0 (1911)												
64203	3F: J6 0-6-0 (1911)												
64205	3F: J6 0-6-0 (1911)												
64226	3F: J6 0-6-0 (1911)												
64268	3F: J6 0-6-0 (1911)												
64271	3F: J6 0-6-0 (1911)												
64274	3F: J6 0-6-0 (1911)												
69432	2P: N1 0-6-2T (1907)	X	X	X	X	X	X	X	X	X	X	Ex Hornsey	
69434	2P: N1 0-6-2T (1907)	X	X	X	X	X	X	X	X	X	X	Ex Hornsey	
69439	2P: N1 0-6-2T (1907)	X	X	X	X	X	X	X	X	X	X	Ex Hornsey	
69443	2P: N1 0-6-2T (1907)												
69447	2P: N1 0-6-2T (1907)												
69448	2P: N1 0-6-2T (1907)												
69449	2P: N1 0-6-2T (1907)												
69454	2P: N1 0-6-2T (1907)												
69459	2P: N1 0-6-2T (1907)												
69464	2P: N1 0-6-2T (1907)												
69474	2P: N1 0-6-2T (1907)												
69478	2P: N1 0-6-2T (1907)												
69479	2P: N1 0-6-2T (1907)												
69482	2P: N1 0-6-2T (1907)												
69483	2P: N1 0-6-2T (1907)							To C. Hill	X	X	X	X	X
69485	2P: N1 0-6-2T (1907)												
67447	2P: C14 4-4-2T (1907)											To Gorton	X
67448	2P: C14 4-4-2T (1907)											To Gorton	X
67450	2P: C14 4-4-2T (1907)											To Gorton	X

Loco	Class	Aug-51	Sep-51	Oct-51	Nov-51	Dec-51	Jan-52	Feb-52	Mar-52	Apr-52	May-52	Jun-52	Jul-52
61031	5MT: B1 4-6-0 (1942)												
61145	5MT: B1 4-6-0 (1942)	X	X	X	Ex Ardsley								
61229	5MT: B1 4-6-0 (1942)												
61230	5MT: B1 4-6-0 (1942)												
61267	5MT: B1 4-6-0 (1942)												
61268	5MT: B1 4-6-0 (1942)												
61294	5MT: B1 4-6-0 (1942)												
61296	5MT: B1 4-6-0 (1942)												
64903	5F: J39 0-6-0 (1926)	X	X	X	X	X	X	X	Ex Ardsley				
64907	5F: J39 0-6-0 (1926)	X	X	X	X	X	X	X	Ex Ardsley				
68892	4F: J50 0-6-0T (1922)												
68895	4F: J50 0-6-0T (1922)												
68897	4F: J50 0-6-0T (1922)												
68898	4F: J50 0-6-0T (1922)												
68902	4F: J50 0-6-0T (1922)												
68906	4F: J50 0-6-0T (1922)												
68908	4F: J50 0-6-0T (1922)												
68912	4F: J50 0-6-0T (1922)												
68922	4F: J50 0-6-0T (1922)												
68923	4F: J50 0-6-0T (1922)												
68932	4F: J50 0-6-0T (1922)												
68933	4F: J50 0-6-0T (1922)												
68934	4F: J50 0-6-0T (1922)												
68940	4F: J50 0-6-0T (1922)												
68941	4F: J50 0-6-0T (1922)												
68942	4F: J50 0-6-0T (1922)												
68943	4F: J50 0-6-0T (1922)												
68944	4F: J50 0-6-0T (1922)												
68959	4F: J50 0-6-0T (1922)												
68969	4F: J50 0-6-0T (1922)												
64170	3F: J6 0-6-0 (1911)												
64203	3F: J6 0-6-0 (1911)												
64205	3F: J6 0-6-0 (1911)												
64226	3F: J6 0-6-0 (1911)												
64268	3F: J6 0-6-0 (1911)												
64271	3F: J6 0-6-0 (1911)								To Ardsley	X	X	X	X
64274	3F: J6 0-6-0 (1911)								To Ardsley	X	X	X	X
69432	2P: N1 0-6-2T (1907)												
69434	2P: N1 0-6-2T (1907)												
69439	2P: N1 0-6-2T (1907)												
69443	2P: N1 0-6-2T (1907)												
69447	2P: N1 0-6-2T (1907)												
69448	2P: N1 0-6-2T (1907)												
69449	2P: N1 0-6-2T (1907)												
69454	2P: N1 0-6-2T (1907)												
69459	2P: N1 0-6-2T (1907)												
69464	2P: N1 0-6-2T (1907)												
69474	2P: N1 0-6-2T (1907)												
69478	2P: N1 0-6-2T (1907)												
69479	2P: N1 0-6-2T (1907)												
69482	2P: N1 0-6-2T (1907)												
69485	2P: N1 0-6-2T (1907)												

Loco	Class	Aug-52	Sep-52	Oct-52	Nov-52	Dec-52	Jan-53	Feb-53	Mar-53	Apr-53	May-53	Jun-53	Jul-53
61031	5MT: B1 4-6-0 (1942)												
61145	5MT: B1 4-6-0 (1942)												
61229	5MT: B1 4-6-0 (1942)												
61230	5MT: B1 4-6-0 (1942)												
61267	5MT: B1 4-6-0 (1942)												
61268	5MT: B1 4-6-0 (1942)												
61294	5MT: B1 4-6-0 (1942)												
61296	5MT: B1 4-6-0 (1942)												
61384	5MT: B1 4-6-0 (1942)	X	Ex Ardsley	To Stratford	X	X	X	X	X	X	X	X	X
64903	5F: J39 0-6-0 (1926)												
64907	5F: J39 0-6-0 (1926)												
68892	4F: J50 0-6-0T (1922)												
68895	4F: J50 0-6-0T (1922)												
68897	4F: J50 0-6-0T (1922)												
68898	4F: J50 0-6-0T (1922)												
68902	4F: J50 0-6-0T (1922)							To Ardsley	X	X	X	X	X
68906	4F: J50 0-6-0T (1922)							To Hornsey	X	X	X	X	X
68908	4F: J50 0-6-0T (1922)												
68912	4F: J50 0-6-0T (1922)												
68922	4F: J50 0-6-0T (1922)												
68923	4F: J50 0-6-0T (1922)												
68932	4F: J50 0-6-0T (1922)												
68933	4F: J50 0-6-0T (1922)												
68934	4F: J50 0-6-0T (1922)												
68940	4F: J50 0-6-0T (1922)												
68941	4F: J50 0-6-0T (1922)										To Ardsley	X	X
68942	4F: J50 0-6-0T (1922)												
68943	4F: J50 0-6-0T (1922)												
68944	4F: J50 0-6-0T (1922)												
68959	4F: J50 0-6-0T (1922)												
68969	4F: J50 0-6-0T (1922)												
64170	3F: J6 0-6-0 (1911)												
64203	3F: J6 0-6-0 (1911)												
64205	3F: J6 0-6-0 (1911)												
64226	3F: J6 0-6-0 (1911)												
64268	3F: J6 0-6-0 (1911)												
69432	2P: N1 0-6-2T (1907)												
69433	2P: N1 0-6-2T (1907)	X	X	X	X	X	X	Ex Hornsey					
69434	2P: N1 0-6-2T (1907)												
69439	2P: N1 0-6-2T (1907)												
69442	2P: N1 0-6-2T (1907)	X	X	X	X	X	Ex Hornsey						
69443	2P: N1 0-6-2T (1907)												
69447	2P: N1 0-6-2T (1907)												
69448	2P: N1 0-6-2T (1907)						W/D	X	X	X	X	X	X
69449	2P: N1 0-6-2T (1907)												
69454	2P: N1 0-6-2T (1907)												
69459	2P: N1 0-6-2T (1907)												
69464	2P: N1 0-6-2T (1907)												
69474	2P: N1 0-6-2T (1907)												
69475	2P: N1 0-6-2T (1907)	X	X	X	X	X	X	Ex Hornsey					
69478	2P: N1 0-6-2T (1907)												
69479	2P: N1 0-6-2T (1907)					W/D	X	X	X	X	X	X	X
69482	2P: N1 0-6-2T (1907)												
69485	2P: N1 0-6-2T (1907)												

Loco	Class	Aug-53	Sep-53	Oct-53	Nov-53	Dec-53	Jan-54	Feb-54	Mar-54	Apr-54	May-54	Jun-54	Jul-54
63920	7F: O4 2-8-0 (1911)	X	X	X	X	Ex Ardsley							
61031	5MT: B1 4-6-0 (1942)												
61145	5MT: B1 4-6-0 (1942)					To Doncaster	X	X	X	X	X	X	X
61229	5MT: B1 4-6-0 (1942)												
61230	5MT: B1 4-6-0 (1942)												
61267	5MT: B1 4-6-0 (1942)												
61268	5MT: B1 4-6-0 (1942)												
61294	5MT: B1 4-6-0 (1942)		To Eastfield	X	X	X	X	X	X	X	X	X	X
61296	5MT: B1 4-6-0 (1942)												
64903	5F: J39 0-6-0 (1926)												
64907	5F: J39 0-6-0 (1926)												
68892	4F: J50 0-6-0T (1922)												
68895	4F: J50 0-6-0T (1922)												
68897	4F: J50 0-6-0T (1922)												
68898	4F: J50 0-6-0T (1922)												
68908	4F: J50 0-6-0T (1922)												
68912	4F: J50 0-6-0T (1922)												
68922	4F: J50 0-6-0T (1922)												
68923	4F: J50 0-6-0T (1922)												
68932	4F: J50 0-6-0T (1922)												
68933	4F: J50 0-6-0T (1922)												
68934	4F: J50 0-6-0T (1922)												
68940	4F: J50 0-6-0T (1922)												
68942	4F: J50 0-6-0T (1922)												
68943	4F: J50 0-6-0T (1922)												
68944	4F: J50 0-6-0T (1922)												
68959	4F: J50 0-6-0T (1922)												
68969	4F: J50 0-6-0T (1922)												
64170	3F: J6 0-6-0 (1911)												
64203	3F: J6 0-6-0 (1911)												
64205	3F: J6 0-6-0 (1911)												
64226	3F: J6 0-6-0 (1911)												
64268	3F: J6 0-6-0 (1911)												
69432	2P: N1 0-6-2T (1907)												
69433	2P: N1 0-6-2T (1907)												
69434	2P: N1 0-6-2T (1907)												
69439	2P: N1 0-6-2T (1907)												
69442	2P: N1 0-6-2T (1907)		W/D	X	X	X	X	X	X	X	X	X	X
69443	2P: N1 0-6-2T (1907)												
69447	2P: N1 0-6-2T (1907)												
69449	2P: N1 0-6-2T (1907)												
69454	2P: N1 0-6-2T (1907)												
69459	2P: N1 0-6-2T (1907)												
69464	2P: N1 0-6-2T (1907)												
69474	2P: N1 0-6-2T (1907)												
69475	2P: N1 0-6-2T (1907)												
69478	2P: N1 0-6-2T (1907)												
69482	2P: N1 0-6-2T (1907)												
69485	2P: N1 0-6-2T (1907)												

Although 0-6-2T's and, to a lesser extent, 4-4-2T's were the usual power for the Leeds local services, there were times when substitutes had to be found as happened when J6 64268 (Bowling Junction) was seen at Holbeck (High Level) whilst being pressed into service on a Leeds - Bradford local passenger. The open lights on the engine's bufferbeam reflects the fact that trains that made limited stops between Leeds and Bradford were granted class A - express passenger - status. (H.C. Casserley)

The fireman of Bowling Junction-based N1 0-6-2 69478 exchanges a few words with the shunter between shunting duties as a nicely lined A1 4-6-2 backs out of platform 3 and makes its way to Copley Hill loco. The foreman shunters were responsible for much of the station's carriage shunting - the shunters doing the actual work - whilst the Inspector, somewhat aloof, drew attention to planned alterations and amendments and observed from a distance. The Station Master and his assistants occupied a different world altogether! (H.C. Casserley)

ALLOCATION & TRANSFERS : BRADFORD (BOWLING JUNCTION) 37C

Loco	Class	Aug-54	Sep-54	Oct-54	Nov-54	Dec-54	Jan-55	Feb-55	Mar-55	Apr-55	May-55	Jun-55	Jul-55
63920	7F: O4 2-8-0 (1911)												
61031	5MT: B1 4-6-0 (1942)												
61229	5MT: B1 4-6-0 (1942)												
61230	5MT: B1 4-6-0 (1942)												
61267	5MT: B1 4-6-0 (1942)												
61268	5MT: B1 4-6-0 (1942)												
61296	5MT: B1 4-6-0 (1942)												
64903	5F: J39 0-6-0 (1926)												
64907	5F: J39 0-6-0 (1926)												
68892	4F: J50 0-6-0T (1922)												
68895	4F: J50 0-6-0T (1922)												
68897	4F: J50 0-6-0T (1922)												
68898	4F: J50 0-6-0T (1922)												
68908	4F: J50 0-6-0T (1922)												
68912	4F: J50 0-6-0T (1922)												
68922	4F: J50 0-6-0T (1922)												
68923	4F: J50 0-6-0T (1922)												
68932	4F: J50 0-6-0T (1922)												
68933	4F: J50 0-6-0T (1922)												
68934	4F: J50 0-6-0T (1922)												
68940	4F: J50 0-6-0T (1922)												
68942	4F: J50 0-6-0T (1922)												
68943	4F: J50 0-6-0T (1922)												
68944	4F: J50 0-6-0T (1922)												
68959	4F: J50 0-6-0T (1922)												
68969	4F: J50 0-6-0T (1922)												
69696	3P: N7 0-6-2T (1914)	X	X	X	X	X	X	X	X	X	X	X	Ex C. Hill
64170	3F: J6 0-6-0 (1911)												
64203	3F: J6 0-6-0 (1911)												
64205	3F: J6 0-6-0 (1911)												
64226	3F: J6 0-6-0 (1911)												
64268	3F: J6 0-6-0 (1911)												
69432	2P: N1 0-6-2T (1907)				W/D	X	X	X	X	X	X	X	X
69433	2P: N1 0-6-2T (1907)					W/D	X	X	X	X	X	X	X
69434	2P: N1 0-6-2T (1907)												
69436	2P: N1 0-6-2T (1907)	Ex C. Hill											W/D
69439	2P: N1 0-6-2T (1907)												
69441	2P: N1 0-6-2T (1907)	X	X	X	X	X	X	X	X	Ex Colwick	W/D	X	X
69443	2P: N1 0-6-2T (1907)												
69447	2P: N1 0-6-2T (1907)												
69449	2P: N1 0-6-2T (1907)									W/D	X	X	X
69451	2P: N1 0-6-2T (1907)	X	X	X	X	X	X	X	X	Ex Colwick			
69454	2P: N1 0-6-2T (1907)							W/D	X		X	X	X
69455	2P: N1 0-6-2T (1907)	X	X	X	X	X	X	X	Ex Hornsey		W/D	X	X
69459	2P: N1 0-6-2T (1907)									W/D	X	X	X
69464	2P: N1 0-6-2T (1907)												
69467	2P: N1 0-6-2T (1907)	X	X	X	X	X	X	X	X	Ex Colwick			
69471	2P: N1 0-6-2T (1907)	Ex C. Hill											
69474	2P: N1 0-6-2T (1907)												
69475	2P: N1 0-6-2T (1907)	To KX	X	X	X	X	X	X	X	Ex C. Hill	W/D	X	X
69478	2P: N1 0-6-2T (1907)												
69482	2P: N1 0-6-2T (1907)	W/D	X	X	X	X	X	X	X	X	X	X	X
69485	2P: N1 0-6-2T (1907)				W/D	X	X	X	X	X	X	X	X

ALLOCATION & TRANSFERS : BRADFORD (BOWLING JUNCTION) 37C

Loco	Class	Aug-55	Sep-55	Oct-55	Nov-55	Dec-55	Jan-56	Feb-56	Mar-56	Apr-56	May-56	Jun-56	Jul-56
63920	7F: O4 2-8-0 (1911)												
61031	5MT: B1 4-6-0 (1942)												
61229	5MT: B1 4-6-0 (1942)												
61230	5MT: B1 4-6-0 (1942)												
61267	5MT: B1 4-6-0 (1942)												
61268	5MT: B1 4-6-0 (1942)												
61296	5MT: B1 4-6-0 (1942)												
64801	5F: J39 0-6-0 (1926)	X	X	X	X	X	X	X	X	X	X	Ex Ardsley	
64903	5F: J39 0-6-0 (1926)												
64907	5F: J39 0-6-0 (1926)												
68892	4F: J50 0-6-0T (1922)												
68895	4F: J50 0-6-0T (1922)												
68897	4F: J50 0-6-0T (1922)												
68898	4F: J50 0-6-0T (1922)												
68908	4F: J50 0-6-0T (1922)												
68912	4F: J50 0-6-0T (1922)												
68922	4F: J50 0-6-0T (1922)												
68923	4F: J50 0-6-0T (1922)												
68932	4F: J50 0-6-0T (1922)												
68933	4F: J50 0-6-0T (1922)												
68934	4F: J50 0-6-0T (1922)												
68940	4F: J50 0-6-0T (1922)												
68942	4F: J50 0-6-0T (1922)												
68943	4F: J50 0-6-0T (1922)												
68944	4F: J50 0-6-0T (1922)												
68959	4F: J50 0-6-0T (1922)												
68969	4F: J50 0-6-0T (1922)												
69696	3P: N7 0-6-2T (1914)									To C. Hill	X	X	X
64170	3F: J6 0-6-0 (1911)												
64203	3F: J6 0-6-0 (1911)									To Ardsley	Ex Ardsley		
64205	3F: J6 0-6-0 (1911)										To Ardsley	Ex Ardsley	X
64226	3F: J6 0-6-0 (1911)									To Ardsley	Ex Ardsley		
64268	3F: J6 0-6-0 (1911)										To Ardsley		X
69434	2P: N1 0-6-2T (1907)												
69439	2P: N1 0-6-2T (1907)				W/D	X	X	X	X	X	X	X	X
69443	2P: N1 0-6-2T (1907)												
69447	2P: N1 0-6-2T (1907)												
69451	2P: N1 0-6-2T (1907)			W/D	X	X	X	X	X	X	X	X	X
69457	2P: N1 0-6-2T (1907)	X	X	X	X	X	X	X	X	Ex Ardsley			
69464	2P: N1 0-6-2T (1907)	W/D	X	X	X	X	X	X	X	X	X	X	X
69467	2P: N1 0-6-2T (1907)												W/D
69471	2P: N1 0-6-2T (1907)								W/D	X	X	X	X
69474	2P: N1 0-6-2T (1907)												
69478	2P: N1 0-6-2T (1907)												

Because it was converted into a maintenance depot for diesel multiple-units as early as February 1958, Bowling Junction (also known as Hammerton Street) was one of the least known of BR's depots. On the basis of allocated engines, the largest shed in the Leeds GN area, its function had been to provide motive power for the Great Northern services from Bradford Exchange; workings that ranged from the rather rural service to Halifax and Keighley via Queensbury to the highly intensive suburban workings to Leeds Central. The shed also worked the Bradford - Kings Cross expresses as far as Wakefield where they merged with the main section from Leeds. A heavy, if local, service of goods workings was also operated with 0-6-0 tender engines being diagrammed to the main line services to Ardsley, Leeds and Wakefield whilst a respectable fleet of J50 0-6-0 tanks took care of the rest.

ALLOCATION & TRANSFERS : BRADFORD (BOWLING JUNCTION) 37C

Loco	Class	Aug-56	Sep-56	Oct-56	Nov-56	Dec-56	Jan-57	Feb-57	Mar-57	Apr-57	May-57	Jun-57	Jul-57
63920	7F: O4 2-8-0 (1911)												
61031	5MT: B1 4-6-0 (1942)												
61229	5MT: B1 4-6-0 (1942)												
61230	5MT: B1 4-6-0 (1942)												
61267	5MT: B1 4-6-0 (1942)											To Wakefield	X
61268	5MT: B1 4-6-0 (1942)											To Wakefield	X
61296	5MT: B1 4-6-0 (1942)											To Wakefield	X
61320	5MT: B1 4-6-0 (1942)	X	X	Ex B. Gdns								To Wakefield	X
64796	5F: J39 0-6-0 (1926)	X	X	X	X	X	X	X	X	X	X	Ex Ardsley	
64801	5F: J39 0-6-0 (1926)												
64872	5F: J39 0-6-0 (1926)	X	X	X	X	X	X	X	X	X	X	Ex Ardsley	
64903	5F: J39 0-6-0 (1926)												
64907	5F: J39 0-6-0 (1926)												
68892	4F: J50 0-6-0T (1922)												
68895	4F: J50 0-6-0T (1922)												
68897	4F: J50 0-6-0T (1922)												
68898	4F: J50 0-6-0T (1922)												
68908	4F: J50 0-6-0T (1922)												
68912	4F: J50 0-6-0T (1922)												
68922	4F: J50 0-6-0T (1922)												
68923	4F: J50 0-6-0T (1922)												
68932	4F: J50 0-6-0T (1922)												
68933	4F: J50 0-6-0T (1922)												
68934	4F: J50 0-6-0T (1922)												
68940	4F: J50 0-6-0T (1922)												
68942	4F: J50 0-6-0T (1922)												
68943	4F: J50 0-6-0T (1922)												
68944	4F: J50 0-6-0T (1922)												
68959	4F: J50 0-6-0T (1922)												
68969	4F: J50 0-6-0T (1922)												
64170	3F: J6 0-6-0 (1911)												
64203	3F: J6 0-6-0 (1911)												
64226	3F: J6 0-6-0 (1911)												
69434	2P: N1 0-6-2T (1907)							To C. Hill	X	X	X	X	X
69443	2P: N1 0-6-2T (1907)												
69447	2P: N1 0-6-2T (1907)		W/D	X	X	X	X	X	X	X	X	X	X
69457	2P: N1 0-6-2T (1907)								To C. Hill	X	X	X	X
69474	2P: N1 0-6-2T (1907)												
69478	2P: N1 0-6-2T (1907)					W/D	X	X	X	X	X	X	X
41251	2MT 2-6-2T (1946)	X	X	X	X	X	Ex Wakefield	To Wakefield	X	X	X	X	X
D3454	0F: Diesel 0-6-0	X	X	X	X	X	X	X	X	X	NEW	To Stourton	X
D3455	0F: Diesel 0-6-0	X	X	X	X	X	X	X	X	X	NEW		
D3456	0F: Diesel 0-6-0	X	X	X	X	X	X	X	X	X	NEW		
D3457	0F: Diesel 0-6-0	X	X	X	X	X	X	X	X	X	X	NEW	

ALLOCATION & TRANSFERS : BRADFORD (BOWLING JUNCTION) 37C

Loco	Class	Aug-57	Sep-57	Oct-57	Nov-57	Dec-57	Jan-58	Feb-58	Mar-58	Apr-58	May-58	Jun-58	Jul-58
90698	8F: WD 2-8-0 (1943)	X	X	X	X	Ex Ardsley	To Low Moor	X	X	X	X	X	X
63920	7F: O4 2-8-0 (1911)							To Ardsley	X	X	X	X	X
61031	5MT: B1 4-6-0 (1942)							To Low Moor	X	X	X	X	X
61131	5MT: B1 4-6-0 (1942)	X	Ex Ardsley					To Low Moor	X	X	X	X	X
61229	5MT: B1 4-6-0 (1942)							To Low Moor	X	X	X	X	X
61230	5MT: B1 4-6-0 (1942)							To Low Moor	X	X	X	X	X
61382	5MT: B1 4-6-0 (1942)	X	Ex Ardsley					To Low Moor	X	X	X	X	X
61383	5MT: B1 4-6-0 (1942)	X	Ex Ardsley					To Low Moor	X	X	X	X	X
64791	5F: J39 0-6-0 (1926)	X	Ex N. Hill					To Low Moor	X	X	X	X	X
64796	5F: J39 0-6-0 (1926)							To Low Moor	X	X	X	X	X
64801	5F: J39 0-6-0 (1926)							To Low Moor	X	X	X	X	X
64872	5F: J39 0-6-0 (1926)							To Low Moor	X	X	X	X	X
64886	5F: J39 0-6-0 (1926)	X	Ex N. Hill					To Low Moor	X	X	X	X	X
64903	5F: J39 0-6-0 (1926)							To Low Moor	X	X	X	X	X
64907	5F: J39 0-6-0 (1926)							To Low Moor	X	X	X	X	X
64947	5F: J39 0-6-0 (1926)	X	Ex Malton					To Low Moor	X	X	X	X	X
68892	4F: J50 0-6-0T (1922)							To Low Moor	X	X	X	X	X
68895	4F: J50 0-6-0T (1922)		To Ardsley	Ex Ardsley				To Low Moor	X	X	X	X	X
68897	4F: J50 0-6-0T (1922)							To Darlington	X	X	X	X	X
68898	4F: J50 0-6-0T (1922)		To Ardsley	X	X	X	X	X	X	X	X	X	X
68908	4F: J50 0-6-0T (1922)							To Low Moor	X	X	X	X	X
68912	4F: J50 0-6-0T (1922)							To Hull (D)	X	X	X	X	X
68922	4F: J50 0-6-0T (1922)							To Low Moor	X	X	X	X	X
68923	4F: J50 0-6-0T (1922)							To Low Moor	X	X	X	X	X
68932	4F: J50 0-6-0T (1922)							To Low Moor	X	X	X	X	X
68933	4F: J50 0-6-0T (1922)							To Low Moor	X	X	X	X	X
68934	4F: J50 0-6-0T (1922)							To Low Moor	X	X	X	X	X
68940	4F: J50 0-6-0T (1922)							To Low Moor	X	X	X	X	X
68942	4F: J50 0-6-0T (1922)							To Low Moor	X	X	X	X	X
68943	4F: J50 0-6-0T (1922)							To Low Moor	X	X	X	X	X
68944	4F: J50 0-6-0T (1922)							To Low Moor	X	X	X	X	X
68959	4F: J50 0-6-0T (1922)		To Ardsley	X	X	X	X	X	X	X	X	X	X
68969	4F: J50 0-6-0T (1922)							To Low Moor	X	X	X	X	X
D8010	4F: 1000HP D/E	X	X	X	X	Ex Devons Rd	To Devons Rd	X	X	X	X	X	X
D8011	4F: 1000HP D/E	X	X	X	X	Ex Devons Rd	To Devons Rd	X	X	X	X	X	X
64170	3F: J6 0-6-0 (1911)							To Low Moor	X	X	X	X	X
64203	3F: J6 0-6-0 (1911)							To Low Moor	X	X	X	X	X
64226	3F: J6 0-6-0 (1911)							To Low Moor	X	X	X	X	X
69443	2P: N1 0-6-2T (1907)				To Ardsley	X	X	X	X	X	X	X	X
69474	2P: N1 0-6-2T (1907)			To Ardsley	X	X	X	X	X	X	X	X	X
D2260	0F: Diesel 0-6-0	X	X	X	X	NEW							
D2261	0F: Diesel 0-6-0	X	X	X	X	NEW							
D2264	0F: Diesel 0-6-0	X	X	X	X	NEW							
D2265	0F: Diesel 0-6-0	X	X	X	X	NEW							
D3455	0F: Diesel 0-6-0												
D3456	0F: Diesel 0-6-0												
D3457	0F: Diesel 0-6-0												

Most of the passenger work was handled by an allocation of fifteen ex-GNR N1 0-6-2T's, the work of which deserves far greater public acclaim than has been given. The service was intensive and the timings were tight whilst the gradients were as tricky as any to be found on any suburban working. How the crews concerned must have looked across to the LMS side of Bradford Exchange and cast glances of envy at the 4MT 2-6-4T's used by Low Moor for its much less exacting local duties. The N1's, which at 2P were nominally only half the power of the Low Moor 2-6-4T's, seemed to be doing twice the work for most of the time.

By the early fifties time, age and effort were beginning to leave their mark on the reliability of the N1's and it was clear that the time was fast approaching for a replacement to be found. A short-lived and somewhat unpopular trial was made using ex-Great Eastern N7 0-6-2T's and push & pull workings on the Leeds service but in the end the N1's managed to hold out until the arrival of diesels in 1954 from which time steam was all but eliminated from the Leeds - Bradford route.

For a few years the depot continued to provide locomotives for goods duties but in February 1958 it became the first BR depot to be devoted entirely to diesel when it was converted to a maintenance depot for diesel railcars; its allocation of steam being transferred to the ex-Lancashire and Yorkshire shed at Low Moor.

1: A1 4-6-2

Copley Hill Loco	07.02	Light	
Leeds	**07.50**	969	
11.40 Kings Cross			
Pass Loco	15.00	Light	
Kings Cross	**15.40**	962	The West Riding
19.19 Leeds	19.50	Light	
19.55 Copley Hill Loco			

2: A1 4-6-2

Copley Hill Loco	10.15	Light	
Leeds	**10.45**	19	Yorkshire Pullman
14.37 Kings Cross			
Top Shed	17.50	Light	
Kings Cross	**18.20**	88	
22.19 Leeds	23.15	Light	
23.20 Copley Hill Loco			

4: B1 4-6-0

Copley Hill Loco	21.30	Light	
Leeds	**22.00**	987	Kings Cross
23.20 Doncaster			
Carr Loco	04.45	Light	
Decoy	**05.00**	1266	21.15 ex KX Goods
09.08 Leeds (Wellington St)	09.15	Light	
09.25 Copley Hill Loco			

25: B1 4-6-0

Copley Hill Loco	01.22	Light	
Leeds	**01.42**	951	
02.30 Doncaster	**02.45**	951	
03.30 Sheffield Vic	03.35	Light	
03.40 Darnall loco	06.00	Light	
06.05 Sheffield Vic	**06.20**	133	
07.03 Doncaster	**07.33**	3022	
08.41 Leeds	09.05	Light	
09.10 Copley Hill Loco	15.00	Light	
15.05 Leeds	**15.40**	3155	
16.50 Doncaster	16.55	Light	
17.00 Carr Loco	19.00	Light	
19.05 Doncaster	**19.24**	102	16.05 ex KX
20.24 Leeds	20.45		
20.50 Copley Hill Loco			

26: B1 4-6-0

Copley Hill Loco	15.35	Light	
15.32 Copley Hill CS	**15.40**	ECS	On Rear
15.48 Leeds	**16.13**	439	
19.12 Cleethorpes	19.30	Light	
19.50 Grimsby Docks	**20.25**	Fish	
00.25 Leeds	00.35	Light	
Steam Heat 01.42			
Leeds	01.50	Light	
01.55 Copley Hill loco			

29: B1 4-6-0

Copley Hill Loco	00.40	Light	
00.45 Leeds	**01.05**	Pcls	March Parcels
02.42 Doncaster	02.50	Light	
02.55 Carr Loco	05.00	Light	
05.05 Doncaster	**05.25**	153	04.20 ex Sheffield
06.53 Leeds	07.47	Light	
07.52 Copley Hill Loco	13.45	Light	
13.50 Leeds	**14.04**	3143	Via Kirkgate
15.21 Doncaster	**16.55**	444	
17.47 Sheffield Vic	17.50	Light	
17.55 Darnall Loco	18.45	Light	
18.50 Sheffield Vic	**19.06**	80	16.30 L'pool - Hull
19.50 Doncaster	**20.30**	ECS	
21.00 Wakefield	21.15	Light	
21.30 Copley Hill Loco			

31: A1 4-6-2

Copley Hill Loco	16.07	Light	
Leeds	**16.36**	131	Queen of Scots
20.04 Kings Cross			
Pass Loco			

32: A1 4-6-2

Pass Loco	08.50	Light	
Kings Cross	**09.20**	40	The White Rose
13.07 Leeds	13.50		
13.55 Copley Hill Loco			

33: A1 4-6-2

Copley Hill Loco	16.53	Light	
Leeds	**17.33**	71	
21.22 Kings Cross			
Pass Loco			

34: A1 4-6-2

Pass Loco	11.20	Light	
Kings Cross	**11.50**	58	Queen of Scots
15.21 Leeds	15.30	Light	
15.35 Copley Hill Loco			

36: B1 4-6-0

Copley Hill Loco	22.15	Light	
22.20 Leeds	**22.35**	3229	Via Kirkgate
23.33 Doncaster	23.40	Light	
23.45 Garden Sidings	01.30	Light	
01.40 Belmont	**02.25**	3006	Goods (F)
04.42 Spring Lane	04.50	Light	
05.05 Copley Hill Loco			

71: B1 4-6-0

Copley Hill Loco	03.18	Light	
03.25 Leeds	**03.43**	970	22.45 ex KX
04.01 Bradford	04.20	Light	
04.45 Leeds	**06.28**	Pcls	
07.23 Bradford	**08.10**	Pcls	
09.24 Ardsley	09.43	Light	
09.50 Copley Hill Loco			

72: N1 0-6-2T

Copley Hill Loco	05.20	Light	
05.25 Copley Hill CS	**05.30**	ECS	07.50 Leeds - KX
05.37 Leeds	**07.50**	Light	Bank 07.50
08.00 Copley Hill CS	**11.30**	ECS	12.30 Leeds - KX
11.39 Leeds	**12.46**	ECS	11.15 ex Doncaster
12.55 Copley Hill CS	**16.13**	ECS	16.43 Leeds - Doncaster
16.20 Leeds	**17.50**	1618	
18.21 Castleford	**18.37**	ECS	
19.11 Copley Hill CS	19.15	Light	
19.20 Copley Hill Loco			

73: J50 0-6-0T

Copley Hill Loco	04.38	Light	
04.40 Copley Hill CS	**04.44**	O/R	07.30 Leeds - KX
04.51 Leeds	**05.30**	ECS	22.45 ex KX
05.37 Copley Hill CS			
Carriage Pilot			
Copley Hill CS	00.55	Light	
01.00 Copley Hill Loco			

74: J50 0-6-0T

Copley Hill Loco	04.15	Light	
04.20 Leeds			
Shunt A/R			
Leeds	**06.22**	ECS	Parcels Vans
06.30 Copley Hill CS	07.10	Light	
07.20 Leeds	**07.45**	ECS	04.20 ex Sheffield
07.52 Copley Hill CS	**09.03**	ECS	10.00 KX ECS
09.10 Leeds			
Shunt A/R			
Leeds	**12.00**	ECS	08.00 ex KX
12.07 Copley Hill CS	**13.23**	ECS	14.04 Leeds - Doncaster
13.30 Leeds			
Shunt A/R			
Leeds	**17.58**	ECS	13.20 ex KX
18.05 Copley Hill CS	**18.31**	ECS	22.00 Leeds - KX
18.38 Leeds			
Shunt A/R			
Leeds	**20.42**	ECS	16.05 ex KX
20.49 Copley Hill CS	**21.35**	ECS	22.35 Leeds - Doncaster
21.45 Leeds			
Shunt A/R			
Leeds	**23.12**	ECS	18.20 ex KX
23.19 Copley Hill CS	23.35	Light	
23.45 Leeds			
Shunt A/R			
Leeds	01.00	Light	
01.05 Copley Hill Loco			

75: N1 0-6-2T

Copley Hill Loco	08.00	Light	
08.10 Leeds	**09.30**	ECS	0400 ex KX
09.40 Copley Hill CS	10.31	Light	
10.41 Leeds	**11.12**	ECS	07.50 Pcls ex Doncaster
11.19 Copley Hill CS	11.35	Light	
11.45 Leeds	**12.19**	ECS	09.23 ex Cleethorpes
12.26 Copley Hill CS	12.40	Light	
12.45 Copley Hill Loco	16.40	Light	
16.45 Copley Hill CS	**16.51**	ECS	17.16 Leeds - Doncaster
16.58 Leeds	**18.40**	ECS	17.13 ex Doncaster
18.47 Copley Hill CS	18.50	Light	
19.00 Leeds	**19.42**	ECS	15.40 ex KX
19.49 Copley Hill CS	**22.36**	ECS	01.42 Leeds - Sheffield
22.43 Leeds	**23.52**	ECS	22.22 ex Doncaster
23.57 Copley Hill CS	00.02	Light	
00.05 Copley Hill Loco			

10G: J50 0-6-0T

Copley Hill Loco	04.35	Light	
04.38 Copley Hill CS	**04.44**	ECS	07.30 Leeds - KX
04.51 Leeds	07.30	Light	
07.35 Wellington St			
Shunt			
Wellington St	17.00	Light	
17.10 Copley Hill CS	**17.31**	ECS	17.45 Leeds - Doncaster
17.38 Leeds	17.47	Light	
17.55 Wellington St			
Shunt			
Wellington St	11.30	Light	
11.40 Copley Hill Loco			

ARDSLEY 1 : B1 4-6-0

Ardsley Loco	09.15	Light	
09.25 Wakefield W	**09.45**	344	Parcels. 07.50 ex Doncaster
11.04 Bradford	11.36	Light	
12.04 Leeds	**12.22**	582	Parcels.
13.41 Bradford	**15.25**	341	Parcels
16.37 Wakefield W	**18.20**	Pcls	
19.30 Bradford	**21.38**	987	KX
22.13 Wakefield W	22.40	Light	
22.50 Ardsley Loco			

ARDSLEY 3 : N1 0-6-2T

Ardsley Loco	15.00	Light	
15.10 Wakefield W	**16.25**	222	ECS
16.28 Wakefield K	**17.00**	222	Via Westgate
17.31 Leeds	17.52	Light	
18.20 Wakefield W	**19.06**	962	15.40 ex KX
19.42 Bradford	**21.09**	669	Parcels
21.47 Leeds	22.05	Light	
22.20 Leeds			

ENGINE DIAGRAMS

In spite of the influx of diesel units in 1955, steam continued to play a major role in operations at Leeds Central and the variety of classes to be seen was as wide as at any ex-LNER main line location. The express services to London were shared between Copley Hill's A1 Pacifics, Doncaster's A3's and A4's from Kings Cross whilst B1 4-6-0's from Doncaster, Copley Hill and Bradford handled the frequent - it is surprising to see how many of them there were - stopping trains to Doncaster and the remaining steam-hauled workings to Bradford. B1's also worked the Bradford portions of the London trains as far as Wakefield; most running over the Tingley branch to Ardsley and then up the main line to Wakefield Westgate where trains would combine. The service between Bradford and Wakefield via Batley and Dewsbury was operated for the most part by diesel railcars.

Leeds Central was also a meeting point with the London Midland whose L&Y trains operated an hourly - there were only a few gaps - express service to West Lancashire; most trains running to Liverpool Exchange via Manchester Victoria with a handful terminating at Southport and Blackpool. LMS motive power was interesting rather than varied and its high point came in the dead of night when a Newton Heath 5XP 'Jubilee' 4-6-0 was sent round from Leeds City to work the 03.25 Leeds Central to Manchester. It was not a working witnessed by very many enthusiasts!

Most of the L&Y trains from Leeds Central were subsidiary portions of Bradford - Liverpool expresses; the two sections being combined at either Low Moor or Halifax. Usually the main engine - invariably a Black 5 4-6-0 - would work the Bradford section leaving the Leeds coaches to be worked by a Low Moor 2-6-4T although a handful of services reversed the process by making the Leeds section the principal component, in which case the Black 5 would make an appearance at Leeds Central. There were several variations on the theme; perhaps the best of which was the Southport 4-6-0 which worked a Liverpool Express as far as Low Moor and was then relieved by another Southport Black 5 for the short leg to Bradford. The Leeds section of this train was worked by a Low Moor Black 5. Variety and interest all round!

LEEDS (FOREIGN) ENGINE DIAGRAMS (1957/8)

DONCASTER 4 : A3 4-6-2

	Carr Loco	18.10	Light	
18.20	Doncaster	18.30	EP	17.15 ex Hull
21.41	Kings Cross	22.10	Light	
22.20	Top Shed	09.50	Light	
10.00	Kings Cross	10.20	952	
14.28	Leeds	15.00	Light	
15.08	Copley Hill loco	16.00	Light	
16.05	Copley Hill CS	16.13	ECS	On Rear
16.20	Leeds	16.43	3165	
17.56	Doncaster	18.00	Light	
18.10	Carr Loco			

DONCASTER 14 : A3 4-6-2

	Carr Loco	01.48	Light	
01.55	Doncaster	02.18	970	22.45 ex KX
03.28	Leeds	04.00	Light	
04.08	Copley Hill loco	07.00	Light	
07.10	Leeds	07.30	961	The West Riding
11.02	Kings Cross	11.20	Light	
11.30	Pasenger Loco	13.00	Light	
13.05	Kings Cross	13.20	70	
17.13	Leeds	17.58	ECS	On Rear
18.05	Copley Hill CS	18.27	Light	
18.38	Wakefield W	19.20	935	KX Parcels
19.53	Doncaster	19.57	Light	
20.00	Carr Loco			

DONCASTER 71 : B1 4-6-0

	Carr Loco	12.30		
12.40	Doncaster	12.55	3048	
14.06	Leeds	14.30	Light	
14.37	Copley Hill Loco	17.15	Light	
17.20	Copley Hill CS	17.30	ECS	On Rear
17.38	Leeds	17.45	3183	
18.53	Doncaster	19.00	Light	
19.10	Carr Loco			

DONCASTER 72 : B1 4-6-0

	Carr Loco	17.20	Light	
17.30	Doncaster	17.44	3052	
18.58	Leeds	19.20	Light	
	Wortley Angle		Turn	
19.38	Leeds	21.00	3209	
22.08	Doncaster	22.15	Light	
22.25	Carr Loco			

DONCASTER 77 : B1 4-6-0

	Carr Loco	06.00	Light	
06.10	Doncaster	06.20	3018	Via Kirkgate
07.33	Leeds	08.00	ECS	Gas Tanks
08.05	Copley Hill CS	08.15	Light	
08.20	Copley Hill Loco	09.15	Light	
09.25	Leeds	10.09	3115	
11.01	Doncaster	11.05	Light	
11.15	Carr Loco	(17.20)		

DONCASTER 78 : B1 4-6-0

	Carr Loco	10.50	Light	
11.00	Doncaster	11.15	3030	
12.32	Leeds	13.00	Light	
13.10	Copley Hill Loco	13.55	Light	
14.00	Leeds	14.25	ECS	Postal vans
14.32	Copley Hill CS	15.32	ECS	16.13 Clee
15.39	Leeds	17.16	3167	
18.11	Doncaster	18.15	Light	
18.25	Carr Loco			

DONCASTER 80 : B1 4-6-0

	Carr Loco	02.35	Light	
02.45	Doncaster (West Yd)	02.58	Pcls	Via Kirkgate
04.38	Leeds	05.00	Light	
05.08	Copley Hill Loco	07.55	Light	
08.05	Leeds	08.22	3083	Via Kirkgate
09.45	Doncaster	09.50	Light	
10.00	Carr Loco	(10.50)		

DONCASTER 84 : B1 4-6-0

	Carr Loco	16.55	Light	
17.05	Doncaster	17.13	30.46	
18.18	Leeds	18.45	Light	
18.50	Copley Hill Loco	19.45	Light	
19.50	Wellington St	20.05	1343	London Goods
22.26	Decoy	22.30		
22.40	Carr Loco			

DONCASTER 89 : B1 4-6-0

	Carr Loco	07.30	Light	
07.40	Doncaster	07.50	3024	Pcls via Kirkgate
10.15	Leeds	11.33	ECS	08.32 ex Liverpool
11.40	Copley Hill CS	12.01	Light	
14.02	Carr Loco	(16.55)		

IMMINGHAM 54 : B1 4-6-0

	Immingham loco	08.15	Light	
09.00	Cleethorpes	09.23	302	
12.03	Leeds	12.19	ECS	On Rear
12.26	Copley Hill CS	12.40	Light	
15.28	Immingham loco			

KINGS CROSS 1 : A4 4-6-2

	Top Shed	03.30	Light	
03.40	Kings Cross	04.00	936	
09.06	Leeds	09.31	Light	
09.40	Copley Hill Loco	11.45	Light	
11.55	Leeds	12.30	35	11.45 Harrogate
16.25	Kings Cross	16.40	Light	
16.50	Top Shed			

KINGS CROSS 3 : A4 4-6-2

	Top Shed	07.30	Light	
07.40	Kings Cross	08.00	948	
11.44	Leeds	12.02	Light	
12.10	Copley Hill Loco	15.00	Light	
15.08	Leeds	15.35	985	The White Rose
19.19	Kings Cross	19.40	Light	
19.50	Top Shed			

KINGS CROSS 38 : A4 4-6-2

	Top Shed	16.50	Light	
17.00	Kings Cross	17.20	84	The Yorkshire Pullman
21.14	Leeds	21.28	Light	
21.35	Copley Hill Loco	(09.30)		

KINGS CROSS 39 : A4 4-6-2

	Copley Hill Loco	09.30		
09.40	Leeds	10.00	971	
13.45	Kings Cross	14.05	Light	
14.15	Top Shed			
	Kings Cross	20.20	108	
22.22	Grantham	22.23	Light	
22.30	Grantham Loco	23.45	Light	
23.50	Grantham	00.04	259	Fish
02.35	KX Goods	02.40	Light	
02.45	Top Shed	(16.50)		

SOWERBY BGE 6 : 4MT 2-6-4T

	Sowerby Bge Loco	05.45	Light	
	Sowerby Bridge	05.58	Pass	
06.28	Bradford	08.15	Liverpool	
08.22	Low Moor			
	Shunt			
	Low Moor	09.35	07.00 ex Southport	
09.58	Leeds	10.55	Liverpool	
11.16	Low Moor	11.32	Light	
11.50	Sowerby Bge Loco			

LOW MOOR 2 : 5MT 4-6-0

	Low Moor Loco	06.14	Light	
06.22	Bradford	07.15	34	
10.44	Southport	10.55	Light	
11.05	Southport loco	12.50	Light	
13.00	Southport	13.10	57	
15.30	Bradford	16.00	Light	
16.08	Low Moor	16.54	611	14.30 ex Liverpool
17.16	Leeds	17.29	Light	
17.56	Low Moor	18.41	647	16.30 ex Liverpool
19.06	Leeds	19.30	Light	
	Wortley Angle		Light	Turn
19.50	Leeds	20.50	708	Manchester
21.15	Low Moor	21.20	Light	
21.25	Low Moor Loco			

LOW MOOR 8 : 2MT 2-6-2T

	Low Moor Loco	04.30	Light	
04.40	Bradford	05.21		
07.04	Penistone	07.23		
08.47	Bradford	09.00	ECS	
09.10	Broomfield CS	09.48	Light	
09.56	Low Moor	10.41	535	08.32 ex Liverpool
11.01	Leeds	11.45	Light	
12.06	Low Moor Loco	14.20	Light	
14.28	Bradford	14.55	1218	
16.24	Penistone	17.15	2172	
18.57	Bradford	19.28	Light	
19.36	Low Moor			
	Shunt			
	Low Moor	20.45	Light	
20.50	Low Moor Loco			

LOW MOOR 11 : 4MT 2-6-4T

	Low Moor Locc	04.25	Light	
04.35	Bradford	04.58	Fish	
05.08	Bridge Street	05.30	Light	
05.40	Bradford	06.23	1147	
07.04	Huddersfield	07.15	ECS	
07.19	Lockwood	07.48	ECS	
08.15	Headfield Jcn	08.35	Light	
08.55	Low Moor	09.27	7	07.00 ex Southport
09.33	Bradford			
	Pilot			
	Bradford	12.15	Light	
12.25	Low Moor Locc	13.17	Light	
13.20	Low Moor	13.47	583	11.30 ex Liverpool
14.08	Leeds	15.55	616	Liverpool
16.16	Low Moor	17.48	973	15.30 ex Liverpool
18.16	Leeds	18.55	144	Southport
19.17	Low Moor	19.25	Light	
19.30	Low Moor Loco			

LOW MOOR 14 : 4MT 2-6-4T

	Low Moor Locc	07.35		
	Low Moor	08.12	501	
08.34	Leeds	09.46	511	ECS
10.10	Low Moor	10.30	Light	
10.35	Low Moor Locc	14.55	Light	
15.07	Halifax	15.55	1228	
17.13	Stockport			
	Pilot			
	Stockport	19.28	2210	
21.20	Bradford	22.05	Light	
22.15	Low Moor Loco			

LOW MOOR 15 : 4MT 2-6-4T

	Low Moor Locc	06.45	Light	
06.52	Bradford	08.00	1166	
08.45	Huddersfield	09.10	ECS	
09.43	Headfield Jcn	10.30	Light	
11.03	Low Moor Locc	13.05	Light	
13.33	Leeds	13.55	590	Liverpool
14.17	Low Moor	14.20	Light	
14.25	Low Moor Locc	15.10	Light	
15.15	Low Moor	15.29	57	13.10 Southport
15.52	Leeds	17.55	654	
18.18	Low Moor	18.25	Light	
18.30	Low Moor Loco			

LOW MOOR 17 : 4MT 2-6-4T

	Low Moor Locc	03.00	Light	
03.10	Halifax	03.30	Pcls	
03.41	Low Moor	04.09	Pcls	
04.48	Leeds			
	pilot			
	Leeds	08.55	530	Liverpool
09.15	Low Moor	09.20	Light	
09.25	Low Moor Locc	11.30	Light	
11.35	Low Moor	11.49	329	09.40 Liverpool
12.06	Leeds	12.55	574	Liverpool
13.15	Low Moor	13.20	Light	
13.30	Low Moor Loco			

LOW MOOR 20 : 4MT 2-6-4T

	Low Moor Locc	06.14	Light	
06.22	Bradford	07.10	1149	
07.52	Huddersfield			
	Pilot			
	Huddersfield	12.13	2104	
13.22	Bradford	13.40	Light	
13.48	Low Moor Locc	16.20	Light	
16.25	Low Moor	17.41	973	15.30 Liverpool
17.48	Bradford	18.59	1185	Pilot
19.58	Huddersfield			
	Pilot			
	Huddersfield	21.10	2216	
21.57	Bradford	22.35	Light	
22.43	Low Moor	23.23	699	20.30 Liverpool
23.41	Leeds	00.15	Light	
00.37	Low Moor Loco			

LIVERPOOL (BANK HALL) 2: 5MT 4-6-0

	Bank Hall	12.00	Light	
12.05	Liverpool (Ex	12.30	1216	
14.54	Low Moor	14.55	Light	
15.00	Low Moor loco	16.11	Light	Turn
16.40	Leeds	17.11	640	
19.32	Liverpool (Ex	20.00	Light	
20.05	Bank Hall			

SOUTHPORT2 5MT 4-6-0

	Southport Loco	06.30	Light	
06.40	Southport	07.00	7	
08.04	Manchester (V)	08.10	7	
09.27	Low Moor	09.30	Light	
09.35	Low Moor loco	10.45	Light	
10.53	Bradford	11.15	548	
13.32	Liverpool	16.30	647	
18.31	Low Moor	18.32	Light	
	Low Moor loco	(05.55)		

SOUTHPORT1 5MT 4-6-0

	Low Moor loco	05.55	Light	
06.00	Low Moor	06.28	475	
06.51	Leeds	07.55	500	
08.17	Low Moor	08.28	500	
10.23	Liverpool Ex	10.47	Light	
10.53	Bank Hall loco	13.35	Light	
13.42	Liverpool Ex	14.30	611	
16.52	Bradford	17.26	Light	
17.34	Low Moor	18.36	647	16.30 Liverpool
18.42	Bradford	19.15	144	
19.22	Low Moor	19.28	144	
20.45	Manchester (V)	21.00	144	
21.57	Southport	22.10	Light	
22.15	Southport Loco	(06.30)		

NEWTON HEATH 4 5XP 4-6-0

	Manchester Ex	00.20	News	News
01.38	Leeds City	02.25	Light	
02.41	Leeds	03.25	462	
05.11	Manchester V	05.25	462	ECS
05.39	Irlam CS	05.50	Light	
06.10	Newton Heath loco			

NEWTON HEATH 17 5MT 4-6-0

	Newton Heath lo	06.15	Light	
06.26	Manchester V	06.50	1162	
07.59	Sowerby Bge	08.17	511	
09.12	Leeds	09.50	Light	
10.00	Copley Hill loco	12.00	Light	
12.05	Copley Hill CS	12.28	ECS	
09.12	Leeds	11.34	ECS	
11.41	Copley Hill CS	12.25	ECS	
12.32	Leeds	13.05	Light	
13.35	Farnley Jcn Loco	21.00	Light	
21.10	Leeds City	22.00	478	Pcls
00.47	Stockport	03.55		Pcls
04.20	Manchester V	04.30	Light	
04.40	Newton Heath loco			

BOWLING JCN 75: B1 4-6-0

	Low Moor Loco	06.10	Light	
06.18	Bradford	07.05	961	Kings Cross
07.39	Wakefield	07.50	Light	
08.20	Bradford			
	local trips			
	Bradford	12.08	35	Kings Cross
12.39	Wakefield	12.50	Light	
13.20	Low Moor	17.00	Light	
17.08	Bradford	18.00	149	Parcels
20.53	Doncaster	22.22	3068	
23.25	Leeds	23.53	Light	
00.05	Low Moor loco			

BOWLING JCN 76: B1 4-6-0

	Low Moor Loco	06.32	Light	
06.40	Bradford	07.19	969	Kings Cross
08.04	Wakefield	08.20	Light	
08.50	Bradford	10.15	19	Pullman
10.32	Leeds	10.47	Light	
	Wortley		turn	
11.10	Leeds	11.50	948	08.00 KX
12.07	Bradford	13.20	ECS	
13.42	Leeds	14.27	Light	
15.00	Low Moor loco			

BOWLING JCN 77: B1 4-6-0

	Low Moor Loco	14.43	Light	
14.52	Bradford	15.13	985	Kings Cross
15.44	Wakefield	17.01	70	13.20 KX
17.39	Bradford	19.20	651	Parcels
20.29	Leeds	21.22	84	Pullman
21.35	Bradford	22.00	Light	
22.10	Low Moor loco			

Loco	Class	Aug-50	Sep-50	Oct-50	Nov-50	Dec-50	Jan-51	Feb-51	Mar-51	Apr-51	May-51	Jun-51	Jul-51
52857	7F 0-8-0 (1912)												
44693	5MT 4-6-0 (1934)	X	X	X	X	NEW							
44694	5MT 4-6-0 (1934)	X	X	X	X	NEW							
44695	5MT 4-6-0 (1934)	X	X	X	X	NEW							
44912	5MT 4-6-0 (1934)												
44951	5MT 4-6-0 (1934)												
44990	5MT 4-6-0 (1934)												
45201	5MT 4-6-0 (1934)												
45207	5MT 4-6-0 (1934)												
45208	5MT 4-6-0 (1934)												
45210	5MT 4-6-0 (1934)	X	X	X	X	Ex H'field							
45219	5MT 4-6-0 (1934)	X	X	Ex H'field									
42726	5MT 2-6-0 (1926)					To Aintree	X	X	X	X	X	X	X
42727	5MT 2-6-0 (1926)					To Aintree	X	X	X	X	X	X	X
42728	5MT 2-6-0 (1926)					To Aintree	X	X	X	X	X	X	X
42732	5MT 2-6-0 (1926)												
42828	5MT 2-6-0 (1926)		To Rose Grove	X	X	X	X	X	X	X	X	X	X
42865	5MT 2-6-0 (1926)					To Mirfield	X	X	X	X	X	X	X
42107	4MT 2-6-4T (1945)												
42108	4MT 2-6-4T (1945)												
42109	4MT 2-6-4T (1945)												
42110	4MT 2-6-4T (1945)												
42111	4MT 2-6-4T (1945)												
42112	4MT 2-6-4T (1945)												
42113	4MT 2-6-4T (1945)												
42114	4MT 2-6-4T (1945)												
42115	4MT 2-6-4T (1945)												
42116	4MT 2-6-4T (1945)												
42188	4MT 2-6-4T (1945)												
42189	4MT 2-6-4T (1945)												
50909	3P 2-4-2T (1898)							W/D	X	X	X	X	X
52561	3F 0-6-0 (1909)	X	X	X	X	X	X	X	X	X	X	X	Ex Wakefield
52590	3F 0-6-0 (1909)											W/D	X
52092	3F 0-6-0 (1889)							W/D	X	X	X	X	X
52104	3F 0-6-0 (1889)												
52166	3F 0-6-0 (1889)	X	X	X	X	X	X	X	X	X	X	X	Ex Mirfield
52237	3F 0-6-0 (1889)												
52309	3F 0-6-0 (1889)												
52410	3F 0-6-0 (1889)												
52411	3F 0-6-0 (1889)												
52427	3F 0-6-0 (1889)				To Bolton	X	X	X	X	X	X	X	X
52461	3F 0-6-0 (1889)												
50736	2P 2-4-2T (1889)	X	X	X	X	X	X	X	X	X	X	Ex H'field	
50762	2P 2-4-2T (1889)	X	X	X	X	X	X	X	X	X	X	Ex Wakefield	
50806	2P 2-4-2T (1889)			To Blackpool	X	X	X	X	X	X	X	X	X
50886	2P 2-4-2T (1889)	X	X	X	X	X	X	X	X	X	X	Ex Wakefield	
51404	2F 0-6-0ST (1877)												

Loco	Class	Aug-51	Sep-51	Oct-51	Nov-51	Dec-51	Jan-52	Feb-52	Mar-52	Apr-52	May-52	Jun-52	Jul-52
52857	7F 0-8-0 (1912)					W/D	X	X	X	X	X	X	X
44693	5MT 4-6-0 (1934)												
44694	5MT 4-6-0 (1934)												
44695	5MT 4-6-0 (1934)												
44912	5MT 4-6-0 (1934)												
44951	5MT 4-6-0 (1934)												
44990	5MT 4-6-0 (1934)												
45201	5MT 4-6-0 (1934)				To Wakefield	X	X	X	X	X	X	X	X
45207	5MT 4-6-0 (1934)												
45208	5MT 4-6-0 (1934)												
45210	5MT 4-6-0 (1934)									To Farnley Jn	Ex Farnley Jn		
45219	5MT 4-6-0 (1934)												
42732	5MT 2-6-0 (1926)	To Aintree	X	X	X	X	X	X	X	X	X	X	X
42107	4MT 2-6-4T (1945)												
42108	4MT 2-6-4T (1945)												
42109	4MT 2-6-4T (1945)												
42110	4MT 2-6-4T (1945)												
42111	4MT 2-6-4T (1945)												
42112	4MT 2-6-4T (1945)												
42113	4MT 2-6-4T (1945)												
42114	4MT 2-6-4T (1945)												
42115	4MT 2-6-4T (1945)												
42116	4MT 2-6-4T (1945)												
42188	4MT 2-6-4T (1945)												
42189	4MT 2-6-4T (1945)												
52561	3F 0-6-0 (1909)												To Goole
52104	3F 0-6-0 (1889)												
52166	3F 0-6-0 (1889)												
52237	3F 0-6-0 (1889)												To Goole
52309	3F 0-6-0 (1889)				To Goole	X	X	X	X	X	X	X	X
52351	3F 0-6-0 (1889)	X	X	X	X	Ex Mirfield							
52410	3F 0-6-0 (1889)				To Goole	X	X	X	X	X	X	X	X
52411	3F 0-6-0 (1889)									To Goole	Ex Goole		
52461	3F 0-6-0 (1889)												
52515	3F 0-6-0 (1889)	X	Ex Mirfield										
52521	3F 0-6-0 (1889)	X	X	X	Ex Wakefield								
50736	2P 2-4-2T (1889)					W/D	X	X	X	X	X	X	X
50762	2P 2-4-2T (1889)			To Wakefield	X	X	X	X	X	X	X	X	Ex Wakefield
50807	2P 2-4-2T (1889)	X	X	X	X	X	X	X	X	X	X	X	Ex Bolton
50818	2P 2-4-2T (1889)	X	X	X	X	X	X	X	X	X	X	Ex N. Heath	
50831	2P 2-4-2T (1889)	X	X	X	X	X	X	X	X	X	X	X	Ex L. Hall
50865	2P 2-4-2T (1889)	X	X	X	X	X	X	X	X	X	X	X	Ex Bolton
50886	2P 2-4-2T (1889)					W/D	X	X	X	X	X	X	X
50892	2P 2-4-2T (1889)	X	X	X	X	X	Ex Mirfield					W/D	x
51404	2F 0-6-0ST (1877)												

Loco	Class	Aug-52	Sep-52	Oct-52	Nov-52	Dec-52	Jan-53	Feb-53	Mar-53	Apr-53	May-53	Jun-53	Jul-53
44693	5MT 4-6-0 (1934)												
44694	5MT 4-6-0 (1934)												
44695	5MT 4-6-0 (1934)												
44912	5MT 4-6-0 (1934)												
44951	5MT 4-6-0 (1934)												
44990	5MT 4-6-0 (1934)												
45207	5MT 4-6-0 (1934)												
45208	5MT 4-6-0 (1934)												
45210	5MT 4-6-0 (1934)												
45219	5MT 4-6-0 (1934)												
40937	4P 4-4-0 (1924)	X	X	X	X	X	X	X	X	Ex Walton	To Blackpool	X	X
41101	4P 4-4-0 (1924)	X	X	X	X	X	X	X	X	Ex Walton		To Bolton	X
41189	4P 4-4-0 (1924)	X	X	X	X	X	X	X	X	Ex Walton		To Bolton	X
42107	4MT 2-6-4T (1945)												
42108	4MT 2-6-4T (1945)												
42109	4MT 2-6-4T (1945)												
42110	4MT 2-6-4T (1945)												
42111	4MT 2-6-4T (1945)												
42112	4MT 2-6-4T (1945)												
42113	4MT 2-6-4T (1945)												
42114	4MT 2-6-4T (1945)												
42115	4MT 2-6-4T (1945)												
42116	4MT 2-6-4T (1945)												
42188	4MT 2-6-4T (1945)												
42189	4MT 2-6-4T (1945)												
52561	3F 0-6-0 (1909)	X	X	Ex Goole									
52104	3F 0-6-0 (1889)												
52166	3F 0-6-0 (1889)												
52345	3F 0-6-0 (1889)	X	X	X	X	ex Wakefield							
52351	3F 0-6-0 (1889)												
52411	3F 0-6-0 (1889)												
52427	3F 0-6-0 (1889)	X	X	X	X	X	X	X	X	X	X	X	Ex Bury
52461	3F 0-6-0 (1889)												
52515	3F 0-6-0 (1889)												
52521	3F 0-6-0 (1889)												
50762	2P 2-4-2T (1889)												
50764	2P 2-4-2T (1889)	X	X	X	X	X	X	X	X	Ex Lostock H.			
50807	2P 2-4-2T (1889)												
50818	2P 2-4-2T (1889)												
50831	2P 2-4-2T (1889)												
50865	2P 2-4-2T (1889)		To Hudd'fld	X	X	X	X	X	X	X	X	X	X
51404	2F 0-6-0ST (1877)												

Loco	Class	Aug-53	Sep-53	Oct-53	Nov-53	Dec-53	Jan-54	Feb-54	Mar-54	Apr-54	May-54	Jun-54	Jul-54
44693	5MT 4-6-0 (1934)												
44694	5MT 4-6-0 (1934)												
44695	5MT 4-6-0 (1934)												
44912	5MT 4-6-0 (1934)												
44951	5MT 4-6-0 (1934)												
44990	5MT 4-6-0 (1934)												
45207	5MT 4-6-0 (1934)												
45208	5MT 4-6-0 (1934)												
45210	5MT 4-6-0 (1934)												
45219	5MT 4-6-0 (1934)												
41101	4P 4-4-0 (1924)	X	X	X	X	X	X	X	X	Ex Bolton			To Southport
41186	4P 4-4-0 (1924)	X	X	X	X	X	X	X	X	Ex Aintree			To Southport
41187	4P 4-4-0 (1924)	X	X	X	X	X	X	X	X	Ex Aintree			To Southport
41189	4P 4-4-0 (1924)	X	X	X	X	X	X	X	X	Ex Bolton			To Southport
42107	4MT 2-6-4T (1945)												
42108	4MT 2-6-4T (1945)												
42109	4MT 2-6-4T (1945)												
42110	4MT 2-6-4T (1945)		To Hudd'fld	X	X	X	X	X	X	X	X	X	X
42111	4MT 2-6-4T (1945)		To Walton	X	X	X	X	X	X	X	X	X	X
42112	4MT 2-6-4T (1945)		To Walton	X	X	X	X	X	X	X	X	X	X
42113	4MT 2-6-4T (1945)		To Walton	X	X	X	X	X	X	X	X	X	X
42114	4MT 2-6-4T (1945)			To Lees	X	X	X	X	X	X	X	X	X
42115	4MT 2-6-4T (1945)			To Lees	X	X	X	X	X	X	X	X	X
42116	4MT 2-6-4T (1945)												
42188	4MT 2-6-4T (1945)												
42189	4MT 2-6-4T (1945)												
52561	3F 0-6-0 (1909)												
52104	3F 0-6-0 (1889)												
52154	3F 0-6-0 (1889)	X	X	X	X	X	X	X	X	Ex Sow Bge			To Wakefield
52166	3F 0-6-0 (1889)												
52343	3F 0-6-0 (1889)	X	Ex N. Heath										
52345	3F 0-6-0 (1889)			To Crewe Wks	X	X	X	X	X	X	X	X	X
52351	3F 0-6-0 (1889)									To Sow Bge	X	X	X
52355	3F 0-6-0 (1889)	X	Ex Sow Bge										
52411	3F 0-6-0 (1889)	To Wakefield	X	X	X	X	X	X	X	X	X	X	X
52427	3F 0-6-0 (1889)			To Lees	X	X	X	X	X	X	X	X	X
52461	3F 0-6-0 (1889)												
52515	3F 0-6-0 (1889)												
52521	3F 0-6-0 (1889)												
50757	2P 2-4-2T (1889)	X	X	X	X	X	X	X	X	Ex Sow Bge			
50762	2P 2-4-2T (1889)					W/D	X	X	X	X	X	X	X
50764	2P 2-4-2T (1889)												
50807	2P 2-4-2T (1889)												
50818	2P 2-4-2T (1889)									To Sow Bge	X	X	X
50831	2P 2-4-2T (1889)												
50869	2P 2-4-2T (1889)	X	Ex Mirfield										
84010	2MT 2-6-2T (1953)	X	NEW										
84011	2MT 2-6-2T (1953)	X	NEW										
84012	2MT 2-6-2T (1953)	X	NEW										
84013	2MT 2-6-2T (1953)	X	NEW										
84014	2MT 2-6-2T (1953)	X	NEW										
84015	2MT 2-6-2T (1953)	X	NEW										
41250	2MT 2-6-2T (1946)	X	X	X	X	X	X	X	X	X	X	X	Ex Wakefield
51404	2F 0-6-0ST (1877)												

Loco	Class	Aug-54	Sep-54	Oct-54	Nov-54	Dec-54	Jan-55	Feb-55	Mar-55	Apr-55	May-55	Jun-55	Jul-55
44693	5MT 4-6-0 (1934)												
44694	5MT 4-6-0 (1934)												
44695	5MT 4-6-0 (1934)												
44912	5MT 4-6-0 (1934)												
44951	5MT 4-6-0 (1934)												
44990	5MT 4-6-0 (1934)												
45207	5MT 4-6-0 (1934)												
45208	5MT 4-6-0 (1934)												
45210	5MT 4-6-0 (1934)												
45219	5MT 4-6-0 (1934)												
45435	5MT 4-6-0 (1934)	X	X	X	X	X	X	X	X	X	X	Ex Wakefield	
42107	4MT 2-6-4T (1945)												
42108	4MT 2-6-4T (1945)												
42109	4MT 2-6-4T (1945)												
42116	4MT 2-6-4T (1945)												
42188	4MT 2-6-4T (1945)												
42189	4MT 2-6-4T (1945)												
42649	4MT 2-6-4T (1935)	X	X	X	X	X	Ex Bury						
42650	4MT 2-6-4T (1935)	X	X	X	X	X	Ex Bury						
52561	3F 0-6-0 (1909)						W/D	X	X	X	X	X	X
52104	3F 0-6-0 (1889)		To Mirfield	X	X	X	X	X	X	X	X	X	X
52120	3F 0-6-0 (1889)	X	X	X	X	X	Ex Wakefield						
52150	3F 0-6-0 (1889)	X	X	X	X	X	Ex Wakefield		W/D	X	X	X	X
52166	3F 0-6-0 (1889)												
52235	3F 0-6-0 (1889)	X	X	X	X	X	Ex Wakefield						
52343	3F 0-6-0 (1889)												
52355	3F 0-6-0 (1889)												
52461	3F 0-6-0 (1889)												
52515	3F 0-6-0 (1889)												
52521	3F 0-6-0 (1889)												
50757	2P 2-4-2T (1889)		To Sow Bge	X	X	X	X	X	X	X	X	Ex Sow Bge	
50764	2P 2-4-2T (1889)												
50807	2P 2-4-2T (1889)										W/D	X	X
50831	2P 2-4-2T (1889)		To Hudd'fld	X	X	X	X	X	X	X	W/D	X	X
50869	2P 2-4-2T (1889)												
84010	2MT 2-6-2T (1953)		To Lees	X	X	X	X	X	X	X	X	X	X
84011	2MT 2-6-2T (1953)						To Bank Hall	X	X	X	X	X	X
84012	2MT 2-6-2T (1953)		To Lees	X	X	X	X	X	X	X	X	X	X
84013	2MT 2-6-2T (1953)						To Bank Hall	X	X	X	X	X	X
84014	2MT 2-6-2T (1953)						To Bank Hall	X	X	X	X	X	X
84015	2MT 2-6-2T (1953)		To Lees	X	X	X	X	X	X	X	X	X	X
41250	2MT 2-6-2T (1946)												
41262	2MT 2-6-2T (1946)	X	Ex Blackpool										
41263	2MT 2-6-2T (1946)	X	Ex Blackpool										
41264	2MT 2-6-2T (1946)	X	Ex Blackpool										
51404	2F 0-6-0ST (1877)												

Loco	Class	Aug-55	Sep-55	Oct-55	Nov-55	Dec-55	Jan-56	Feb-56	Mar-56	Apr-56	May-56	Jun-56	Jul-56
90397	8F : WD 2-8-0 (1943)	X	X	X	X	X	X	X	X	X	X	Ex Goole	
90406	8F : WD 2-8-0 (1943)	X	X	X	X	X	X	X	X	X	X	Ex Wakefield	
44693	5MT 4-6-0 (1934)												
44694	5MT 4-6-0 (1934)												
44695	5MT 4-6-0 (1934)												
44912	5MT 4-6-0 (1934)												
44951	5MT 4-6-0 (1934)												
44990	5MT 4-6-0 (1934)												
45101	5MT 4-6-0 (1934)	X	X	X	X	X	X	Ex Wakefield				To Wakefield	X
45207	5MT 4-6-0 (1934)												
45208	5MT 4-6-0 (1934)												
45210	5MT 4-6-0 (1934)												
45219	5MT 4-6-0 (1934)												
45435	5MT 4-6-0 (1934)			To Wakefield	X	X	X	X	X	X	X	X	X
42107	4MT 2-6-4T (1945)												
42108	4MT 2-6-4T (1945)												
42109	4MT 2-6-4T (1945)												
42116	4MT 2-6-4T (1945)												
42188	4MT 2-6-4T (1945)												
42189	4MT 2-6-4T (1945)												
42622	4MT 2-6-4T (1935)	X	X	X	X	X	X	X	X	X	X	Ex N. Heath	
42649	4MT 2-6-4T (1935)												
42650	4MT 2-6-4T (1935)												
52120	3F 0-6-0 (1889)												
52166	3F 0-6-0 (1889)												
52235	3F 0-6-0 (1889)												
52343	3F 0-6-0 (1889)											W/D	X
52355	3F 0-6-0 (1889)												
52461	3F 0-6-0 (1889)			To Bolton	X	X	X	X	X	X	X	X	X
52515	3F 0-6-0 (1889)												
52521	3F 0-6-0 (1889)												
50757	2P 2-4-2T (1889)												
50764	2P 2-4-2T (1889)											W/D	X
50831	2P 2-4-2T (1889)	X	X	X	Ex Hudd'fld								
50869	2P 2-4-2T (1889)			W/D	X	X	X	X	X	X	X	X	X
41250	2MT 2-6-2T (1946)												
41262	2MT 2-6-2T (1946)												
41263	2MT 2-6-2T (1946)												
41264	2MT 2-6-2T (1946)												
51404	2F 0-6-0ST (1877)												

V2 2-6-2's were not as common on West Riding expresses as they were on East Coast services but that is not to say they were unknown, especially on the diagrams covered by Carr loco, Doncaster. 60935 of Doncaster emerges from Stoke tunnel and gets ready for the racing stretch to Peterborough with an up Leeds express in June 1951.

ALLOCATION & TRANSFERS : BRADFORD (LOW MOOR) : 25F													
Loco	Class	Aug-56	Sep-56	Oct-56	Nov-56	Dec-56	Jan-57	Feb-57	Mar-57	Apr-57	May-57	Jun-57	Jul-57
90126	8F : WD 2-8-0 (1943)	X	Ex N. Heath										
90397	8F : WD 2-8-0 (1943)												
90406	8F : WD 2-8-0 (1943)												
44693	5MT 4-6-0 (1934)												
44694	5MT 4-6-0 (1934)												
44695	5MT 4-6-0 (1934)												
44912	5MT 4-6-0 (1934)												
44951	5MT 4-6-0 (1934)												
44990	5MT 4-6-0 (1934)												
45207	5MT 4-6-0 (1934)												
45208	5MT 4-6-0 (1934)												
45210	5MT 4-6-0 (1934)	To Bank Hall	X	X	X	X	X	X	X	X	X	X	X
45219	5MT 4-6-0 (1934)												
42107	4MT 2-6-4T (1945)												
42108	4MT 2-6-4T (1945)												
42109	4MT 2-6-4T (1945)												
42116	4MT 2-6-4T (1945)												
42188	4MT 2-6-4T (1945)												
42189	4MT 2-6-4T (1945)												
42622	4MT 2-6-4T (1935)												
42649	4MT 2-6-4T (1935)												
42650	4MT 2-6-4T (1935)												
47335	3F 0-6-0T (1924)	X	X	X	X	X	X	X	X	X	X	Ex Normanton	
47249	3F 0-6-0T (1899)	X	X	X	X	X	X	X	X	X	X	Ex Stourton	
52089	3F 0-6-0 (1889)	x	x	x	x	x	x	x	Ex N. Heath				
52120	3F 0-6-0 (1889)										To Mirfield		X
52166	3F 0-6-0 (1889)		W/D	X	X	X	X	X	X	X	X	X	X
52235	3F 0-6-0 (1889)												W/D
52355	3F 0-6-0 (1889)												
52413	3F 0-6-0 (1889)	X	X	X	X	X	X	X	X	X	X	Ex L. Darwer To R. Grove	
52461	3F 0-6-0 (1889)	X	X	X	X	X	X	X	X	X	X	Ex Bolton	
52515	3F 0-6-0 (1889)												
52521	3F 0-6-0 (1889)										W/D	X	X
50757	2P 2-4-2T (1889)												
50831	2P 2-4-2T (1889)												
50855	2P 2-4-2T (1889)	Ex Bolton											
41250	2MT 2-6-2T (1946)												
41262	2MT 2-6-2T (1946)												
41263	2MT 2-6-2T (1946)												
41264	2MT 2-6-2T (1946)												
51404	2F 0-6-0ST (1877)												

ALLOCATION & TRANSFERS : BRADFORD (LOW MOOR) : 25F

Loco	Class	Aug-57	Sep-57	Oct-57	Nov-57	Dec-57	Jan-58	Feb-58	Mar-58	Apr-58	May-58	Jun-58	Jul-58
48080	8F 2-8-0 (1935)	X	X	X	X	X	X	X	X	X	Ex Royston		
48162	8F 2-8-0 (1935)	X	X	X	X	X	X	X	X	X	Ex Royston		
48265	8F 2-8-0 (1935)	X	X	X	X	X	X	X	X	X	Ex Royston		
48394	8F 2-8-0 (1935)	X	X	X	X	X	X	X	X	X	Ex Wakefield		
90126	8F : WD 2-8-0 (1943)											To Darlington	X
90397	8F : WD 2-8-0 (1943)											To Darlington	X
90406	8F : WD 2-8-0 (1943)											To Darlington	X
90698	8F : WD 2-8-0 (1943)	X	X	X	X	X	Ex Bowling Jn						
90711	8F : WD 2-8-0 (1943)	X	X	X	X	X	X	X	X	X	Ex Ardsley		
61020	5MT: B1 4-6-0 (1942)	X	X	X	X	X	X	X	X	X	X	Ex Darlington	
61023	5MT: B1 4-6-0 (1942)	X	X	X	X	X	X	X	X	X	X	Ex Darlington	
61031	5MT: B1 4-6-0 (1942)	X	X	X	X	X	X	Ex Bowling Jn					
61039	5MT: B1 4-6-0 (1942)	X	X	X	X	X	X	X	X	X	X	X	Ex Darlington
61040	5MT: B1 4-6-0 (1942)	X	X	X	X	X	X	X	X	X	X	X	Ex Darlington
61049	5MT: B1 4-6-0 (1942)	X	X	X	X	X	X	X	X	X	X	X	Ex Darlington
61061	5MT: B1 4-6-0 (1942)	X	X	X	X	X	X	X	X	X	X	Ex Darlington	
61131	5MT: B1 4-6-0 (1942)	X	X	X	X	X	X	Ex Bowling Jn					
61229	5MT: B1 4-6-0 (1942)	X	X	X	X	X	X	Ex Bowling Jn					
61230	5MT: B1 4-6-0 (1942)	X	X	X	X	X	X	Ex Bowling Jn					
61382	5MT: B1 4-6-0 (1942)	X	X	X	X	X	X	Ex Bowling Jn					
61383	5MT: B1 4-6-0 (1942)	X	X	X	X	X	X	Ex Bowling Jn					
44693	5MT 4-6-0 (1934)												
44694	5MT 4-6-0 (1934)												
44695	5MT 4-6-0 (1934)												
44912	5MT 4-6-0 (1934)												
44951	5MT 4-6-0 (1934)												
44990	5MT 4-6-0 (1934)												
45207	5MT 4-6-0 (1934)												
45208	5MT 4-6-0 (1934)												
45219	5MT 4-6-0 (1934)												
64791	5F : J39 0-6-0 (1926)	X	X	X	X	X	X	Ex Bowling Jn					
64796	5F : J39 0-6-0 (1926)	X	X	X	X	X	X	Ex Bowling Jn					
64801	5F : J39 0-6-0 (1926)	X	X	X	X	X	X	Ex Bowling Jn					
64872	5F : J39 0-6-0 (1926)	X	X	X	X	X	X	Ex Bowling Jn					
64886	5F : J39 0-6-0 (1926)	X	X	X	X	X	X	Ex Bowling Jn					
64903	5F : J39 0-6-0 (1926)	X	X	X	X	X	X	Ex Bowling Jn					
64907	5F : J39 0-6-0 (1926)	X	X	X	X	X	X	Ex Bowling Jn					
64947	5F : J39 0-6-0 (1926)	X	X	X	X	X	X	Ex Bowling Jn				To Hull (D)	X
42107	4MT 2-6-4T (1945)												
42108	4MT 2-6-4T (1945)												
42109	4MT 2-6-4T (1945)												
42116	4MT 2-6-4T (1945)												
42188	4MT 2-6-4T (1945)												
42189	4MT 2-6-4T (1945)												
42622	4MT 2-6-4T (1935)												
42649	4MT 2-6-4T (1935)												
42650	4MT 2-6-4T (1935)												
43101	4MT 2-6-0 (1947)	Ex Ardsley										To Ardsley	X
68892	4F : J50 0-6-0T (1922)	X	X	X	X	X	X	Ex Bowling Jn				To Stockton	X
68895	4F : J50 0-6-0T (1922)	X	X	X	X	X	X	Ex Bowling Jn					
68908	4F : J50 0-6-0T (1922)	X	X	X	X	X	X	Ex Bowling Jn			To Middlesbro	X	X
68922	4F : J50 0-6-0T (1922)	X	X	X	X	X	X	Ex Bowling Jn					
68923	4F : J50 0-6-0T (1922)	X	X	X	X	X	X	Ex Bowling Jn					
68932	4F : J50 0-6-0T (1922)	X	X	X	X	X	X	Ex Bowling Jn					
68933	4F : J50 0-6-0T (1922)	X	X	X	X	X	X	Ex Bowling Jn					
68934	4F : J50 0-6-0T (1922)	X	X	X	X	X	X	Ex Bowling Jn	To Darlington	X	X	X	X
68940	4F : J50 0-6-0T (1922)	X	X	X	X	X	X	Ex Bowling Jn					
68942	4F : J50 0-6-0T (1922)	X	X	X	X	X	X	Ex Bowling Jn			To Middlesbro	X	X
68943	4F : J50 0-6-0T (1922)	X	X	X	X	X	X	Ex Bowling Jn					
68944	4F : J50 0-6-0T (1922)	X	X	X	X	X	X	Ex Bowling Jn					
68969	4F : J50 0-6-0T (1922)	X	X	X	X	X	X	Ex Bowling Jn					
44062	4F 0-6-0 (1924)	Ex Mirfield											
40155	3P 2-6-2T (1935)	X	Ex Wakefield										
64170	3F : J6 0-6-0 (1911)	X	X	X	X	X	X	Ex Bowling Jn					
64203	3F : J6 0-6-0 (1911)	X	X	X	X	X	X	Ex Bowling Jn	To Wakefield	X	X	Ex Wakefield	
64226	3F : J6 0-6-0 (1911)	X	X	X	X	X	X	Ex Bowling Jn					
47335	3F 0-6-0T (1924)											To Mirfield	X
47405	3F 0-6-0T (1924)	X	X	X	X	X	X	X	X	X	Ex Normanton		
47446	3F 0-6-0T (1924)	X	X	X	X	X	X	X	X	X	Ex Normanton		
47635	3F 0-6-0T (1924)	X	X	X	X	X	X	X	X	X	Ex Normanton		
47249	3F 0-6-0T (1899)	To Sow Bge	X	X	X	X	X	X	X	X	X	X	X
52089	3F 0-6-0 (1889)												
52355	3F 0-6-0 (1889)												
52461	3F 0-6-0 (1889)												
52515	3F 0-6-0 (1889)												
43579	3F 0-6-0 (1885)	X	X	X	X	X	X	X	X	X	X	Ex Wakefield	
50757	2P 2-4-2T (1889)												
50831	2P 2-4-2T (1889)												
50855	2P 2-4-2T (1889)												
41250	2MT 2-6-2T (1946)												
41253	2MT 2-6-2T (1946)	X	X	X	X	X	X	Ex Wakefield					
41262	2MT 2-6-2T (1946)												
41263	2MT 2-6-2T (1946)												
41264	2MT 2-6-2T (1946)												
46483	2MT 2-6-0 (1946)	X	X	X	X	X	X	Ex Wakefield					
51404	2F 0-6-0ST (1877)												

Bradford had no less than three motive power depots: one on the Midland Railway at Manningham (and outside the scope of this book), another at Bowling Junction - often referred to as Hammerton Street - for the Great Northern and one at Low Moor to look after the interests of the ex-Lancashire & Yorkshire which ran from Bradford Exchange to Manchester Victoria and beyond with a branch running from Low Moor to Leeds. It is interesting to note that although the Great Northern and Lancashire & Yorkshire were closely connected in both Leeds and Bradford, there was little inclination to economise by combining resources and even Bradford Exchange was divided into operationally separate halves in order to keep the two systems apart. This, of course, was not untypical of British practice with company distinctions being perpetuated for twenty years (and more) after nationalisation.

Low Moor had a higher proportion of passenger traffic than most sheds on the goods-orientated Lancashire & Yorkshire since much of Bradford's goods needs were served relatively locally, involving a small fleet of around eight Barton-Wright 0-6-0's which tripped as ordered between Bradford and the yards on the Manchester - Wakefield main line. The handful of express goods trains worked by Low Moor had been handled by 'Crab' 2-6-0 locomotives until their replacement by Black 5 4-6-0's in early BR days.

The backbone of the shed's work was the long established hourly express service between Bradford and Liverpool which was shared with Bank

Introduced in 1898 for the suburban lines of the West Riding, the Great Northern C12 4-4-2T's could still be see at Leeds half a century later although much of their work had been taken over by N1 and J50 locomotives.   In or around 1950, (6)7353 coasts into Holbeck (High Level) with a Leeds Central - Castleford service.   (H.C. Casserley)

In many respects, a personification of the area. An ex-Great Northern N1 0-6-2T 69436 (Copley Hill) runs into Holbeck with a Leeds - Bradford local in or about 1950.   For many, it was rather a sad day when diesel multiple units took over the local services. (H.C. Casserley)

Loco	Class	Aug-58	Sep-58	Oct-58	Nov-58	Dec-58	Jan-59	Feb-59	Mar-59	Apr-59	May-59	Jun-59	Jul-59
48080	8F 2-8-0 (1935)												
48162	8F 2-8-0 (1935)	To Stourton	X	X	X	X	X	X	X	X	X	X	X
48265	8F 2-8-0 (1935)		To Mirfield	X	X	X	X	X	X	X	X	X	X
48394	8F 2-8-0 (1935)												
48702	8F 2-8-0 (1935)	X	Ex Mirfield										
90333	8F : WD 2-8-0 (1943)	X	X	Ex Wakefield									
90711	8F : WD 2-8-0 (1943)												
62047	6F: K1 2-6-0 (1949)	X	X	X	X	X	X	X	X	X	X	Ex Stockton	
62065	6F: K1 2-6-0 (1949)	X	X	X	X	X	X	X	X	X	X	Ex Stockton	
61020	5MT: B1 4-6-0 (1942)												
61023	5MT: B1 4-6-0 (1942)												
61031	5MT: B1 4-6-0 (1942)		To Darlington	X	X	X	X	X	X	X	X	X	X
61039	5MT: B1 4-6-0 (1942)												
61040	5MT: B1 4-6-0 (1942)								To Wakefield	X	X	X	X
61049	5MT: B1 4-6-0 (1942)												
61061	5MT: B1 4-6-0 (1942)		To Darlington	X	X	X	X	X	X	X	X	X	X
61131	5MT: B1 4-6-0 (1942)							To Wakefield	X	X	X	X	X
61198	5MT: B1 4-6-0 (1942)	X	X	X	X	X	X	X	X	X	X	Ex Darlington	
61229	5MT: B1 4-6-0 (1942)		To Darlington	X	X	X	X	X	X	X	X	X	X
61230	5MT: B1 4-6-0 (1942)												
61274	5MT: B1 4-6-0 (1942)	X	X	X	X	X	X	X	X	X	X	Ex Darlington	
61382	5MT: B1 4-6-0 (1942)		To Darlington	X	X	X	X	X	X	X	X	X	X
61383	5MT: B1 4-6-0 (1942)												
61387	5MT: B1 4-6-0 (1942)	X	X	X	X	X	X	X	X	X	X	Ex Darlington	
44693	5MT 4-6-0 (1934)												
44694	5MT 4-6-0 (1934)												
44695	5MT 4-6-0 (1934)												
44824	5MT 4-6-0 (1934)	X	X	X	X	X	X	X	Ex Crewe (S)				
44912	5MT 4-6-0 (1934)												
44951	5MT 4-6-0 (1934)												
44990	5MT 4-6-0 (1934)												
45207	5MT 4-6-0 (1934)												
45208	5MT 4-6-0 (1934)												
45219	5MT 4-6-0 (1934)												
64791	5F: J39 0-6-0 (1926)												
64796	5F: J39 0-6-0 (1926)											To Ardsley	X
64801	5F: J39 0-6-0 (1926)												
64817	5F: J39 0-6-0 (1926)	X	X	X	X	X	X	Ex Sunderland					
64872	5F: J39 0-6-0 (1926)												
64886	5F: J39 0-6-0 (1926)												
64903	5F: J39 0-6-0 (1926)												
64907	5F: J39 0-6-0 (1926)												
64919	5F: J39 0-6-0 (1926)	X	X	X	X	X	X	Ex Sunderland					
42084	4MT 2-6-4T (1945)	X	X	X	X	X	X	X	X	Ex Scarbro			
42107	4MT 2-6-4T (1945)												
42108	4MT 2-6-4T (1945)												
42109	4MT 2-6-4T (1945)												
42116	4MT 2-6-4T (1945)												
42188	4MT 2-6-4T (1945)												
42189	4MT 2-6-4T (1945)												
42622	4MT 2-6-4T (1935)												
42649	4MT 2-6-4T (1935)												
42650	4MT 2-6-4T (1935)												
42311	4MT 2-6-4T (1927)	X	X	X	X	X	X	X	X	X	X	Ex Sow Bge	
42380	4MT 2-6-4T (1927)	X	X	X	X	X	X	X	X	X	X	Ex Sow Bge	
42411	4MT 2-6-4T (1927)	X	X	X	X	X	Ex N. Hill						
43053	4MT 2-6-0 (1947)	X	X	X	X	X	X	X	X	X	X	Ex Hull (D)	
68895	4F: J50 0-6-0T (1922)												
68908	4F: J50 0-6-0T (1922)	X	X	X	X	X	X	Ex Thornaby					
68912	4F: J50 0-6-0T (1922)	X	X	X	X	X	X	Ex Goole					
68922	4F: J50 0-6-0T (1922)												
68923	4F: J50 0-6-0T (1922)												
68932	4F: J50 0-6-0T (1922)												
68933	4F: J50 0-6-0T (1922)												
68940	4F: J50 0-6-0T (1922)		W/D	X	X	X	X	X	X	X	X	X	X
68943	4F: J50 0-6-0T (1922)												
68944	4F: J50 0-6-0T (1922)												
68969	4F: J50 0-6-0T (1922)												
44062	4F 0-6-0 (1924)												
40155	3P 2-6-2T (1935)	To Ardsley	X	X	X	X	X	X	X	X	X	X	X
64170	3F: J6 0-6-0 (1911)												
64203	3F: J6 0-6-0 (1911)												
64226	3F: J6 0-6-0 (1911)												
47405	3F 0-6-0T (1924)												
47446	3F 0-6-0T (1924)												
47635	3F 0-6-0T (1924)												
47255	3F 0-6-0T (1899)	X	X	X	X	X	Ex Manningham						
52089	3F 0-6-0 (1889)								To Mirfield	X	X	X	X
52355	3F 0-6-0 (1889)	To Wakefield	X	X	X	X	X	X	X	X	X	X	X
52461	3F 0-6-0 (1889)												
52515	3F 0-6-0 (1889)								To Mirfield	X	X	X	X
43579	3F 0-6-0 (1885)												
50757	2P 2-4-2T (1889)	W/D	X	X	X	X	X	X	X	X	X	X	X
50831	2P 2-4-2T (1889)	W/D	X	X	X	X	X	X	X	X	X	X	X
50855	2P 2-4-2T (1889)	W/D	X	X	X	X	X	X	X	X	X	X	X
41250	2MT 2-6-2T (1946)												
41253	2MT 2-6-2T (1946)												
41262	2MT 2-6-2T (1946)												
41263	2MT 2-6-2T (1946)												
41268	2MT 2-6-2T (1946)	To Wakefield	X	X	X	X	X	X	X	X	X	X	X
41274	2MT 2-6-2T (1946)	X	X	X	X	X	X	X	X	X	X	Ex Royston	
46483	2MT 2-6-0 (1946)											To Wakefield	X
51404	2F 0-6-0ST (1877)	To Mirfield	X	X	X	X	X	X	X	X	X	X	X

Hall, Liverpool, and Southport.   It was rare to see anything other than a Black 5 4-6-0 on any of the services and the main element of variety came with the Leeds coaches which were worked separately from Low Moor to Leeds Central; LMS 2-6-4T's being the mainstay although 5MT 4-6-0's were booked to some of the Leeds workings.   Low Moor 2-6-4T's also covered many of the stopping services that ran between Bradford Exchange and Huddersfield, Penistone and Stockport.

In spite of the heavy gradients, many of the turns were capable of being worked by engines very much smaller than the large 2-6-4T's - for years many of the services had been in the hands of nothing larger than a 2P 2-4-2T - and in 1953 a number of 2-6-4T's were replaced by the highly capable

| ALLOCATION & TRANSFERS : BRADFORD (LOW MOOR) : 25F | | | | | | | | | | | | |
Loco	Class	Aug-59	Sep-59	Oct-59	Nov-59	Dec-59	Jan-60	Feb-60	Mar-60	Apr-60	May-60	Jun-60	Jul-60
48080	8F 2-8-0 (1935)							To Stourton	X	X	X	X	X
48394	8F 2-8-0 (1935)							To Stourton	X	X	X	X	X
48702	8F 2-8-0 (1935)							To Stourton	X	X	X	X	X
90068	8F : WD 2-8-0 (1943)	X	X	X	Ex Wakefield								
90200	8F : WD 2-8-0 (1943)	X	X	X	Ex Wakefield								
90236	8F : WD 2-8-0 (1943)	X	X	X	Ex Wakefield								
90322	8F : WD 2-8-0 (1943)	X	X	X	X	X	X	Ex Mirfield					
90333	8F : WD 2-8-0 (1943)												
90351	8F : WD 2-8-0 (1943)	X	X	X	X	X	X	Ex Mirfield					
90397	8F : WD 2-8-0 (1943)	X	X	X	X	X	X	Ex Mirfield					
90711	8F : WD 2-8-0 (1943)												
62047	6F: K1 2-6-0 (1949)	To York	X	X	X	X	X	X	X	X	X	X	X
62065	6F: K1 2-6-0 (1949)	To York	X	X	X	X	X	X	X	X	X	X	X
61020	5MT: B1 4-6-0 (1942)				To Wakefield	X	X	X	X	X	X	X	X
61023	5MT: B1 4-6-0 (1942)				To Ardsley	X	X	X	X	X	X	X	X
61039	5MT: B1 4-6-0 (1942)				To Ardsley	X	X	X	X	X	X	X	X
61049	5MT: B1 4-6-0 (1942)				To Mirfield	X	X	X	X	X	X	X	X
61198	5MT: B1 4-6-0 (1942)	To York	X	X	X	X	X	X	X	X	X	X	X
61230	5MT: B1 4-6-0 (1942)				To Mirfield	X	X	X	X	X	X	X	X
61274	5MT: B1 4-6-0 (1942)												
61383	5MT: B1 4-6-0 (1942)												
61387	5MT: B1 4-6-0 (1942)												
44693	5MT 4-6-0 (1934)												
44694	5MT 4-6-0 (1934)												
44695	5MT 4-6-0 (1934)												
44824	5MT 4-6-0 (1934)		To Holbeck	X	X	X	X	X	X	X	X	X	X
44912	5MT 4-6-0 (1934)												
44951	5MT 4-6-0 (1934)												
44990	5MT 4-6-0 (1934)												
45207	5MT 4-6-0 (1934)												
45208	5MT 4-6-0 (1934)												
45219	5MT 4-6-0 (1934)												
64791	5F: J39 0-6-0 (1926)												
64801	5F: J39 0-6-0 (1926)												
64817	5F: J39 0-6-0 (1926)		.										
64872	5F: J39 0-6-0 (1926)												
64886	5F: J39 0-6-0 (1926)												
64903	5F: J39 0-6-0 (1926)												
64907	5F: J39 0-6-0 (1926)												
64919	5F: J39 0-6-0 (1926)												
42084	4MT 2-6-4T (1945)												
42107	4MT 2-6-4T (1945)												
42108	4MT 2-6-4T (1945)												
42109	4MT 2-6-4T (1945)												
42116	4MT 2-6-4T (1945)												
42188	4MT 2-6-4T (1945)												
42189	4MT 2-6-4T (1945)												
42622	4MT 2-6-4T (1935)				To Wakefield	X	X	X	X	X	X	X	X
42649	4MT 2-6-4T (1935)				To Copley H.	X	X	X	X	X	X	X	X
42650	4MT 2-6-4T (1935)				To Copley H.	X	X	X	X	X	X	X	X
42311	4MT 2-6-4T (1927)												
42324	4MT 2-6-4T (1927)	X	X	X	X	X	X	X	X	X	Ex Mirfield		
42380	4MT 2-6-4T (1927)			To Sow Bge	X	X	X	X	X	X	Ex Sow Bge		
42411	4MT 2-6-4T (1927)			To Sow Bge	X	X	X	X	X	X	Ex Sow Bge		
43053	4MT 2-6-0 (1947)				To W. H'pool	X	X	X	X	X	X	X	X
68895	4F: J50 0-6-0T (1922)								W/D	X	X	X	X
68908	4F: J50 0-6-0T (1922)												
68912	4F: J50 0-6-0T (1922)		W/D	X	X	X	X	X	X	X	X	X	X
68922	4F: J50 0-6-0T (1922)												
68923	4F: J50 0-6-0T (1922)												
68932	4F: J50 0-6-0T (1922)												
68933	4F: J50 0-6-0T (1922)										To Wakefield	X	X
68943	4F: J50 0-6-0T (1922)												
68944	4F: J50 0-6-0T (1922)												
68948	4F: J50 0-6-0T (1922)	X	Ex Selby										
68959	4F: J50 0-6-0T (1922)	X	X	X	X	X	X	X	X	X	Ex Wakefield		
68969	4F: J50 0-6-0T (1922)								W/D	X	X	X	X
44062	4F 0-6-0 (1924)												
40147	3P 2-6-2T (1935)	X	X	X	X	X	X	X	X	X	Ex Sow Bge		
40190	3P 2-6-2T (1935)	X	X	X	X	X	X	X	X	X	Ex Sow Bge		
64170	3F: J6 0-6-0 (1911)												
64203	3F: J6 0-6-0 (1911)												
64226	3F: J6 0-6-0 (1911)												
47405	3F 0-6-0T (1924)												
47446	3F 0-6-0T (1924)												
47635	3F 0-6-0T (1924)												
47255	3F 0-6-0T (1899)												
52461	3F 0-6-0 (1889)												
43579	3F 0-6-0 (1885)				To Wakefield	X	X	X	X	X	X	X	X
41250	2MT 2-6-2T (1946)												
41253	2MT 2-6-2T (1946)												
41262	2MT 2-6-2T (1946)							To Hull (D)	X	X	X	X	X
41263	2MT 2-6-2T (1946)												
41264	2MT 2-6-2T (1946)	X	X	X	X	X	X	X	X	X	Ex Mirfield		
41274	2MT 2-6-2T (1946)												
46413	2MT 2-6-0 (1946)	X	X	X	Ex Wakefield								
46435	2MT 2-6-0 (1946)	X	X	X	Ex Wakefield								

LMS and BR 2MT 2-6-2T's. It should be noted that the 2-4-2T's did not give in without a fight and survived in traffic until Summer 1958.

Although Low Moor was not directly affected by the dieselisation of the Leeds - Bradford local service, the indirect affect was considerable when in early 1958, Bowling Junction (Hammerton Street) was rebuilt as a maintenance depot for diesel multiple-units and its steam work transferred to Low Moor. The immediate result was that Low Moor's allocation of engines increased overnight from thirty-five to sixty-nine although the sharing of the depot did not mean a merging of work since the former GN engines continued to be used on the same workings that they had operated from Bowling Junction whilst the L&Y diagrams continued to operate as they always had. This was in spite of the fact that the North Eastern Region had - nominally - taken control of all the railways in the West Riding although the various components continued to operate more or less in isolation right up to the mid-1960's. It took more than the grouping and nationalisation to bury the individuality of British railway tradition.